AF806082

Creative Economy

Series editors

Stephen Hill
Kazuo Nishimura
Tadashi Yagi

Editorial Board

Nobuko Kawashima
Sebastine Lechevalier
Yoshifumi Nakata
Andy Pratt
Masayuki Sasaki
Toshiaki Tachibanaki
Makoto Yano
Roberto Zanola

As the global economy has developed, we have seen severe competition and polarisation in income distribution. With this drastic change in the economic system, creativity with a high market value has come to be considered the main source of competiveness. In addition to the improvement of competitiveness, however, we are required to work toward fairness in society.

This series covers research on creative economies that are based on humanity and spirituality to enhance the competitiveness, sustainability, peace, and fairness of international society. We define a creative economy as a socio-economic system that promotes those creative activities with a high market value and leads to the improvement of society's overall well-being.

Through this series, we intend to propose various policy recommendations that contribute to the prosperity of international society and improve the well-being of mankind by clarifying the concrete actions that are needed.

More information about this series at http://www.springer.com/series/13627

Sigrid Hemels · Kazuko Goto
Editors

Tax Incentives for the Creative Industries

Springer

Editors
Sigrid Hemels
Erasmus School of Law
Erasmus University Rotterdam
Rotterdam, Zuid-Holland
The Netherlands

Kazuko Goto
Setsunan University
Neyagawa, Osaka
Japan

ISSN 2364-9186 ISSN 2364-9445 (electronic)
Creative Economy
ISBN 978-981-287-831-1 ISBN 978-981-287-832-8 (eBook)
DOI 10.1007/978-981-287-832-8

Library of Congress Control Number: 2016959747

© Springer Science+Business Media Singapore 2017
This work is subject to copyright. All rights are reserved by the Publisher, whether the whole or part of the material is concerned, specifically the rights of translation, reprinting, reuse of illustrations, recitation, broadcasting, reproduction on microfilms or in any other physical way, and transmission or information storage and retrieval, electronic adaptation, computer software, or by similar or dissimilar methodology now known or hereafter developed.
The use of general descriptive names, registered names, trademarks, service marks, etc. in this publication does not imply, even in the absence of a specific statement, that such names are exempt from the relevant protective laws and regulations and therefore free for general use.
The publisher, the authors and the editors are safe to assume that the advice and information in this book are believed to be true and accurate at the date of publication. Neither the publisher nor the authors or the editors give a warranty, express or implied, with respect to the material contained herein or for any errors or omissions that may have been made.

Printed on acid-free paper

This Springer imprint is published by Springer Nature
The registered company is Springer Nature Singapore Pte Ltd.
The registered company address is: 152 Beach Road, #22-06/08 Gateway East, Singapore 189721, Singapore

Preface

To find the origins of this book, we have to go back to the winter of 2004 when we first met at the Rotterdam Art Center Witte de With, where we both participated in one of Arjo Klamer's special seminars on cultural economics. Klamer, the well-known Professor of Cultural Economics at Erasmus University Rotterdam, introduced us to each other saying that he was sure we had mutual interests: Kazoko Goto being a researcher in cultural economics with a public finance background and Sigrid Hemels, a tax specialist who, at that time, had just completed her Ph.D. research on tax incentives for the arts and culture in the Netherlands.

Arjo Klamer was right. What followed was an academic and personal friendship built over more than a decade with joint publications and mutual research visits to the Netherlands and Japan, enabled by financial support from the Japan Society for the Promotion of Science (JSPS) and Saitama University. During Sigrid's JSPS short-term fellowship in Japan in November 2014, we met over dinner with Prof. Tadashi Yagi of Doshisha University, Kyoto, and talked with him about the possibility of writing a book on tax incentives for the creative industries. This book is the result of that dinner.

We thank the editors of the Creative Economy series who gave us this opportunity. Furthermore, we are grateful to three anonymous peer reviewers for their useful comments on our book proposal: we hope that we have addressed your points satisfactorily. We are also very grateful to our co-authors who enthusiastically joined this project notwithstanding their busy schedules: Renate Buijze, Raymond Luja, and Dick Molenaar. Without their specific expertise, this book could not have been as comprehensive as it is now. Last but not least, we would like to thank everybody at Springer who has been involved in the production of this book, especially Juno Kawakami, Misao Taguchi and Sudeshna Das, who were always very patient and helpful. We hope our readers will enjoy this book and benefit as much from reading it as we did from writing and discussing it.

Amsterdam, Kyoto
Fall 2016

Sigrid Hemels
Kazuko Goto

Contents

Editors and Contributors

About the Editors

Sigrid Hemels received her Ph.D. from Leiden University in the Netherlands in 2005. She is Full Professor of Tax Law, Erasmus School of Law (ESL), Erasmus University Rotterdam; programme leader of the ESL Research Programme Fiscal Autonomy and Its Boundaries; and head of the ESL Department of Tax Law. She is also senior professional support lawyer at the Amsterdam office of Allen & Overy LLP and a member of the supervisory boards of several Dutch cultural institutions. Dr. Hemels frequently publishes and lectures, both in the Netherlands and abroad, on various tax topics, including tax incentives for charities, art, and cultural heritage.

Kazuko Goto received her Ph.D. in Economics from Kyoto University in 1998. She was Professor at Saitama University, 2004–2014, and visiting professor at Erasmus University Rotterdam, 2004–2005. At present, she is Professor at Setsunan University in Osaka, where she has been since 2014. She was an executive board member of the Association for Cultural Economics International, 2006–2012. Professor Goto also was editor in chief of *Bunka Keizaigaku* (Cultural Economics), 2006–2010, and was president of the Japan Association for Cultural Economics, 2010–2012. She has been an executive board member of the Japan Institute of Public Finance since 2016.

Contributors

Renate Buijze is a Ph.D. candidate at the Erasmus School of Law (ESL). Her research focuses on cross-border philanthropy and specifically the tax incentives for giving to the arts. With a Master's degree in Cultural Economics and cultural entrepreneurship from the Erasmus School of History, Culture, and Communication, she has an interdisciplinary scope on research.

Raymond Luja is Professor of Comparative Tax Law at Maastricht University, the Netherlands, where he heads the Department of Tax law. He is also expert counsel to Loyens & Loeff N.V., Amsterdam, where he deals with issues of fiscal state aid. He holds Master's degrees in Fiscal Economics and in Law. In 2003 he received a Ph.D. from Maastricht University after defending his thesis "Assessment and Recovery of Tax Incentives in the EC and the WTO: A View on State Aids, Trade Subsidies and Direct Taxation". Dr. Luja frequently publishes in the area of state aid and harmful tax competition and lectures in this field at various universities and institutions in Europe.

Dick Molenaar is a researcher of tax law at the Erasmus School of Law (ESL) of Erasmus University Rotterdam, the Netherlands. His research field is the tax aspects of performing artists, arts, culture, media, and sports. He is also a partner with All Arts Tax Advisers in Rotterdam, the Netherlands. In 2006, he defended his Ph.D. thesis "Taxation of International Performing Artistes" at the Erasmus University Rotterdam, the Netherlands. Dr. Molenaar has published extensively, both in the Netherlands and abroad, on various topics from his research field. He is also a member of the International Association of Entertainment Lawyers (IAEL) and of the International Tax Entertainment Group (ITEG). In addition, he is a member of the supervisory board of several Dutch cultural institutions.

Contributors

Renate Buijze Department of Tax Law, Erasmus School of Law, Erasmus University Rotterdam, Rotterdam, The Netherlands

Kazuko Goto Faculty of Economics, Setsunan University, Neyagawa, Osaka, Japan

Sigrid Hemels Department of Tax Law, Erasmus School of Law, Erasmus University Rotterdam, Rotterdam, The Netherlands; Allen & Overy, Amsterdam, The Netherlands

Raymond Luja Department of Tax Law/Maastricht Centre for Taxation, Maastricht University, Maastricht, The Netherlands; Loyens & Loeff N.V., Amsterdam, The Netherlands

Dick Molenaar Department of Tax Law, Erasmus School of Law, Erasmus University Rotterdam, Rotterdam, The Netherlands; All Arts Tax Advisers, Rotterdam, The Netherlands

Abbreviations

AO	Abgabenordnung (Tax Code, Germany)
ATR	Animation Tax Relief (UK)
AUD	Australian Dollar
AV	Audiovisual
AVMS Directive	Audiovisual Media Services Directive (EU: Directive 2010/13/EU of 10 March 2010) OJ L 95, 15.4.2010, p. 1–24
AWR	Algemene Wet inzake Rijksbelastingen (General State Taxes Act, Netherlands)
BEPS	Base Erosion and Profit Shifting
CA	Charities Act 2011 (UK)
CAD	Canadian Dollar
CCIP	Customs Code Implementing Provisions (EU)
CGI	Code Général des Impôts (General Taxes Act, France)
Chap.	Chapter
CITR	Creative Industry Tax Reliefs (UK)
CTA	Corporation Tax Act 2009 (UK)
DCMS	Department for Culture Media and Sports (UK)
EC	European Commission
ECCC	European Convention on Cinematographic Co-Production
ECJ	European Court of Justice
EEA	European Economic Area
EFC	European Foundation Centre
EStG	Einkommensteuergesetz (Income Tax, Germany)
EU	European Union
EUR	Euro
FA95	Finance Act 1995 (Ireland)
FA12	Finance Act 2012 (UK)
FE	Fundatio Europea; European Foundation
FIMI	Film in Malaysia Incentive
FTR	Film Tax Relief (UK)

G20	Group of twenty major economies
GATS	General Agreement in Trade in Services
GATT	General Agreement on Tariffs and Trade
GBER	General Block Exemption Regulation (Commission Regulation (EU) No 651/2014 of 17 June 2014 declaring certain categories of aid compatible with the internal market in application of Articles 107 and 108 of the Treaty, OJ L 187/1 of 26 June 2014)
GDP	Gross Domestic Product
GVA	Gross Value Added
HMRC	Her Majesty's Revenue and Customs (UK's tax and customs authority)
HS code	Harmonized Commodity Description and Coding System
HTR	High-end Television Tax Relief (UK)
IAS	International Accounting Standards
IB	Wet inkomstenbelasting 2001 (Personal Income Tax Act 2001, the Netherlands)
IBP	International Budget Partnership
IEP	Irish Pound
IHTA	Inheritance Tax Act 1984 (UK)
IMF	International Monetary Fund
IP	Intellectual Property
IRC	Internal Revenue Code (USA)
IRR	Internal Rate of Return
ITA	Income Tax Act 2007 (UK)
ITAA	Income Tax Assessment Act 1997 (Australia)
ITR	Income Tax Regulations (Canada)
JSPS	Japan Society for the Promotion of Science
KBFUS	King Baudouin Foundation United States
LB	Wet op de loonbelasting 1964 (Wage tax Act 1964, the Netherlands)
LIS	Ley del Impuesto sobre Sociedades (Corporation Tax Act, Spain)
LOB	Limitation On Benefits
LP	Limited Partnership
MERCOSUR	Mercado Común del Sur
NGO	Non-governmental organisation
NPO	Non Profit Organisation
NPO Law	特定非営利活動促進法 (Law to Promote Specified Nonprofit Activities, Japan)
OECD	Organisation for Economic Co-operation and Development
OIDMTC	Ontario Interactive Digital Media Tax Credit
OJ	Official Journal of the European Union
OTR	Orchestra Tax Relief (UK)
p.	Page

Para.	Paragraph
PBE	Public Benefit Pursuing Entity
PDV Offset	Post, Digital and Visual effects Offset
pp.	Pages
PPT	Principal Purpose Test
PSRI	Pay Related Social Insurance (Ireland)
QAPE	Qualifying Australian Production Expenditure
R&D	Research & Development
RST	Retail Sales Tax
SAC	Significant Australian Content
SCM Agreement	Agreement on Subsidies and Countervailing Measures
Sect.	Section
SGEI	Services of General Economic Interest
SME	Small and Medium sized Enterprises
SW	Successiewet 1956 (Gift and Inheritance Act, the Netherlands)
TCA	Taxes Consolidation Act, 1997 (Ireland)
TFEU	Treaty on the Functioning of the European Union
TGE	Transnational Giving Europe
TRIP	Tax Rebate for International Production (crédit d'impôt en faveur de la production de films étrangers en France)
TTR	Theatre Tax Relief (UK)
TUIR	Testo Unico delle Imposte sui Redditi (Income Tax Act, Italy)
TV	Television
UK	United Kingdom
UN	United Nations
UNCTAD	United Nations Conference on Trade and Development
UNESCO	United Nations Educational, Scientific and Cultural Organization
US	United States
USA	United States of America
USD	US Dollar
VAT	Value Added Tax
VAT Directive	Council Directive 2006/112/EC of 28 November 2006 on the common system of value added tax (as amended)
VFX	Visual effects
VGTR	Video Games Tax Relief (UK)
Vpb	Wet op de vennootschapsbelasting 1969 (Corporate income tax Act 1964, the Netherlands)
WIB92	Wetboek van de Inkomstenbelastingen 1992 (Income Tax Act 1992, Belgium)
WIPO	World Intellectual Property Organizations
WTO	World Trade Organization
ZV	Zollverordnung (Customs Regulation, Switzerland)
#	Number of

Chapter 1
Introduction

Sigrid Hemels

Abstract This chapter explains the background and structure of this book.

Keywords Tax incentives · Creative industries

1 What This Book Is About and How It Builds on Previous Research

The creative industries have been studied by academics from various backgrounds and disciplines, and this sector has also attracted attention from policy makers for both economic and cultural reasons. A highly relevant question for public policy makers who have decided they want to support the creative industries is which instrument to use for this purpose. This book focuses on one instrument in the public policy toolbox which has not always been given as much attention as the other tools, but which has become rather important for the creative industries: support through measures in tax legislation—in other words, tax incentives. Schuster (2006), pp. 1257, 1286 noted that in tax incentives, more than in direct subsidies, experimentation and variety can be found. Furthermore, with decreasing government budgets for direct subsidies, tax incentives are often perceived by politicians and those within the sector as alternatives outside the budget, even though this is a misconception, especially from the standpoint of the government as a whole. The public policy tenet made famous by Friedman (1975) that there is no such thing as a free lunch applies here, too. Still, this is a powerful force behind pleas for the introduction of new tax incentives for the creative industries all over the world.

S. Hemels (✉)
Department of Tax Law, Erasmus School of Law,
Erasmus University Rotterdam, Rotterdam, The Netherlands
e-mail: hemels@law.eur.nl

S. Hemels
Allen & Overy, Amsterdam, The Netherlands

© Springer Science+Business Media Singapore 2017
S. Hemels and K. Goto (eds.), *Tax Incentives for the Creative Industries*,
Creative Economy, DOI 10.1007/978-981-287-832-8_1

Most of the literature on tax incentives for the creative industries focuses on the USA and other English-speaking countries. Research in this field is usually done from an economist's perspective. Furthermore, most attention has been given to a specific sub-sector of the creative industries, namely, the non-profit charitable part that includes museums and the arts in general. This can probably be explained in part by the fact that the most important contributions in this field have been made by the American cultural economist J.M. Schuster, who focused on the role of tax policy in cultural policy. Starting with his doctoral thesis (Schuster 1979), he pioneered research on tax incentives as a cultural policy instrument. His thesis was not published at the time, but, thanks to open access, is now easily available online. It resulted in the standard reference work *Patrons Despite Themselves: Taxpayers and Arts Policy* (Feld et al. 1983). Both focused on the arts and the USA from an economist's perspective. Schuster (2006), p. 1263 noted that

> Schuster has been the most consistent contributor to the (American) literature on the role of tax policy in cultural policy.

We agree with this observation, but would like to point out that this might also have influenced the focus of research on this topic. Schuster (2006), p. 1293 did some comparative research but remarked that:

> there is also a need for comparative research on the forms of incentives and their relationship to various national contexts.

In order to get a full picture, it is important not only to focus on the American and English literature, but also to consider experiences in other countries and non-English sources. Besides, in the globalized world we live in today, transactions are often not restricted to one country, but cross borders. This is especially the case for the creative industries as they are, in part, highly mobile and not bound to any one territory. This gives rise to a new dimension and the question of whether tax incentives can cross borders as well. Furthermore, given the steady growth and increased importance of the more commercial part of the creative industries, both in economic terms and in policy discussions, it makes sense to broaden the scope of research from the non-profit arts and culture part of the creative industries to the more commercial for-profit part of the sector. Many countries provide tax incentives not only for the non-profit part of the creative industries, but also for commercial parts as well. Examples include tax incentives for films, the art market, and copyright. In this context, tax incentives may be used as tools for tax competition between countries to attract and stimulate the growth of particular sub-sectors of the creative industries. For such incentives, economic motivations may dominate over cultural motivations.

Finally, it is important to study tax incentives for the creative industries not only from an economic perspective, but also from a legal perspective. Tax legislation and international treaties can have a strong influence on the design of tax incentives. They explain certain features of a tax incentive offered in a country and may restrict policy makers in the design and application of certain tax incentives for the creative industries.

For all of these reasons, this book combines insights from cultural economics, public finance, and tax law. It provides an accessible and comprehensive introduction to the application of tax incentives in the creative industries. In order to meet this objective, we adopted a rather broad definition of "creative industries," and rather than focusing on a single country, we have included perspectives and examples from various countries around the world.

2 Structure of This Book

We have divided this book into three parts. It begins with a theoretical part that discusses the theoretical context within which tax incentives for the creative industries function. In the second part of the book, we focus on various examples of tax incentives for specific sub-sectors of the creative industries. This discussion builds on the theoretical framework developed in the first part. In Part III we conclude with a short discussion on the theoretical framework developed in Part I, viewed in relation to the cases presented in Part II, in order to arrive at some general conclusions regarding tax incentives for the creative industries.

2.1 Part I: Theoretical Framework

The logical starting point of our discussion is establishing a definition of the creative industries as a foundation on which the remainder of the book can be built. After a review of various possible definitions, Kazuko Goto (Chap. 2) develops a definition based on three characteristic features of the creative industries:

1. They have cultural and economic aspects relating to cultural policy goals as well as economic policy goals.
2. They are a combination of art and commerce.
3. They contain both nonprofit and for-profit organizations.

Following this definition, for purposes of this book the creative industries include the non-profit arts and cultural heritage which are targets of traditional cultural policy, as well as more commercial activities, including the audiovisual industry, copyright, and the art market.

After having established this definition, Kazuko Goto (Chap. 3) discusses the rationale of governments for providing support to the creative industries. Why do governments intervene in the market for these goods and services? She considers cultural policy motivations and economic theory to explain this phenomenon. From the perspective of cultural policy, reasons for financially supporting the creative industries include the furtherance of excellence, innovation, and access; recognition and celebration of national, regional, or local identity; promotion of continuity; and furtherance of diversity. These may be defined in economic terms as positive externalities. Reasons from the perspective of economic policy include the contributions of the creative industries to the economy; perceived positive externalities; the desire to redress free rider behavior; the difficulties some creative industries face for increasing productivity when costs increase (Baumol's cost disease; Baumol and Bowen (1966)); and the desire to reduce the negative effects of the cost structure of many creative industries, where there is a combination of high sunk and fixed costs and low marginal costs. Governments predominantly intervene in the market for creative goods and services for cultural reasons, even though these may run counter to economic efficiency at times.

The rationale behind government support for the creative industries thus having been established, Sigrid Hemels (Chap. 4) focuses on one of the instruments used by governments to provide this support: tax incentives. She develops the following definition of tax incentives for the creative industries used in this book:

> A provision in tax legislation that departs from the benchmark tax structure and favors creative industries, resulting in a reduction or postponement of tax income for the government.

Furthermore, she gives an overview of various designs of these incentives and discusses why tax experts are usually not in favor of this policy tool. This book takes the perspective that tax incentives are not necessarily better or worse than other policy instruments, but that the most appropriate instrument should be determined based on both the policy objective and fiscal policy considerations. The OECD (2010) identified several conditions under which tax incentives are most likely to be successful. In addition to these OECD conditions, cultural or creative policy objectives might result in tax incentives being more appropriate than other government tools. That being said, it is acknowledged that tax incentives are not always controlled, accounted for, and evaluated in the same way as direct subsidies and that tax incentives are inferior to direct subsidies in that respect.

As previously mentioned, alongside an economic perspective, this book adopts a legal perspective to understand and analyze tax incentives. Raymond Luja (Chap. 5) provides key building blocks for this analysis. He addresses the question of the extent to which individual states are free to design their tax incentives for the creative industries according to their liking, with a particular focus on the EU. He points out that in today's globalized and digitalized world in which the creative industries operate, several regulatory restrictions influence the design and application of certain tax incentives. These include restrictions imposed by guidelines on harmful tax competition, the fight of several international organizations, including the OECD, against tax evasion and profit shifting, and, in the EU context, the prohibition of state aid. Such regulations restrict the options of governments to provide aid to the creative industries. This is especially the case for tax incentives aimed at the more commercial and international sub-sectors of the creative industries such as the audiovisual industry and copyrights.

However, not only the commercial parts of the creative industries are affected by international rules and regulations. The nonprofit part can also operate on an international scale and has to come to grips with these international provisions. Renate Buijze (Chap. 6) addresses this issue in her discussion of tax incentives that cross borders, taking up the example of tax incentives for charitable giving. She notes that several cultural organizations raise funds abroad and then find themselves confronted with tax barriers, as many countries restrict tax incentives to domestic charities. She provides an overview of current solutions initiated either by governments or private organizations, which help arts organizations to overcome these barriers. Furthermore, she discusses the crucial factors that determine the effectiveness of these solutions.

2.2 Part II: Tax Incentives for Specific Sub-sectors of the Creative Industries

The theoretical part is followed by Part II, which focuses on tax incentives for specific sub-sectors of the creative industries. This part presents insightful examples from various countries to illustrate the application of these tax incentives.

Sigrid Hemels (Chap. 7) discusses tax incentives that can be found in many countries and have been the focus of most researchers in this field, namely, tax incentives for museums and cultural heritage, the nonprofit part of the creative industries. First, she discusses tax incentives for donations, shows that various designs are used, and questions whether the general assumption that the USA has the most generous tax incentives in this respect is correct. Her discussion also includes exemptions for charities, tax incentives for volunteers, the possibility of paying tax with art and heritage objects, wealth tax exemptions for objects given on loan to cultural organizations, and tax incentives for the restoration and maintenance of monuments.

Next, Sigrid Hemels discusses the tax incentives for what is probably the most commercial, international, and powerful part of the creative industries: the audiovisual industry (Chap. 8). She observes that, especially in the Americas and Europe, many countries provide tax incentives for films. Competition to attract this business can be fierce between countries, and even between lower levels of government within federal states such as the USA. She suggests that countries without a big home market can no longer support a film industry without offering incentives. Notwithstanding the fact that economic reasons are very important for introducing these incentives, cultural and political reasons are also prominent, especially when countering the dominance of the USA. Politicians seem to be rather receptive to lobbies advocating such incentives. Hemels discusses these incentives, which are aimed either at producers and investors or at consumers of films, in relation to the specific features of the film industry. Furthermore, she discusses tax incentives for adjacent sectors such as television, videogames, phonographic recordings, and music videos.

Sigrid Hemels then discusses the art market (Chap. 9), which is a sub-sector of the creative industries that, at least in part, has become rather global. Part of the art market is extremely international, competitive, and commercial and part of it is more local in its focus. She points out that several countries apply tax incentives to the sale or acquisition of certain works of art. These incentives can reduce the net and gross prices of art. She notes that important incentives in this respect are reduced VAT and customs levies on works of art. However, the definition of "art" that is applied is rather restrictive and conservative and is, therefore, not always in line with what art experts consider to be art. She gives examples of court cases involving various works of art, including those of Brancusi, Moholy-Nagy, and Viola. She also addresses the incentives that are provided in so called free ports.

Another international and highly mobile part of the creative industries is copyright. Dick Molenaar defines copyright as the legal result of the creative process (Chap. 10). He points out that tax incentives for copyright can be motivated by various reasons such as positive economic effects and support of artists. By giving various examples, he illustrates that incentives can take many different forms, ranging from exemption of artists to special IP boxes and R&D tax deductions. Furthermore, he addresses the measures countries have taken to prevent double taxation of royalty income in cross-border situations, the EU Directive on royalty income, and the limits that are currently being set by the international anti-base erosion and profit shifting project.

Next, Dick Molenaar analyzes tax incentives for artists (Chap. 11). These incentives usually have a national focus. They can take the form of financial support measures for artists with low incomes such as an exemption of artists' income and the possibility of using works of art to pay taxes. Another reason for introducing such incentives is the promotion a country's national culture. In the EU, fundamental freedoms and rules pertaining to state aid must be considered when designing such incentives. Molenaar also covers tax incentives from which artists derive indirect benefits, such as tax incentives aimed at the performing arts.

3 Who Should Read This Book?

As this book combines academic and practical approaches, we believe that it will be of relevance both to researchers and students studying the creative industries, as well as policy makers and readers involved in the creative industries who are seeking an in depth and up to date overview of this alternative way for governments to support the creative industries. The book may be used by policy makers contemplating the introduction of new tax incentives to find best practices and to make arguments against implementing incentives that do not seem to have worked well in other countries. It will also help researchers and students to understand the peculiarities of the design of certain tax incentives and the legal restrictions that countries face when designing tax incentives. Last but not least, we hope this book will inspire further research on this fascinating aspect of the cultural industries.

References

Baumol WJ, Bowen WG (1966) Performing arts: the economic dilemma. The Twentieth Century Fund, New York

Feld AL, O'Hare M, Schuster JMD (1983) Patrons despite themselves: taxpayers and arts policy. New York University Press, New York

Friedman M (1975) There's no such thing as a free lunch. Open Court, La Salle

OECD (2010) Tax expenditures in OECD Countries. OECD, Paris

Schuster JMD (1979) Income taxes and the arts: tax expenditures as cultural policy. Massachusetts Institute of Technology, Cambridge. http://dspace.mit.edu/handle/1721.1/70147#files-area. Accessed 12 July 2016

Schuster JM (2006) Chapter 36: tax incentives in cultural policy. In: Ginsburg VA, Throsby D (eds) Handbook of the economics of art and culture. North-Holland (Elsevier), Amsterdam, pp 1254–1298

Part I
Theoretical Context of Tax Incentives for the Creative Industries

Chapter 2
Defining Creative Industries

Kazuko Goto

Abstract This chapter explores various categorizations and definitions of creative industries and develops a definition for the purposes of this book: to discuss tax incentives governments have implemented for the creative industries and explore their rationale and effects. This definition characterizes creative industries by three features. First, creative industries contain cultural and economic aspects relating to cultural policy goals such as cultural diversity and access to culture, as well as economic policy goals. Second, creative industries are a combination of art, in the narrow sense, and commerce: the combination of a specific form of creativity, cultural content creation, and its delivery. Third, creative industries are defined to include both nonprofit and for-profit organizations.

Keywords Creativity · Creative industry · Cultural industry · Copyright industry · Cultural policy · Cultural diversity · Access · Economic policy · Nonprofit organizations · For-profit organizations

1 Introduction

In 1994, the Office for the Arts of the Australian government used the term cultural industry in the cultural policy document *Creative Nation*. In 1997, the UK Department for Culture Media and Sport (DCMS) used the term creative industries when naming the Creative Industries Task Force and, in 1998, in the *Creative Industries Mapping Documents*. After this, the term gained wide acceptance, although there are still variations in terminology. Besides creative industry, the terms cultural industry and copyright industry are also used. In this book, we will use the term creative industries.

K. Goto (✉)
Faculty of Economics, Setsunan University, Osaka, Japan
e-mail: k-goto@econ.setsunan.ac.jp

© Springer Science+Business Media Singapore 2017
S. Hemels and K. Goto (eds.), *Tax Incentives for the Creative Industries*,
Creative Economy, DOI 10.1007/978-981-287-832-8_2

The meaning given to the term creative industries varies. After the UK DCMS, among others, the United Nations Conference on Trade and Development (UNCTAD), the United Nations Educational, Scientific and Cultural Organization (UNESCO), and World Intellectual Property Organization (WIPO) introduced different definitions and scopes for the creative industries. Despite the fact that these definitions largely overlap, the differences between them make it difficult to make quantitative international comparisons of creative industries. Still, it is meaningful to explore differences in definitions to understand their theoretical background and to come to a useful definition for the purposes of this book.

A common characteristic that appears in all definitions is that, as UNCTAD (2010), p. 23 noted, the creative economy has a multitude of dimensions, and that it contributes to economic, social, cultural and sustainable development goals. This book mainly focuses on economic and cultural aspects of creative industries.

This chapter will discuss several definitions and classifications of the creative industries, including their theoretical and empirical background (Sect. 2). In Sect. 3, the characteristics of the creative industries are analyzed and presented as the building blocks of the definition used in this book.

2 Various Definitions of Creative Industries and Their Background

The definitions, terminology, and classifications used for creative industries are diverse. The differences can often be explained by differences in focus. For example, UNCTAD is interested in world trade, whereas UNESCO is interested in promotion of culture, and WIPO is interested in intellectual property rights. The terminology used often reflects this main focus: UNESCO uses the term cultural industry, whereas WIPO uses copyright industry. Many classifications of cultural goods and creative industries relate to statistical data and aim to give an estimation of the scale of creative industries and their contribution to the economy in terms of, for example, GDP, employment and international trade.

Below we discuss several definitions and classifications which have been developed over the past 30 years.

2.1 UNESCO

Article 4(5) of the 2005 UNESCO Convention on the Protection and Promotion of the Diversity of Cultural Expressions defined cultural industries as industries producing and distributing cultural goods or services. UNESCO deliberately uses the term "cultural" industries, rather than "creative" based on the following (UNESCO 2009, p. 19):

> Many countries have used the term 'creative' to describe these industries, but many industries within a creative 'sector' may not be creative. The definition and measurement of creativity is in itself subject to much debate. Creative industries usually cover a broader scope than traditional artistic domains with the inclusion, for example, of all ICT industries or research and development. The framework addresses this issue by allowing the inclusion of some specific creative industries (design and advertising) as a separate domain.

Article 4(4) of the 2005 UNESCO Convention defined cultural goods and services as those goods and services, which at the time they are considered as a specific attribute, use or purpose, embody or convey cultural expressions, irrespective of the commercial value they may have. Cultural activities may be an end in themselves or they may contribute to the production of cultural goods and services.

In 1986, UNESCO developed a framework for cultural statistics. This framework influenced many countries that were trying to establish cultural statistics. The framework outlined by UNESCO (1986, pp. 6–7) included the following categories:

0. Cultural heritage
1. Printed matter and literature
2. Music
3. Performing arts
4. Visual arts
5. Cinema and photography
6. Radio and television
7. Socio-cultural activities
8. Sports and games
9. Environment and nature

In 2009, UNESCO proposed a new framework for cultural statistics. This framework is based on a hierarchical model comprised of cultural domains and related domains. The cultural and related domains are (UNESCO 2009, p. 24):

A. Cultural and Natural Heritage;
B. Performance and Celebration;
C. Visual Arts and Crafts;
D. Books and Press;
E. Audio-visual and Interactive Media;
F. Design and Creative Services;
G. Tourism (related domain);
H. Sports and recreation (related domain)

Certain domains are regarded as transversal because they can be applied to all of the cultural and related domains. These transversal domains are:

- Intangible Cultural Heritage
- Education and training
- Archiving and preservation
- Equipment and supporting materials.

2.2 Eurostat

In 1997, Eurostat introduced common cultural statistics for the EU. It defined several categories of cultural goods to estimate their import and export. Eurostat (2016), p. 98 gives the following definition of cultural goods:

> 'Cultural goods' are the products of artistic creativity that convey artistic, symbolic and aesthetic values; examples are antiques, works of art, books, newspapers, photos, films and music. The category includes CDs, DVDs and video games and consoles, as media enabling access to cultural content. It also includes musical instruments, which are not cultural goods in themselves, but represent means of artistic expression. 'Cultural goods' exclude products of large scale manufacturing even if they facilitate access to cultural content (e.g. TV sets or CD players).

2.3 UK DCMS

DCMS (1998) defined the purpose of the 1998 UK Creative Industries Mapping Documents as raising awareness of the creative industries, the contribution they make to the economy and the issues they face. DCMS (1998) defined creative industries as those industries that have their origin in individual creativity, skill, and talent, and that have a potential for wealth and job creation through the generation and exploitation of intellectual property. This definition stresses the importance of both cultural aspects (individual creativity, skill, and talent) and economic aspects (intellectual property and economic growth).

Based on this definition DCMS worked closely with stakeholders to determine which occupations and industries should be considered to be creative. Through consultation, the creative occupations were identified. Next, the proportion of creative jobs for each industry was calculated. This was used as a measurement of creative intensity. Industries with creative intensity above a specified threshold were considered creative industries. Under these criteria, the following industries were characterized as creative industries: advertising, architecture, the art and antiques market, crafts, design, designer fashion, film and video, interactive leisure software, music, performing arts, publishing, software and computer services, television and radio.

The creative economy as defined by DCMS includes the contribution of all who are in creative occupations outside the creative industries as well as all who are employed in the creative industries. In this definition, the creative industry is a subset of the creative economy. The creative industry includes only those working in the creative industries themselves and may include both persons in creative occupations or those in other roles such as finance.

2.4 MERCOSUR

MERCOSUR tried to offer practical means to measure the flow of cultural goods in South American countries. As listed by UNCTAD (2010), p. 107, three categories of cultural goods were defined by MERCOSUR:

1. Characteristic goods: typical goods and services from the cultural field that manifest the creation, expression, interpretation, conservation, and transmission of symbolic content (CDs, films, books, etc.)
2. Related goods: interdependent products that serve as inputs and capital for the production of characteristic products (printing paper, video cassettes, microphones, etc.)
3. Auxiliary goods: these goods include marketing, distribution, and related products that enable end users to consume culture (television sets, music players, video projectors, etc.).

These three categories were combined into a matrix with what was regarded as the three core cultural industries: phonographic recordings, publishing, and the audio-visual industry (UNCTAD 2010, pp. 107–108).

2.5 WIPO

Intellectual property and copyright play important roles in the creative industries. Under the DCMS definition of creative industries, intellectual property is a principal source of economic growth and job creation. The UNESCO classification also includes intellectual property as an important cultural service. In 2003, WIPO published the *Guide on Surveying the Economic Contribution of the Copyright-Based Industries*. WIPO (2015), p. 30 defines copyright industries as those industries which function under the protection of copyright and related rights. It defines cultural industries as those industries whose products have culturally significant content which is reproduced on an industrial scale. According to WIPO (2015), p. 30 the term creative industries normally has a wider meaning and includes, besides the copyright and cultural industries, all cultural or artistic production, whether live or produced as an individual unit. WIPO (2015), p. 31

mentions that the terms "cultural" and "creative" industries are often used together, and that the distinction between these two is often very fine.

2.6 UNCTAD

UNCTAD (2008), p. 4 summarized the UNCTAD definition of the creative economy as follows:

> The creative economy is an evolving concept based on creative assets potentially generating economic growth and development. It can foster income generation, job creation and export earnings, while promoting social inclusion, cultural diversity, and human development. It embraces economic, cultural and social aspects interacting with technology, intellectual property, and tourism objectives. It is a set of knowledge-based economic activities with a development dimension and cross-cutting linkages at macro and micro levels to the overall economy. It is a feasible development option calling for innovative multidisciplinary policy responses and inter-ministerial actions. At the heart of the creative economy are the creative industries.

UNCTAD (2008), p. 13 gave the following UNCTAD definition of the creative industries:

The creative industries:

- are the cycles of creation, production and distribution of goods and services that use creativity and intellectual capital as primary inputs;
- constitute a set of knowledge-based activities, focused on but not limited to arts, potentially generating revenues from trade and intellectual property rights;
- comprise tangible products and intangible intellectual or artistic services with creative content, economic value and market objectives;
- are at the cross-road among the artisan, services and industrial sectors; and
- constitute a new dynamic sector in world trade.

The classification of UNCTAD (2010), pp. 106–116 is based on the Harmonized Commodity Description and Coding System (HS) code, which was made to standardize the classification of international trade commodities. The HS code classification for creative goods and services includes various domains and subgroups. For example "heritage" is a domain and "art crafts goods" is a subgroup. This classification includes the following domains and subgroups:

1. Heritage: Art crafts goods, other personal, cultural, and recreational services
2. Arts: Performing arts goods and visual arts goods
3. Media: Publishing goods, audio-visual goods, audio-visuals, and related services
4. Functional creation: Design goods, new media goods, advertising, market research and public opinion services, research and development services, architectural, engineering and other technical services, personal, cultural, and recreational services

UNCTAD (2010), p. 111 points out that the UNESCO classification is better at capturing the experience of countries in the global north, while the UNCTAD classification better reflects opportunities for countries in the global south. The majority of products in the UNCTAD classification falls into the design and arts and crafts categories, as developing countries have higher market shares and more international trade opportunities in these sectors.

3 Definition of Creative Industries Based on Cultural Economics Theory

Taking into account the definitions and classifications discussed in the previous section, this section focuses on the characteristics of the creative industries in order to derive a useful definition of creative industries for the purposes of this book.

3.1 Economic and Cultural Dimensions

Creativity, talent, and skills are sources of creative industries. According to Towse (2011), p. 126 the dominant view is that, rather than wealth driving creativity, future wealth and economic growth relies on creativity and the creative industries. She views creativity as the engine of economic growth.

In the 2005 UNESCO Convention on the Protection and Promotion of the Diversity of Cultural Expressions, cultural diversity is explicitly related to the cultural industries. Article 6(2)(c) of this convention cites measures aimed at providing independent domestic cultural industries and activities in the informal sector effective access to the means of production, dissemination and distribution of cultural activities, goods and services as measures that countries may adopt to protect and promote the diversity of cultural expressions within their territory.

Throsby (2010), p. 16 defined cultural goods as follows:

1. They require some input of human creativity in their production.
2. They are vehicles for symbolic messages to those who consume them. That is, they are more than simply utilitarian, insofar as they serve some larger communicative purpose.
3. They contain, at least potentially, some intellectual property that is attributable to the individual or group producing the good and service.

Creativity and intellectual property can be targets of both cultural and economic policy,[1] while the symbolic meaning relating to identity can be a target of cultural policy.

[1]When we refer to economic policy, this includes industrial policy.

The first characteristic of creative industries is, therefore, that those industries have cultural and economic dimensions.

3.2 Art and Commerce

Creativity as such does not distinguish the creative industries from other industries as most human actions require creativity. For example, inventing new medicines requires a lot of creativity, but the pharmaceutical industry is not regarded as a creative industry. Thus, the link is not so much with creativity as such, but with a specific form of creativity: cultural content creation. According to Towse (2011), p. 127 the economic characteristics of cultural content production makes the creative industry different from other industries.

Caves (2000), pp. 1–2, 10–17 used contract theory and transaction cost economics to analyze the economic organization of the creative industries. He defines the creative industries as a combination of art and commerce. In other words, production of creative goods consists of two distinct aspects, content creation and its delivery. Content creation is the responsibility of the artist and delivery that of the businessperson. However, both aspects are often combined. For example, museums and cultural heritage are a combination of cultural content creation and provision of various goods and services in a competitive market. According to Caves (2000), p. 1, creative industries supply goods and services that are broadly associated with cultural, artistic or entertainment value. They include book and magazine publishing, the visualarts, the performing arts, sound recordings, cinema and TV films, fashion, toys, and games.

Throsby (2010), pp. 91–93 explained the combination of art and commerce in a different way. He proposed a concentric circle model of cultural industries. The core of the concentric circle contains purely creative ideas and activities, whereas the periphery circle contains commercial activities. The model comprises the following four circles:

1. Core creative arts: literature, music, performing arts, visual arts;
2. Other core cultural industries: Film, museums, galleries, libraries, photography;
3. Wider cultural industries: Heritage services, publishing and printed media, sound recording, television and radio, video, and computer games;
4. Related industries: Advertising, architecture, design, fashion.

According to Throsby, the cultural industry combines cultural and industry features. The dual cultural and industrial characteristic of the model is caused by the fact that it distinguishes between the cultural value and the economic value yielded by cultural goods and services.

The second feature of creative industries is, therefore, that creative industries are a combination of art and commerce, in other words, a combination of cultural content creation and its delivery.

3.3 Nonprofit and For-Profit

Cultural activities are conducted by both nonprofit and commercial organizations. In the domain of the arts, many arts organizations are formed as nonprofit organizations. In contrast, many organizations that deliver the content (for example, record companies, book publishers, and cinemas) are for-profit organizations.

Generally, until the 1990s, cultural policy and cultural economics focused on the arts and cultural heritage, i.e., the nonprofit sector. The concept of the creative economy revised some of the central issues in cultural economics. The most important revision was the reconstruction of boundaries between the cultural and non-cultural sectors. Cultural economics did not focus on sectors such as software, design, advertisement, marketing, and services. As Cowen (2011), p. 120 observes, these activities have been integrated with the arts in the narrow sense of the word. Throsby (2010), pp. 2–5 points out that the scope of cultural policy has extended from the arts and heritage to film, television, printed media, fashion, design, architecture, tourism, urban and regional development, international trade and more. He observes a related economic transformation of the economic environment in which cultural goods are produced, distributed, and consumed. This transformation has been caused by globalization and the digital revolution. Together, increased cross border movements of capital and labor, the emergence of a global market, and the internationalization of communication have led to the transmission of cultural symbols and messages around the world. Consequently, the creative industries both include the nonprofit arts and cultural heritage, which are targets of traditional cultural policies, and more commercial activities, including the audio-visual industry and the art market.

Therefore, the third feature of creative industries is that those industries contain both nonprofit and for-profit organizations.

4 Conclusion

Creativity, as such, does not distinguish the creative industries from other industries. It is a specific form of creativity, cultural content creation, that makes the creative industries different. Towse (2011), p. 125 notes that the creative industries combine the creative and performing arts with cultural industries, which variously include advertising, architecture, the art and antiques market, crafts, design, fashion, film, games, heritage services, museums, libraries, Internet, publishing, software, television, radio, and video.

Various definitions and classifications of the creative industries exist. This book does not follow a specific classification or definition of creative industries. Instead, creative industries are defined in this book by the following three characteristics:

1. Creative industries have cultural and economic aspects relating to cultural policy goals such as cultural diversity and access to culture, as well as economic policy goals.
2. Creative industries are a combination of art, in the narrow sense, and commerce, i.e., a combination of cultural content creation and its delivery.
3. Creative industries contain both nonprofit and for-profit organizations.

References

Baumol WJ (2011) Application of welfare economics. In: Towse R (ed) A handbook of cultural economics, 2nd edn. Edward Elgar, Cheltenham

Caves R (2000) Creative industries, contract between art and commerce. Harvard University Press, Cambridge

Cowen T (2011) Creative economy. In: Towse R (ed) A handbook of cultural economics, 2nd edn. Edward Elgar, Cheltenham

DCMS (1998) Creative industries mapping documents 1998. https://www.gov.uk/government/publications/creative-industries-mapping-documents-1998. Accessed 6 Sep 2016

DCMS (2001) Creative industries mapping documents 2001. https://www.gov.uk/government/publications/creative-industries-mapping-documents-2001. Accessed 6 Sep 2016

Eurostat (2016) Culture statistics. Publications Office of the European Union, Luxembourg. http://ec.europa.eu/eurostat/documents/3217494/7551543/KS-04-15-737-EN-N.pdf/648072f3-63c4-47d8-905a-6fdc742b8605. Accessed 29 Sep 2016

Office for the Arts (1994) Creative nation: commonwealth cultural policy. http://apo.org.au/node/29704. Accessed 6 Sep 2016

Throsby D (2010) The economics of cultural policy. Cambridge University Press, Cambridge

Towse R (2011) Creative industries. In: Towse R (ed) A handbook of cultural economics, 2nd edn. Edward Elgar, Cheltenham

UNCTAD (2008) Creative economy report 2008. http://unctad.org/en/docs/ditc20082cer_en.pdf. Accessed 17 Sep 2016

UNCTAD (2010) Creative economy report 2010. http://unctad.org/en/Docs/ditctab20103_en.pdf. Accessed 17 Sep 2016

UNESCO (1986) The UNESCO framework for cultural statistics. Statistical commission and economic commission for Europe, UNESCO, conference of European statisticians. Third joint meeting on cultural statistics, 17–20 March 1986. CES/AC/44/11. 13 February 1986. http://www.uis.unesco.org/culture/Documents/unesco-fcs-1986-en.pdf. Accessed 29 Sep 2016

UNESCO (2009) UNESCO framework for cultural statistics, UNESCO, Institute for Statistics, Montreal. http://www.uis.unesco.org/culture/Documents/framework-cultural-statistics-culture-2009-en.pdf. Accessed 29 Sep 2016

WIPO (2003) Guide on surveying the economic contribution of the copyright-based industries. WIPO Geneva

WIPO (2015) Guide on surveying the economic contribution of the copyright-based industries. WIPO Geneva http://www.wipo.int/edocs/pubdocs/en/copyright/893/wipo_pub_893.pdf. Accessed 29 Sep 2016

Chapter 3
Why Do Governments Financially Support the Creative Industries?

Kazuko Goto

Abstract This chapter discusses the reasons why governments financially support the creative industries, both from the point of view of cultural policy and economic theory. Cultural policy reasons for financial support of the creative industries include the furtherance of excellence, innovation, and access; recognition and celebration of national, regional, or local identity; promotion of continuity; and furtherance of diversity. Economic policy reasons include the contribution of the creative industries to the economy; perceived positive externalities; the desire to redress free rider behavior; the difficulties some creative industries face for increasing productivity when costs increase; and the desire to reduce the negative effects of the cost structure of many creative industries, where there is a combination of high sunk and fixed costs and low marginal costs.

Keywords Cultural policy · Economic policy · Innovation · Identity · Diversity · Market failures · Externalities · Free rider behavior · Public goods · Impure public goods · Baumol's cost disease · Sunk costs · Fixed costs · Marginal costs · Economies of scale

1 Introduction

In an optimally efficient market, the price mechanism ensures that resources are perfectly allocated, resulting in an optimal balance between demand and supply. However, in most societies the market outcome is not regarded as being the most optimal outcome in all sectors of the economy. This is caused by so called market failures: situations in which the allocation of goods and services is not efficient. A reason for such market failure can be that benefits or drawbacks for society are not taken into account. If the competitive market equilibrium does not lead to an

K. Goto (✉)
Faculty of Economics, Setsunan University, Neyagawa, Osaka, Japan
e-mail: k-goto@econ.setsunan.ac.jp

© Springer Science+Business Media Singapore 2017
S. Hemels and K. Goto (eds.), *Tax Incentives for the Creative Industries*,
Creative Economy, DOI 10.1007/978-981-287-832-8_3

efficiency maximizing outcome, a government may decide to intervene in the market to redress market failures and to increase efficiency.

Furthermore, an efficient market outcome, might, in the view of a government, not be a desirable outcome. Perceived distributional problems can also be a reason for government intervention in a market. For example, the distribution of resources among economic actors under the market outcome may be perceived as unfair. In order to correct this, governments can decide to implement policies to redistribute income and wealth. For example, one might be of the opinion that the market outcome results in too little income for the majority of artists. Also, a government might believe that an efficient market outcome is not the most desired outcome in terms of diversity of products and goods, and thus have a political reason to intervene.

In Chap. 2 it was discussed that one of the features of creative industries is that they have cultural and economic aspects and are a target of both cultural and economic policy. Not surprisingly, the reasons governments use to justify intervention in the market for the creative industries can also be characterized as cultural policy reasons and economic policy reasons, or a combination of both. The latter is the result of cultural policy having expanded from the arts and cultural heritage to a broader spectrum of cultural and creative industries, including commercial activities.

This chapter focuses on the reasons governments may have to financially support the creative industries. Section 2 discusses the cultural policy reasons and Sect. 3 outlines the economic policy reasons. Section 4 briefly draws attention to the interplay between cultural and economic policy goals before this chapter is concluded in Sect. 5.

2 Cultural Policy Reasons for Interference

Throsby (2010), pp. 42–45 distinguishes the following cultural policy objectives:

1. Furtherance of excellence, innovation, and access;
2. Recognition and celebration of national, regional, or local identity;
3. Promotion of continuity; and
4. Furtherance of diversity.

Throsby (2010), p. 173 observes a shift in the emphasis which is put on these policy goals since the Second World War. During the 1950s and 1960s, cultural policy was mostly concerned with the production and consumption of the arts: the furtherance of excellence, innovation and access. During the Cold War, culture was interpreted as identity. Incentives for films produced in the domestic language and cultural heritage policy can be explained by this policy objective. From the 1970s to the 1990s, culture and development were linked. Education was believed to ensure continuity of knowledge and skills from one generation to the next. Furthermore, cultural heritage was regarded as a bequest to the next generation. In the most recent phase, cultural diversity that embraces democracy and human rights was added to cultural policy objectives.

These cultural policy objectives are also used by governments as a reason to intervene in the market for products of the creative industries.

3 Economic Policy Reasons for Interference

This section analyzes the economic policy reasons for government support of the creative industry. Governments emphasize the contribution of the creative industries to the economy and rationalize their interventions in the market of the creative industries by the need to address various market failures which are discussed below.

3.1 Contribution of the Creative Industries to the Economy

In many advanced economies, the creative economy is regarded as being important for generating economic growth, employment, innovation, and trade. Throsby (2010), pp. 93–95 points out that there are various ways to estimate the economic contribution of creative industries. One is to use macro statistics to estimate the gross value of production, value added, fixed capital formation, employment, exports, and so on. Throsby warns that these statistics can be misused if the aim is simply to substantiate the economic impact of creative industries to promote policy interventions. The second way Throsby (2010), p. 94 distinguishes is to use standard methods of industrial organization theory. The traditional approach is to evaluate the structure, conduct, and performance characteristics of industries. Caves (2000) applied this approach. The third alternative is an input-output analysis to analyze inter-industrial relationships. Various goods and services are bought and sold between sectors of the creative industries and between creative industries and other industries. Furthermore, individuals switch between working in the creative industries and in other industries. Another important link between industries is the transfer of knowledge. Throsby (2010), pp. 95–97 gives as an example that the creative industries, especially those built around new digital technologies, are a significant source of innovation. Creative ideas and knowledge are transferred from creative businesses to firms in other industries. Input–output analysis can depict the ways in which output is produced and distributed in the economy and can capture the direct, indirect, and induced effects of external stimuli. Unfortunately, the availability of data is a constraint for an input-output analysis of the cultural sector.

Notwithstanding the difficulties in estimating the contribution of the creative industries for the economy, several attempts to quantify the creative industry have been made. Even though one has to be cautious when interpreting the figures, these data at least give some idea about the size and growth of the creative industries.

UNCTAD (2008), pp. 4–5 estimated that from 2000 to 2005 international trade in creative goods and services increased at an annual rate of 8.7%. The value of world export of creative products reached $424 billion in 2005. UNCTAD (2010), p. 128 stated that in 2008, total exports of all creative industry products reached $592 billion, with an annual growth rate of 14% since 2002. The value of creative services exports rose from $62 billion to $185 billion, growing annually by 17% from 2002 to 2008. UNCTAD (2010), p. 28 stated that in OECD countries the creative industries have grown at an annual rate of more than twice that of the service industries overall and more than four times that of manufacturing. While these results are compelling, it must be mentioned that UNCTAD used a very broad definition of the creative industries in this comparison.

China headed the UNCTAD (2010), p. 132 list of the world's 20 leading exporters of creative goods in 2002 and 2008. The USA, Germany, Italy, the UK, France, and the Netherlands were close to the top. UNCTAD (2010), pp. 28–29 estimated that the creative industries contributed around 2.6% of the total GDP of the EU, providing jobs to around 5 million people.

In the UK, DCMS periodically publishes the Creative Industries Economic Estimates. These are official statistics used to measure the direct economic contribution of the creative industries to the UK economy. DCMS (2016), pp. 5–6 reports the following key findings on the role of the creative industries in the UK economy.[1] The gross value added of the creative industries was £84.1 billion in 2014 and accounted for 5.2% of the UK economy. The broader creative economy was worth £133.3 billion in 2014, accounting for 8.2% of the UK economy. The creative industries increased by 8.9% between 2013 and 2014, whereas overall growth in the UK economy was 4.6%. Between 1997 and 2014, the gross value added of the creative industries increased by 6% each year, compared to 4.3% for the UK economy overall. The creative economy as a whole grew by 25% between 2011 and 2014, at a rate faster than for the total UK economy, which grew 12.1% over this period. This rise has primarily been led by the growth of the creative industries. The number of jobs in the creative industries (both creative and support jobs), increased by 5.5% between 2013 and 2014 to 1.8 million jobs. Total employment in the creative economy across the UK increased by 5% between 2013 and 2014 to 2.8 million jobs, compared with a 2.1% increase in the total number of jobs in the wider UK economy over the same period. The value of services exported by the UK creative industries in 2013 was £17.9 billion, a 3.5% increase compared with 2012. Exports of services from the creative industries accounted for 8.7% of total exports of services for the UK in 2013.

These figures give an idea of the economic potential and scale of the creative economy. Several governments see the role of creative industries in the economy and have decided to support them. It is important for governments to have an estimate of the contribution of creative industries to their economy when making

[1]Please refer to Sect. 2.3 of Chap. 2 for the UK definitions of creative industry and creative economy.

policy decisions. To rationalize government support, direct, indirect, and induced economic impacts are brought forward. However, it has to be questioned whether similar economic impacts would have occurred anyway if governments had supported other fields instead of the creative industries. Besides, economic impacts are often estimated without accounting for the costs of supportive policies. Notwithstanding the fact that economic impact should be regarded carefully, it cannot be denied that governments use this argument to justify their support of the creative industries.

3.2 *Positive Externalities*

The classic example of market failures (i.e., problems that cause a market to deliver an outcome that does not maximize efficiency) are externalities. An externality occurs whenever the actions of one party make another party worse or better off, yet the first party neither bears the costs nor receives the benefits of doing so. Externalities can arise either from the production of goods or from their consumption. Externalities can be negative (pollution, for example) or positive (for example, maintenance of a monument by its owner). Externalities present a classic justification for government intervention. When one party's actions affect another party and the first party is not fully compensated by the other for this effect, then the market has failed and government intervention is potentially justified.

A government can not only take into account costs and benefits of individual actors in the economy, but also the costs and benefits of other actors. In other words: government can ensure that positive or negative externalities are taken into account. A government may regard the demand or the supply of certain goods that results from the market mechanism as being too low or too high. A government may choose to address such a market failure by implementing policies to encourage the consumption or production of goods with perceived positive externalities (merit goods) and discourage those with negative externalities (demerit goods).

The rationale for public support for the arts has been discussed in cultural economics for a long time. Baumol (2011), pp. 9–11 summarizes several arguments which have been brought forward to rationalize this support: equal opportunities to enjoy the arts, ensuring output diversity, the external benefit of education, public good properties of cultural products, the infant stage of cultural organizations, the merit character of cultural products, and the need to invest for future generations.

There is much debate on positive externalities in relation to the creative industries. Baumol (2011), pp. 10–11 mentions that the externalities of artistic activities are not entirely clear. He observes that the claim that persons with interests in the arts are generally "better" members of society is not easy to prove or even to make explicit. He dismisses the notion that new art enterprises and artists merit public assistance because society benefits from such aid in the long run as an ancient argument, which has elicited much skepticism from economists. Furthermore, he compares the claim that even if a society does not value the arts sufficiently for itself it may want to do so for future generations, to the King of Naples who supported the opera on condition that he never be asked to attend. Baumol also mentions the merit good argument that the arts deserve public support simply because they are worthy. This resembles the title of a Dutch 1990's television program, which is difficult to translate in English: "Art… because it is obligatory" (*Kunst… omdat het moet*). According to Baumol (2011), p. 11 economists generally seem to feel that none of these arguments constitute an overwhelming case for extensive support of the arts, the basic objection being that while cultural activity offers benefits, other human activities do as well.

Arguments regarding positive externalities of art and culture regularly have paternalistic characteristics and are closely linked to cultural policy objectives. As these arguments are influential in the political debate, they have to be taken into account as explanations for the phenomenon of government support to the arts, even though these political arguments may not always be sound from a theoretical point of view.

The impact of creative industries on other sectors in the economy is also used as an argument to support these industries. For example, audiences who visit museums and theaters may also visit surrounding hotels, restaurants and cafés. These businesses enjoy positive externalities of museums and theaters for free, but museums and theatres cannot charge surrounding businesses for these benefits. Furthermore, additional demand for the products of creative industries can induce additional supply in creative industries and other industries. This is called the multiplier effect of creative industries. Also, through mobility of the creative workforce and knowledge transfer, other industries can develop new ideas and may improve productivity. Furthermore, creative industries are expected to promote the national image and national brand to attract tourism and increase exports. These may all be reasons governments use to stimulate the growth of the creative industries.

3.3 Redress Free Rider Behavior

For public goods,[2] the price mechanism does not function optimally. This is caused by two specific characteristics of public goods. First of all, these goods are non-excludable. This means that individuals who do not pay for the good cannot be excluded from the enjoyment of the good. Second, public goods are non-rival. This means that the consumption of the good by one individual does not reduce the possibility of others to consume the good. The reason that the price mechanism does not work well for public goods is that because of non-excludability, even without paying for these goods, individuals can enjoy them. This makes individuals reluctant to pay for these goods. This is called the free rider problem: when an investment has a personal cost but a common benefit, individuals will underinvest.

---

[2]An alternative term for public goods is collective goods. In this book we will use the term public goods.

By intervening in the market by providing subsidies or commissions to producers of public goods or by producing these goods themselves, governments can oblige individuals to pay for these goods through general taxes, which allows governments to make sure these goods are produced and paid for.

Classic examples of such public goods are dams, dikes and national defense. However, pure public goods are rare because there are few goods that are both non-excludable and non-rival. Often, enjoyment of a good is harmed if too many people want to enjoy it. For example, if too many people want to see a Rembrandt exhibition, not everybody can be admitted to the museum to enjoy the paintings. Similarly, quite often it is possible to exclude individuals from the enjoyment of a good. For example, the enjoyment of world heritage in Venice and the canals in the city center of Amsterdam can be priced individually by erecting gates and ticket offices at the borders of these cities.

However, the costs to exclude people from the enjoyment of the good might be very high. Such goods, might, therefore, not qualify as pure public goods, but do meet the definition of an impure public good. Impure public goods satisfy the two characteristics of public goods to some extent but not fully. Many products from the non-profit side of the cultural industries meet this definition of impure public goods, which may give governments a justification to intervene in these markets to make sure free rider behavior will not lead to underinvestment in these products.

3.4 Difficulty to Increase Productivity When Costs Increase

Cultural economics theory provides one of the rationales for government support of arts organizations, namely that when they are faced with ever increasing costs, it is difficult for these organizations to increase their productivity because technological innovation does not play a major role in improving productivity in these sectors. For example, you need as many actors and as much time for a performance of a Shakespeare play now as in Shakespeare's time. This analysis of the productivity lag was first made by Baumol and Bowen (1966) and has become known under the name "Baumol's cost disease." They observed that costs in the live performing arts increase relative to costs in the economy as a whole because of general wage increases even though productivity improvements in the arts lag behind. As a result, costs per unit of output in the live performing arts increase.

Caves (2000), p. 242 observed that after World War II orchestras regularly faced deficits which were caused by increasing costs. Orchestras and theaters found it hard to improve their productivity because these are labor-intensive industries, whereas, for example, manufacturing industries such as the automobile industry can improve their productivity through technological innovation. This productivity gap between cultural activities and other industries makes art organizations inefficient and leads to operating losses and deficits. For this reason and in order to meet cultural policy objects, governments may intervene in these markets to make sure that, despite commercial deficits, the products will still be produced.

Baumol (2013), pp. 20–25 explored whether or not this cost disease is cured in the digital economy. He found that it is not. In any economy, the productivity growth rate of labor intensive activities, such as police protection, health care, or the performing arts will be lower than average. It is difficult to reduce the time and effort devoted to these activities without damaging their quality.

Caves (2000), pp. 255–260 points out various ways of mitigating the effect of the cost disease in the performing arts. One strategy is a long-run approach to increase economies of scale through longer seasons. For example, by the late 1920s, the average play ran 70 performances, whereas by the 1960s, the average run had increased to 150 plays. A second adjustment is the selection of plays: producers select those plays most likely to attract an audience and succeed. Caves found that in the 20th century the average run length for hits increased by 37%, whereas the average run length of flops increased by only 18%. Even though producers have little ability to predict success, flops are typically identified early in the run and closed down. Risks could further be reduced by selling successful Broadway scripts to Hollywood and thus offsetting losses on theatre productions with income from film rights.

These examples suggest that the cost disease in cultural activities can be overcome by various commercial activities such as longer runs of selected hits and the production of blockbusters. However, these strategies may result in less supply of experimental productions and art that is perceived as being more difficult and less likely to become a commercial success. If such productions are not produced anymore or only to a much smaller extend, this might result in a reduction in the diversity of the supply of the performing arts. Governments might deem this an undesirable result and along with other cultural policy reasons may decide to intervene in these markets.

3.5 High Fixed and Sunk Costs

Shapiro and Varian (1998) characterize the creative industries as having high fixed and sunk costs. Fixed costs are costs that do not change with an increase or decrease in the amount of goods or services produced. Sunk costs are costs that have already been incurred and cannot be recovered when an activity is withdrawn. Examples of sunk costs are transportation and advertisement costs for an exhibition that is cancelled. All sunk costs are fixed, although not all fixed costs are necessarily sunk: for example, showcases that are not used for a cancelled exhibition may be sold, in which way these fixed costs can be (partly) recovered.

Many of the costs incurred in creative activities are both fixed and sunk. It does not matter whether 10 people or 1,000 people attend an orchestra performance, the wage costs for the members of the orchestra remain the same: they are fixed and, if the orchestra members have tenure, sunk. If fixed and sunk costs are high, the average cost of production can be decreased by increasing the scale of production. The costs of the orchestra performance per member of the public decreases when the number of attendees increases: the efficiency of goods with high fixed costs is much higher if it is used by many, rather than by few people. Fixed costs thus induce economies of scale. A producer who is able to cover the fixed costs and enters the market first, takes advantage of the economies of scale and can make the barrier of new entry high. Towse (2010), p. 386 points out that, in general, the larger the enterprise, the greater its investment in physical and human capital assets. This makes it more difficult for a competitor to enter the market. This problem is increased by the fact that one never knows whether entering a market will prove to be successful and whether the fixed costs can be recovered. Nobody can predict the success of creative products. A few will win and get a massive reward, but the majority will fail as is illustrated in the music industry where there are a few superstars and many struggling artists. Small differences in talent are magnified in large earnings differences.

These characteristics of the creative industries induce monopolies or oligopolies: only one or a few producers dominate the market. Examples of such industries are new media industries, where consumers are attracted to the bigger networks such as Facebook and are reluctant to leave such established networks for newcomers as less people are involved in new social media. This dynamic produces a "winner-take-all" effect. Thus, high fixed and sunk costs can be a barrier to market entry. In economic theory, a competitive market increases efficiency and incentivizes innovation. This might be a reason for a government to intervene in creative industries and mitigate the problem of high fixed and sunk costs. This can be done through regulation, such as anti-trust legislation, which is not the focus of this book, or through financial interventions.

Furthermore, a government may be of the opinion that the monopolies and oligopolies that result from high fixed costs adversely affect diversity. A government may also believe that high fixed costs lead to a focus on quantity, such as the number of visitors, instead of on quality. In short, the effects of high fixed costs may adversely affect cultural policy objects and can thus induce governments to support the creative industries.

3.6 Low Marginal Costs

In addition to high fixed and sunk costs, Shapiro and Varian (1998) observed that creative industries are characterized by very low or even zero marginal costs. Marginal costs reflect the change in total costs resulting from the production of one additional unit. A good example is the market for reproductions of creative works such as books, photos and audiovisual products. Technology has made the marginal costs of reproducing or copying such creative goods almost zero. This might induce free riding and makes it difficult for a producer to get a price that enables him to recover the sunk costs. This can be a reason for governments to intervene in these markets. In many cases, such interventions are done through regulation such as the introduction and protection of copyrights or intellectual property rights such as patents. This kind of government intervention is not the focus of this book. However, governments can also intervene with financial incentives to redress this problem, for example, through a price subsidy for each product sold, such as a reduced VAT rate.

4 Interplay Between Cultural and Economic Policy Goals

In the creative industries, economic policy and cultural policy come together. In the introduction of the Australian Creative Nation publication, Office for the Arts (1994) explicitly linked cultural policy to economic policy:

> This cultural policy is also an economic policy. Culture creates wealth. Broadly defined, our cultural industries generate 13 billion dollars a year. Culture employs. Around 336,000 Australians are employed in culture-related industries. Culture adds value, it makes an essential contribution to innovation, marketing and design. It is a badge of our industry. The level of our creativity substantially determines our ability to adapt to new economic imperatives. It is a valuable export in itself and an essential accompaniment to the export of other commodities. It attracts tourists and students. It is essential to our economic success.

However, sometimes economic policy goals and cultural policy goals can be in conflict. For example, from an economic point of view free trade of cultural products may be promoted, whereas from a cultural point of view a country might prefer protectionism to ensure cultural diversity within that country. Throsby (2010), pp. 158–160 mentions that in relation to the GATT, more specifically as regards audiovisual products such as films, it was debated whether cultural goods should be treated as commercial merchandise or whether it should be taken into account that these goods convey cultural messages and are essential for the national identity, which would justify a cultural exception. From an economic point of view, this cultural exception would lead to market distortion and economic inefficiencies.

In fact, in this respect even cultural policy objects may conflict. Those who support a cultural exception insist that having a wide range of domestically produced cultural products is important for cultural diversity. In contrast, those who are against cultural exceptions stress that imports promote cultural diversity of goods and services.

It will not always be possible to reconcile these conflicting policy objects. In such cases a political decision must be made, which might result in a reduction in economic efficiency to increase, for example, cultural diversity.

5 Conclusion

Cultural policy generally aims to stimulate artistic excellence, innovation, access, identity, and diversity. Economic policy generally aims to redress market failures and to stimulate economic growth, employment, innovation, and trade. Both policy objects provide reasons for governmental support to the creative industries. At times, these policy aims conflict as in the case of cultural diversity and free trade. However, the reasons for government support are often aligned, especially given that cultural policy reasons often provide the underlying rationale to redress a market failure. In this regard it has to be noted that not all government interventions can be rationalized on the basis of economic theory. In the end, it is a political decision to support the creative industries.

References

Baumol WJ, Bowen WG (1966) Performing arts: the economic dilemma. The Twentieth Century Fund, New York

Baumol WJ (2011) Application of welfare economics. In: Towse R (ed) A handbook of cultural economics, 2nd edn. Edward Elgar, Cheltenham, pp 9–18

Baumol WJ (2013) Reining in those unstoppably rising cost. In: Towse R, Handke C (eds) Handbook on the digital creative economy. Edward Elgar, Cheltenham, pp 20–25

Caves RE (2000) Creative industries: contracts between art and commerce. Harvard University Press, Cambridge

DCMS (2016) Creative Industries Economic Estimates. https://www.gov.uk/government/uploads/system/uploads/attachment_data/file/523024/Creative_Industries_Economic_Estimates_January_2016_Updated_201605.pdf. Accessed 17 Sept 2016

Office for the Arts (1994) Creative nation: Commonwealth cultural policy. http://apo.org.au/node/29704. Accessed 6 Sept 2016

Shapiro C, Varian Hal R (1998) Information rules, a strategy guide to the network economy. Harvard Business School Press, Boston

Throsby D (2010) The economics of cultural policy. Cambridge University Press, Cambridge

Towse R (2010) A text book of cultural economics. Cambridge University Press, Cambridge

UNCTAD (2008) Creative economy report 2008. http://unctad.org/en/docs/ditc20082cer_en.pdf. Accessed 17 Sept 2016

UNCTAD (2010) Creative economy report 2010. http://unctad.org/en/Docs/ditctab20103_en.pdf. Accessed 17 Sept 2016

Chapter 4
Tax Incentives as a Creative Industries Policy Instrument

Sigrid Hemels

Abstract The primary function of tax legislation is to raise a budget for government expenditure. Tax incentives can also be used to achieve creative industries policy goals. This book defines tax incentives as a provision in tax legislation that departs from the benchmark tax structure and favors creative industries, resulting in a reduction or postponement of tax income for the government. Tax incentives must be considered relative to alternative policy tools such as spending programs, regulations and information campaigns. Many tax experts are not in favor of tax incentives. Some of their arguments apply to direct subsidies as well, but others are more specific to tax incentives. Even though tax incentives are not without fault, the OECD has formulated conditions for successful tax incentives. Not only fiscal policy arguments but also creative industries policy objectives are of importance when deciding on the most appropriate instrument. From the latter perspective, tax incentives have several benefits. A prerequisite for the effective and efficient use of tax incentives is that they are accounted for, controlled and evaluated in the same way as direct subsidies. As this is currently not always the case, tax incentives are, in that respect, inferior to direct subsidies.

Keywords Bench mark tax structure · Exemption · Allowance · Credit · Rate relief · Tax deferral · Fairness · Complexity · Tax expenditure budget · Sunset legislation

---

S. Hemels (✉)
Department of Tax Law, Erasmus School of Law,
Erasmus University Rotterdam, Rotterdam, The Netherlands
e-mail: hemels@law.eur.nl

S. Hemels
Allen & Overy, Amsterdam, The Netherlands

© Springer Science+Business Media Singapore 2017

S. Hemels and K. Goto (eds.), *Tax Incentives for the Creative Industries*,
Creative Economy, DOI 10.1007/978-981-287-832-8_4

1 Introduction

As was discussed in Chap. 3, governments can have various policy reasons to interfere in the markets for the creative industries. Governments can apply several instruments to achieve policy goals, including policy goals in the field of the creative industries. Such instruments include:

1. Legislation, for example the requirement of a permit or certain qualifications to practice in a given field in the creative industries;
2. Information campaigns and nudging, for example, a Danish Design campaign to promote the consumption of Danish design;
3. Fines or levies: for example a fine for pornographic movies or a high import duty or sales tax rate for such films.
4. Subsidies:
   - Direct subsidies, guarantees and loans, for example, government grants for artists and guarantees or cheap loans for creative startups;
   - Tax incentives, for example, a tax deduction for film producers.

In this book, we focus on the instrument of tax incentives. This concept is discussed in this chapter as it relates to creative industries policy. I start with a discussion of the terminology and the definition of the concept of tax incentives (Sect. 2). Next, the possible forms of tax incentives are analyzed (Sect. 3). It is observed that by definition the calculation of the costs of tax incentives is an estimate (Sect. 4). The reasons why tax experts are usually not in favor of tax incentives are analyzed (Sect. 5) followed by the OECD conditions for successful tax incentives (Sect. 6). However, not only the fiscal policy perspective should be taken into account; creative policy objectives might make a tax incentive a more suitable instrument than a direct subsidy (Sect. 7). Subsequently, I discuss how to determine whether to introduce a tax incentive or a direct subsidy (Sect. 8) and then come to a conclusion (Sect. 9).

2 Terminology and Definition

The primary function of tax legislation is to raise a budget for government expenditure. However, tax legislation can also be used to achieve certain policy goals. This is the secondary or ancillary function of tax legislation. Tax legislation can, for example, be used to discourage the consumption of certain goods or services by imposing a higher tax on them. Tax legislation can also be used to give rewards for desired behavior: a tax incentive. In such cases, a tax provision functions as an alternative for a direct government subsidy. The tax incentive concept was developed in recognition of the fact the tax system can be used to achieve similar goals to public spending programs (Whitehouse 1999, p. 28). Various terms have been used for this concept (Sect. 2.1). The definition of the concept was developed between the late 1960s and the end of the 1980s (Sect. 2.2). The most controversial part of the definition is the benchmark that should be used to distinguish a tax incentive from other provisions (Sect. 2.3).

2.1 *Terminology*

According to Surrey (1973), p. vii he was the first to use the term 'tax expenditures' in 1967, when he was Assistant Secretary of the Treasury for Tax Policy of the USA. Surrey used this terminology to express the fact that direct subsidies and tax incentives are two sides of the same coin. The term 'tax expenditure' highlights the similarity with direct expenditures. For government, a tax expenditure is a loss in revenue (OECD 2010, p. 12) that reduces the government budget in a similar way as direct expenditures. The term 'tax expenditure' is especially useful when studying these provisions in the context of the government budget, government expenses and the link with the budgetary function of taxation. Synonyms such as 'tax incentive', 'tax concession', 'tax relief', 'tax aid', 'tax break', 'fiscal incentive', 'indirect subsidy' and 'tax subsidy' express the connection with direct subsidies. This wording is useful when the focus of the analysis is on the beneficiary, the objective of the tax provision and the ancillary function of taxation. However, the meaning of the terms is the same, and various authors use different terms. In this book, we will primarily use 'tax incentive', as our focus is on the use of tax provisions to achieve policy goals in the field of the creative industries.

2.2 *Definition*

The definition of a tax incentive has evolved, especially in the 1970s and 1980s. Surrey and Sunley (1976), pp. 16–17 formulated a definition that was primarily aimed at the income tax:

> A special item in the income tax - such as a special exclusion or exemption - that represents a deliberate departure from accepted concepts of net income and the regular rate structure in order to affect the private sector in a way that is often accomplished by direct expenditures.

Later this definition was generalized, for example by Willis and Hardwick (1978), p. 1:

> A tax expenditure is an exemption or relief which is not part of the essential structure of the tax in question but has been introduced into the tax code for some extraneous reason.

and the Committee on Fiscal Affairs of the OECD (1984), p. 7:

> A departure from the generally accepted or benchmark tax structure which produces a favorable tax treatment of particular types of activities or groups of taxpayers.

In 1976, the Dutch Ministry of Finance decided to appoint a committee to study tax expenditures, which committee published its report in 1987 (Ministerie van Financiën 1987, p. 11) and gave a definition of tax incentives that is still used by the Ministry:

> A tax incentive is a government expenditure constituted by a loss or deferral of tax income which results from a provision in the tax legislation insofar as this provision is not in accordance with the primary structure of the law.

The OECD (2010), p. 12 uses the definition by Anderson (2008), slide 4:

> Provisions of tax law, regulation or practices that reduce or postpone revenue for a comparatively narrow population of tax payers relative to a benchmark tax.

In these later definitions, the relationship with direct expenditures is omitted. Kraan (2004), p. 130 still includes a reference to direct expenditures:

> A tax expenditure can be defined as a transfer of public resources that is achieved by reducing tax obligations with respect to a benchmark tax, rather than by a direct expenditure.

I prefer definitions that omit the link with direct subsidies, as the possible existence of a counterpart in the form of a direct subsidy is not an essential characteristic of a tax incentive. A provision can be a tax incentive even if the policy objective is not often accomplished by direct expenditures.

From these definitions the following major elements can be deduced to define tax incentives for the creative industries:

1. a provision in tax legislation, regulation or practice;
2. a reduction or postponement of tax income for the government;
3. a favorable tax treatment of creative industries activities or groups of taxpayers consuming, producing or favoring the creative industries;
4. a departure from the benchmark structure of the tax legislation.

These four elements can be joined in the following definition of tax incentives for the creative industries that we will use in this book:

> A provision in tax legislation that departs from the benchmark tax structure and favors creative industries, resulting in a reduction or postponement of tax income for the government.

These four elements are used in this book to decide whether a provision is a tax incentive for the creative industries. The first element is rather straightforward, as it is a formal criterion: is the measure included in tax legislation, tax regulation or tax practices. Direct subsidies, such as measures included in other legislation, regulations and practices other than taxes, are beyond the scope of this book. The second element is also not too difficult to assess, as it usually follows from the design of a provision whether it increases or decreases the government budget, or has a neutral effect. Because of this criterion, tax provisions that discourage certain behavior and can, therefore, lead to an increase of government tax income are outside the scope of this book. To establish whether the third element is met, the definition of creative industries is crucial. In this book we use the definition developed in Chap. 2. The last element is most problematic as it requires a normative definition of the benchmark from which the incentive deviates. As we will see in the next paragraph, some tax measures may not be readily classified as part of the benchmark or as an exception to it (Whitehouse 1999, p. 29).

2.3 Benchmark

In discussions regarding the definition of tax incentives, the biggest issue is defining the benchmark or basic tax structure from which the incentive is a deviation. Structural elements of a tax system should not be recorded as tax expenditures, whereas programmatic features should be (OECD 2010, p. 12). Kraan (2004), p. 131 describes the identification of tax expenditures as a classification exercise: dividing the provisions of the tax laws into a benchmark tax and a series of deviations from that benchmark tax.

Stevers (1978), p. 35 pointed out that the debate about what is and what is not part of the benchmark is often caused by the implicit idea that tax incentives should be abolished and, if necessary, replaced with direct subsidies. This makes the definition of the benchmark, at least in part, a political issue. For example, in the USA, some writers have argued that the deduction of gifts is not a tax incentive on the grounds that an item of revenue received by a taxpayer and given away to charity does not increase the taxpayer's net worth as it stops being available for the consumption of the donor, but instead becomes available for consumption by all (Simon 1987, p. 73). It this reasoning the gift deduction would be part of the benchmark structure. However, very few economists and law scholars support this view (O'Hagan 2011, pp. 410, 412). Also governments and organizations such as the OECD do consider gift deduction a tax incentive.

Notwithstanding the political discussion, academics have managed to find a way to define an unbiased benchmark structure. They came to the conclusion that using a general, normative, 'ideal' structure as the benchmark, such as the Haig-Simons definition of income,[1] is not productive. Views of the appropriate normative tax base—the monetary sum in the hands of private households to which the tax ought to be applied—not only differ between national tax systems, but also between interpretations of the same national tax system by citizens and politicians (Kraan 2004, p. 131).

Japan does use a kind of normative benchmark in its definition of "Special Tax Measures": provisions that take exception to Japan's fundamental tax principles (equity, neutrality, and simplicity) to pursue a different policy objective (OECD

[1]The Haig-Simons or accretion definition of income states that income is the difference in wealth of a household between two points in time, plus the value of consumption during that period (Kraan 2004, p. 131).

2010, pp. 16, 93). However, in most countries a positive approach is taken, in which the specific tax structure of a specific country at a given time is used, instead of using a normative tax base. This means that what constitutes a tax incentive in one country does not necessarily have to be a tax incentive in another country as the benchmark tax structure might differ (OECD 2010, p. 16).

McDaniel (1976), p. 245 summarized the questions whose answers, together with the technical rules to implement them, form the benchmark structure of a selected tax:

1. What is the base of the tax?
2. What rates are to be applied?
3. What is the taxable unit?
4. What is the time period for determination of tax liability?

Whitehouse (1999), p. 28 added an international element to the definition of the benchmark:

> In general, this norm includes the tax rate structure, accounting conventions, administrative provisions and provisions relating to international fiscal obligations.

The OECD (2010), p. 12 refers to a benchmark definition by Kraan (2004) that includes all elements of Whitehouse (1999), but adds "the deductibility of compulsory payments". However, I prefer the broader concepts of the tax base and taxable unit instead of naming specific deviations such as the deductibility of certain payments.

If a tax provision deviates from the benchmark structure of a certain country defined using these questions and provides a benefit, it is a tax incentive. Other authors such as Christiaanse (1977), p. 70 Surrey (1981), p. 36 and Ministerie van Financiën (1987), p. 13 have used similar questions in determining the benchmark structure. McDaniel (1976) acknowledged that different countries may give different answers to these questions. He gave the example where country A may decide to treat an individual as the basic taxable unit for income tax purposes and country B may instead treat a (married) couple as this basic unit. The same is true for a particular country in different periods of time. For example, in the Netherlands, until 1 January 1973, a married couple was treated as the taxable unit for income tax purposes (i.e. the income of the wife was considered to form part of the husband's income), whereas nowadays the individual spouse is considered to be the taxable unit for most sources of income.

Using these elements means that an economical or theoretical notion is not the basis of the benchmark structure, but the actual structure of a tax. Therefore, this approach does not universally answer the question of what the benchmark structure of a tax is, but it does provide an answer for a particular jurisdiction at a given time. This dynamic notion of the benchmark structure fits with the dynamics of tax law in general and is therefore useful in determining whether or not something is a tax incentive (a deviation from this benchmark structure), in a particular country at a given time. A drawback is that the possible use of different benchmarks by different countries reduces the comparability of figures between countries (Whitehouse 1999, p. 30).

This definition of the benchmark stipulates that determining whether a tax provision is or is not a tax incentive is not an exact science. The choices we have made in this book to regard a provision as a tax incentive can, of course, be debated. In any case, we would like to stress that classifying a provision as a tax incentive does not give any information on the desirability of this provision. I would like to quote Surrey and McDaniel (1985), pp. 5–6 in this respect:

> The classification of an item as a tax expenditure is purely informative, just as the presence of an item in the direct budget of a government is informative; it is simply a way of announcing that the item is not part of the normative tax structure. This being so it is appropriate to ask whether the presence of those items in the tax system is desirable or undesirable, given the existing budget policy, tax policy, and other relevant criteria.

That a provision is a tax incentive is, in itself, not a reason to abolish it. In the words of Fieldstein (1980), p. 122:

> It would (…) be a perversion of logic to seek to eliminate tax expenditures instead of trying to improve the legislative and administrative process.

3 Forms

Tax incentives can take various forms depending on the tax they are included in. In this section I will list some common forms without trying to be exhaustive. All forms are illustrated with examples of tax incentives for the creative industries.

3.1 Exemptions

A very common form of a tax incentive is to exempt from the tax base certain items (objective exemption) or exclude as taxable units (subjective exemption) persons or entities that would, according to the general rules, be included in the tax base or taxable units, respectively. For example, certain kinds of income, wealth or capital gains can be exempt from personal and corporate income tax or from wealth tax. An example is the exemption of income of artists up to a certain maximum in Ireland (I refer to Chap. 10 for a discussion of this incentive). Such tax incentives can also be found in consumer taxes such as sales taxes. For example, in the Canadian province of British Columbia, books are exempt from provincial sales tax.[2] A tax exemption cannot only regard certain items of the tax base, but also certain tax-payers. For example, certain non-profit organizations such as museums can be exempt from corporate income tax in, for example, the USA[3] and Japan.[4]

---

[2]Section 16 Provincial Sales Tax Exemption and Refund Regulation.

[3]Section 501(c)(3) IRC.

[4]Article 46-2 NPO Law.

3.2 Allowances

Allowances are deductions from the tax base. These can be defined as provisions that allow the deduction of items from the tax base that would usually not reduce the tax base. Such provisions are usually found in income and wealth taxes. These can be expenditures that are under the regular rules regarded as non-deductible consumptive expenses and not costs related to earning the income such as gifts and maintenance costs for monuments. This does not mean that these deductions must always be linked to real expenditures. The tax incentive can also take the form of an additional deduction. For example, the UK creative industry tax reliefs allow qualifying companies to claim a larger deduction of corporate income tax when calculating their taxable profits (I refer to Sect. 3.4.3 of Chap. 8 for a discussion of these incentives).

3.3 Tax Credits

Unlike a deduction of the tax base, a tax credit does not reduce the taxable base. Instead, it reduces the tax liability, the amount of tax to be paid. Especially when a tax has a progressive rate (a tax rate that increases at a higher level of income), it makes a difference whether a tax incentive has the form of an income deduction or of a tax credit. Unlike an income deduction, a tax credit is indifferent to the income of the taxpayer. I can illustrate this using as an example a Dutch taxpayer with an income of €60.000 taxed at a rate of 52% and another Dutch taxpayer with an income of €35.000 taxed at a rate of 42%. Both taxpayers donate €1000 to a theatre, which is a registered charity in the Netherlands. For the sake of the example, I assume that the full €1000 is deductible. In the Netherlands, gift deduction takes the form of an income deduction. This means that the high-income individual has a benefit of €520 from his gift to the theatre, whereas the individual with a lower income receives a benefit of only €420. This could be regarded as undesirable from an equity point of view. This equity problem can be solved if the tax incentive is modeled as a tax credit. If the tax credit would, for example, be 45%, both the high income taxpayer and the low income taxpayer would have a benefit of EUR 450. For a discussion of various tax incentives for donations I refer to Sect. 2 of Chap. 7.

3.4 Reduced Rates

Rate relief, a reduced tax rate, can be applied to certain taxpayers or certain transactions. Such incentive can be included in any kind of tax, as every tax has a tax rate. For example, Annex III of the European VAT Directive provides for a list of supplies of goods and services to which EU Member States may apply reduced

VAT rates. This list includes the supply of books, admission to shows, theatres, circuses, fairs, amusement parks, concerts, museums, zoos, cinemas, exhibitions and similar cultural events and facilities, the reception of radio and television broadcasting services and the supply of services by writers, composers and performing artists, or of the royalties due to them.

3.5 Tax Deferral

Tax legislation stipulates when the tax is due, for example when income is received, a payment is made or a transfer of ownership has been finalized. A tax incentive can delay the moment when the tax has to be paid: a tax deferral. Unlike an exemption, which has the effect that no tax has to be paid at all (annulment) a deferral has only the effect that the tax has to be paid later (postponement). A deferral gives liquidity benefit to the taxpayer. An example was the former Dutch arbitrary depreciation of film investments. Where other investments had to be depreciated (e.g. the costs of the investments were deducted) over the course of the economic lifespan of the investment, film investments could be depreciated at will, for example, in the first year of investment. The investor in a film could thus reduce his taxable profit in the year of the investment. Because he was not able to depreciate the film investment in later years any further, the taxable profits in those years would be higher than if the arbitrary depreciation had not been applied, resulting in a higher tax liability in later years.

4 Calculating the Costs of Tax Incentives

As I mentioned before, tax incentives reduce government budget. This means that after the introduction of a tax incentive, either direct government spending must be cut, taxes must be raised or the budget must otherwise be brought back to the original amount if costs are not cut, for example by taking out loans (Schuster 1979, pp. 75–77). In any case, tax incentives are not ‘free lunches’. Whereas the costs of direct expenditures can relatively easily be assessed, this is not the case for tax incentives. The OECD (2010), p. 12 comments:

> Since tax expenditures are not actual outlays, the amounts “spent” are notional: that is, they are based on assumptions and estimates as to how tax payers would behave under particular conditions.

Therefore, by definition the costs of tax incentives are estimates. Kraan (2004), pp. 136–137, Anderson (2008), slide 5 and the OECD (2010), pp. 13–14 distinguish three different methods to estimate the costs of tax incentives:

1. Initial revenue loss (gain): the amount by which tax revenue is reduced (increased) as a consequence of the introduction (abolition) of a tax incentive,

based upon the assumption of unchanged behavior of taxpayers and unchanged revenues from other taxes.
2. Final revenue loss (gain): the amount by which tax revenue is reduced (increased) as a consequence of the introduction (abolition) of a tax incentive, taking into account the change in behavior and the effects on revenues from other taxes as a consequence of the introduction (abolition).
3. Outlay equivalence: the direct expenditure that would be required in pre-tax terms to achieve the same after-tax effect on taxpayers' incomes as the tax incentive, if the direct expenditure is accorded the tax treatment appropriate to that type of subsidy or transfer in the hands of the recipient.

Whitehouse (1999), p. 29 observed that usually the initial revenue loss method is used to calculate tax incentives. Kraan (2004), p. 137 noted that this is the easiest, but also the least realistic method. Not only will taxpayers often change their behavior in reaction to a tax incentive, usually such change in behavior is the intention of the government when introducing a tax incentive. However, he also mentions that many governments seem to assume that the accuracy that might be gained using a more realistic method is generally not worth the efforts. It is very difficult to predict and calculate behavioral effects without introducing too many variables in the equation.

In any case, these observations mean that costs of tax incentives cannot be perceived as exact figures, but must always be treated as estimates.

5 Why Many Tax Experts Are not in Favor of Tax Incentives

The OECD (2010), p. 14 observed that tax expenditures have been a serious concern of budget and tax analysts for almost half a century. Several theoretical and practical allegations against tax incentives have been identified, for example by the OECD (2010), pp. 25–34. When proposing or advocating a tax incentive for the creative industries, these arguments must be taken into account and weighed against the alleged benefits of using a tax incentive instead of other instruments for the specific policy goal. Below, various reasons as to why many tax experts are not in favor of tax incentives are analyzed. Some arguments contain valid concerns that should be taken into account, others do not seem to be specific for tax incentives, but would also apply to direct subsidies.

5.1 Fairness

OECD (2010), p. 26 mentions that it is alleged that the tool of tax incentives tends towards unfair results, both in the likelihood that undeserving groups of taxpayers obtain them, and in the operation of tax expenditures once they have been enacted. A preliminary remark regarding the argument of fairness is that this is not a clear-cut concept. What one person might perceive as being fair, for example, income aid for artists, another person may not recognize as such. Fairness is a subjective concept with a meaning that may differ between societies, people and in time.

Notwithstanding the vagueness of the concept of fairness, lobby groups can have a strong political influence when pleading for tax incentives that can lead to results perceived as being unfair. The benefit of such incentives is large for the small groups who benefit from them, with the costs borne by a large group of anonymous taxpayers (Grampp 1989 pp. 208–216). The interests of the large group are not always duly taken into account by members of parliament. Furthermore, as the costs for each individual group member are rather small, they do not perceive it as worthwhile to oppose the tax incentive. Tax incentives might, therefore, infringe the fairness of a tax system: small, powerful groups with easy access to parliament and the media can secure benefits for themselves that must then be borne by all other taxpayers. These lobby groups can also make it difficult to abolish an ineffective or inefficient tax incentive, as these become perceived as inalienable rights.

However, this is not different for direct subsidies that might also have unfair effects, which might not be abolished because of strong lobby groups and the relatively low costs for each group member of the large anonymous group that has to bear the costs of the subsidy. Furthermore, the OECD (2010), p. 26 observes that it is difficult to judge whether the greater bargaining power of certain groups would be more likely to affect the enactment of tax provisions than spending programs. Nevertheless, it must be observed that from a political point of view, it will likely be easier to advocate a tax cut than a new subsidy (OECD 2010, p. 32). Also, the broader public might be more sympathetic towards not withdrawing a tax cut instead of giving a direct subsidy as the tax cut might be more easily perceived (wrongly) as not costing money to other taxpayers.

Another drawback of specific tax incentives, such as allowances in progressive income tax systems, can be that they infringe upon the ability to pay principle. An example is the gift deduction, from which high-income groups benefit more than low-income groups in a progressive income tax system (I refer to the example in Sect. 3.3). Surrey and McDaniel (1985), p. 87 called this the "upside down effect" of tax incentives. However, this is not an intrinsic feature of tax incentives, but rather a characteristic of allowances in a progressive tax system. By replacing a gift allowance with a tax credit for gifts, the problem would be solved while keeping a tax incentive in place. Also the OECD (2010), p. 26 observes that the upside down effect can be defeated by using non-wastable tax credits: tax credits that are fixed regardless of income and that are payable in full even if the credits exceed the amount of tax liability.

Furthermore, direct subsidies can also effect a redistribution to high-income groups. This is, for example the case for direct subsidies for performing arts, such as opera and concerts, as the audience for these art forms are mainly high-income groups who, therefore, benefit more than lower-income groups from the direct subsidies given by many European governments to these art forms.

In my view, fairness concerns are, therefore, not a good reason to generally dismiss tax incentives as policy tools, given the fact that these concerns can either be addressed by using a different form for the tax incentive or are inherent to the policy goal and would not be different if a direct subsidy were used. However, when enacting a tax incentive, these concerns must be taken into account. The legislator, when choosing a policy tool and considering a tax incentive, must be aware of the consequences that a lobby can have for the division of the tax burden between citizens and companies and of the effects of the design of a tax incentive.

5.2 *Complexity*

Many authors (for example, Surrey 1971, p. 146; Christiaanse 1977, p. 74; OECD 1984, p. 14) have observed that tax incentives increase the complexity of the tax system. In the Netherlands, this has been a reason for several tax professors to propose the abolishment of gift deductions (Heithuis 2013; Kavelaars 2014; Van Weeghel 2015).

Although tax incentives can increase the complexity of a tax system, a complex society leads to complex legislation, and direct subsidy legislation can be complex as well. From the perspective of the government as a whole, it is not an improvement to replace a tax incentive by a direct subsidy if this results in slightly reduced complexity of the tax legislation but seriously increased complexity of subsidy legislation and administration. Looking at only the complexity of the tax system while ignoring substitution effects in other legislation and practices does not lead to constructive solutions from the perspective of society as a whole. The pure tax perspective is too narrow in this regard. For this reason, complexity is not an argument in itself to dismiss tax incentives as a tool of government policy. However, when designing or evaluating a tax incentive, its complexity in comparison with policy alternatives must be taken into account.

5.3 *Neutrality*

Some tax experts are of the opinion that tax legislation may only be used to obtain budget for the government (the primary function of taxation). Furthermore, taxation should in their opinion be as neutral as possible, that is, tax legislation should interfere in the economy as little as possible. However, this seems to be more a political opinion than an academic argument. In this vision, the market outcome is the best outcome in which the government should not interfere. However, Wagner (1880), pp. 285–288 already pointed out that the division of wealth and income before taxation is not necessary just. The actual aversion of the proponents of the neutrality argument does not seem to regard the tax incentive as such, but rather the policy objective pursued by the tax incentive. They would probably also oppose a direct subsidy with the same purpose. For example, when Kavelaars (2014) argues:

> Why should a taxpayer pay more tax because his neighbor donates to the Red Cross?

he is not, as he intends, arguing against the gift deduction, but against government support for the Red Cross in general. He mixes the means with the object.

Furthermore, taxation is not an object in itself. Taxation gives the government the means to finance its policy, which is by definition interference in the economy. Tax policy is an integral part of the financial and social-economic government policy, not a separated phenomenon. Mann (1947), p. 13 stated in this respect that taxation must be "de-provincialized". Furthermore, taxes have always been used for other policy objectives. Manvel (1971) observed:

> Tax incentives have a long background antedating by far American history. The use of government's revenue-raising authority not only to obtain resources, but also to attempt to influence human activities goes back to the dawn of history.

Therefore, the neutrality argument is also not a reason to dismiss tax incentives as a policy argument.

5.4 Difficult to Calculate Costs

Whereas it will usually be possible to assess the costs of direct subsidies, the costs of tax incentives can only be estimated and are usually calculated with a ceteris paribus method that does not reflect the reality of behavioral reactions to policy changes. Furthermore, where subsidies can be capped, for example by "first come, first served" or selection mechanisms, this is much harder for a tax incentive. Usually tax incentives are open-ended, making it even harder to estimate and assess the costs. This uncertainty about the real costs of the tax incentive makes it difficult to make budget decisions and evaluate the costs of these measures. Even though it is not always easy to estimate beforehand the effect and costs of a direct subsidy either, this calculation problem is a true drawback of tax incentives in comparison with direct subsidies.

However, it must be noted that tax incentives do not necessarily need to be open ended. For example, the UK Cultural Gifts Scheme and Acceptance in Lieu of Tax Scheme, which is discussed in Chap. 7, Sects. 2.3 and 6, must operate within a £40 million annual limit for both schemes. Eight months into each financial year, the Arts Council must provide a report on the progress of the two schemes, setting out what proportion of the annual limit has been used to date. Furthermore, on the first working day of each month, a report is provided illustrating the current financial position for both schemes (Department for Culture, Media and Sport 2015).

Therefore, it is not an inherent characteristic of tax incentives that they are open ended, but instead a question of the design of the tax incentive. That being said, it is not always easy to transform a tax incentive in a closed end incentive as this might lead to an additional administrative burden.

5.5 *Effectiveness and Efficiency*

Tax incentives that can be included in the tax law without many requirements and exclusions are for the most part easy for both the tax administration and taxpayers to handle. Such incentives should not impose significant additional administrative burdens. However, simple incentives will usually have a broad scope and are difficult to target at special groups. This reduces the effectiveness and efficiency of these tax incentives. An example is a reduced VAT rate for theatre performances as is allowed by the EU VAT Directive (Annex III, sub 7). Once the definition of a theatre performance is established, this is rather simple to execute, both for the tax administration and for theatres. However, this tax incentive applies to all consumers and all producers: including consumers with high income, consumers who are insensitive to the price of a ticket and commercial performances. This might not be the objective of the government policy. It is easier to target a direct subsidy, for example by using discount cards for low-income consumers such as students, and subsidies for specific performances. If this is the actual policy objective, the tax incentive is much more expensive than a direct subsidy would be and is a waste of government resources. Also the European Commission (1997), p. 15 underlined that from a theoretical standpoint VAT is a neutral multi-stage broad based consumer tax, which is as such not best suited as a means of selectively providing favorable treatment for certain social and cultural activities, for example. The EC regarded it a fact in economic terms that other means such as direct subsidies are much more effective and efficient and do not cause as many undesirable side-effects.

However, if the scope of a tax incentive is rather broad, the wide application is not a problem. For example, if the policy objective is to stimulate charitable gifts among all taxpayers and it is established that these gifts are price-elastic, a tax incentive for such gifts can be effective and efficient.

5.6 *Invisibility Undermines Budgetary Principles and Functions*

In general, tax incentives have the drawback that, compared with direct subsidies, there is less information and less democratic control on these expenditures than on direct subsidies, which are accounted for in the annual budget. Often, it is even required by national constitutions that direct subsidies are included in a yearly government budget, for example in the Netherlands (article 105), Japan (articles 85 and 86) and the Philippines (articles VI, sect. 29 and VII sect. 22). In general, a government budget is the financial plan of a government for a given period, usually for a fiscal year, which shows what the resources are and how they will be generated and used over the fiscal period. Usually, the budget has to be adopted by parliament. The budget is the government's key instrument for promoting its socio-economic objectives.

5.6.1 Functions of the Budget

The budget has four very important functions in a democracy (Kraan 2004, p. 122):

1. The authorization function: adoption of the budget by Parliament authorizes spending of money by the government. Through adoption of the budget, the government obtains legislative authorization for its expenditures and to finance these through taxes, levies and loans.
2. The allocation function: the budget enables to compare and trade off all expenditures and revenues and changes therein.
3. The macroeconomic function: the budget enables decisions to be made on the economy from totals and composition of expenditure, revenues and the deficit. This can, for example, include spending rules that impose caps on certain forms of government expenditures and rules for the use of revenues that were not included in the budget.
4. The administrative function: the budget enables to control the lawfulness (correctness and exhaustiveness) and efficiency (are objects being reached at the lowest costs) of the expenditures.

Kraan (2004), pp. 122–123 distinguishes three prerequisites for all budget functions to be fulfilled:

1. The universality principle: all expenditures and all revenues must be included in the budget.
2. The unity principle: all revenues to be collected and all expenditures to be made during a certain period of time must be included in a single document.
3. The specificity principle: expenditures and revenues must be specified separately in the budget ("gross recording") and at a level of detail required by the budgetary authorities.

5.6.2 Tax Incentives and the Budget

Tax incentives reduce government income. These are, therefore, implicitly reflected in the budget in the amount of government income to be collected, but are not explicitly accounted for as an expenditure. This makes it difficult to reconcile tax incentives with the three basic principles mentioned in the previous section: tax incentives are not included as an expenditure (universality), for that reason not all expenditures are visibly included in the budget (unity) or specified (specificity). This hampers the functioning of the budget.

Not explicitly accounting for tax incentives in the budget especially reduces the allocation function, macro-economic function and administrative function of the budget. It is difficult to weigh direct expenditures against tax incentives, as is the purpose of the allocation function of the budget. The OECD (2010), p. 29 observed that tax incentives are seldom presented together with equivalent spending programs. This may have the effect that tax incentives are not effectively evaluated against direct spending options. Regarding the macro-economic function: if tax incentives are not included in the budget it is more difficult to assess total expenditures and to apply fiscal rules such as deficit and balance rules if tax incentives are not included in, for example, an expenditure ceiling. According to the OECD (2010), p. 14 the handling of tax incentives under such rules is critical because a systematically lesser degree of budgetary control on tax incentives, as opposed to direct spending, could direct increasing flows of

> what would - and often should - be 'spending' through the tax system.

Not including tax incentives in the budget also complicates control of the lawfulness and effectiveness of expenditures and thus negatively affects the administrative function of the budget.

Kraan (2004), p. 134 observed that:

> Although there may be good reasons for tax expenditures, it is also important that tax expenditures be subjected to budgetary control in the same way as regular expenditures are.

Not including tax incentives in the budget may give the impression that these are free lunches. This perception is wrong. A tax incentive reduces the tax income of government, creating a need for the government to either increase the tax burden of other taxpayers, obtain other funds, for example loans (thus putting the burden on future generations) and/or increase other taxes to maintain the same level of expenditures, or reduce spending. Also regarding tax incentives there is no such thing as a free lunch. Just as direct subsidies, tax incentives are a cost for the government. Kraan (2004), p. 134 warned that less-rigorous control of tax incentives would create an incentive to enact subsidies and transfers in the form of tax incentives, regardless of any objective considerations that could justify such a choice. Ministries other than the Ministry of Finance often prefer a tax incentive over a direct subsidy as these do not reduce their budget, but affect the revenue of the Ministry of Finance only. In the case of the Ministry of Culture, for example, an ineffective tax incentive for the creative industries might therefore be more attractive than a more effective direct subsidy, which would reduce its budget. For the government as a whole this is, of course, very inefficient as the costs of a direct expenditure would be less than that of the tax incentive.

Kraan (2004), p. 136 emphasizes that it is important for all functions of the budget that tax incentives are assigned to ministries and that individual ministers are made responsible for them together with the Minister of Finance, to avoid the case where tax incentives undermine the efficiency and effectiveness of the tax system. However, to my knowledge, this is not the case in most countries. This is also a drawback from a policy point of view. Usually the Ministry of Finance will not have expertise in the specific policy field (Schuster 1987, p. 32). Furthermore, the primary objective of the Ministry of Finance and the tax administration is to generate revenue, not to decrease revenue. This might result in the tax rationale being dominant over the policy rationale of the tax incentive. This might negatively affect the effectiveness of such incentives.

Furthermore, to be able to effectively apply fiscal rules, such as expenditure ceilings, tax incentives must be included in the total expenditure ceiling or a special ceiling must be set for these tax incentives, including compensation rules for under- and overspending of tax incentives (Kraan 2004, p. 135). If such fiscal rules do not include tax incentives, there is an easy way to circumvent these rules: in the words of the OECD (2010), p. 14 "a back channel for resource allocation".

One has to agree with Kraan (2004), p. 134 that not imposing the same control on tax incentives as on direct subsidies jeopardizes the allocative, macroeconomic and administrative functions of the budget and could endanger the primary revenue collection function of the tax system.

5.6.3 Tax Expenditure Budget

The concept of a "tax expenditure" was, in fact, developed in an attempt to address some of these problems and to make tax incentives more visible, thus reinforcing the functions of the budget. As Whitehouse (1999), p. 28 stated:

> The concept of a 'tax expenditure' was developed in recognition of the fact the tax system can be used to achieve similar goals to public spending programs, but accounting for the costs and benefits of tax measures is often less rigorous and regular than for direct expenditure.

The IMF's Code of Good Practices on Fiscal Transparency (2007), Sect. 3.1.3 states that:

> Statements describing the nature and fiscal significance of central government tax incentives, contingent liabilities, and quasi-fiscal activities should be part of the budget documentation, together with an assessment of all other major fiscal risks.

Additionally, the OECD (2015), p. 8 has included as a principle of good budgetary governance to provide for an inclusive, participative and realistic debate on budgetary choices, by, among other methods, providing clarity about the relative costs and benefits of the wide range of public expenditure programs and tax incentives.

Since the end of the 1960s, various countries have tried to get a better grip on tax incentives by accounting for these incentives in tax expenditure reports. Already, since 1959, Germany has reported regularly on visible and invisible subsidies. In 1967, it became law that every two years a *Subventionsbericht* ('Subsidy report') has to be published.[5] In 1968, the USA published the first tax expenditure report. The US Budget Reform Act of 1974 required that tax expenditures be subjected to scrutiny and controls similar to those applicable to direct expenditure programs (McDaniel 1976, p. 248). Later on, other countries also introduced various kinds of tax expenditure budgets, for example Spain (1978), Canada (1979), the UK (1979), Austria (1979), Portugal (1980) and, in 1981, France, Ireland and Australia (Ministerie van Financiën 1987, p. 192). According to Kraan (2004), p. 130 almost all OECD member countries reported tax expenditures in 1996. Whitehouse (1999), p. 29 reported that in 1999 fourteen OECD countries produced tax expenditure reports. India released its first tax expenditure report with the Union Budget of 2006–2007 (Philips 2012, p. 8). In Japan, tax incentives are not disclosed in a yearly budget (Uemura 2009, p. 4). Uemura (2009), p. 16 is of the opinion that:

> Creation of a tax expenditure budget and its disclosure are essential to increase fiscal transparency of Japan, to recover reliability on finance, and to openly discuss tax expenditures as policies.

Since the Special Taxation Measures Transparent Act of 2010, the Japanese Minister of Finance creates a report that describes the applicability of the Special Taxation Measures each fiscal year, and Cabinet submits the report to the Diet. However, this act is not enough for the Special Measures to be accounted for and controlled by Parliament.

It is important to note that tax expenditure reports can be very different. The information in these overviews varies widely. This is illustrated by the answers on question 45 of the International Budget Survey that gives the following information on the use of tax expenditure reports in the 100 countries that were examined in 2012 (IBP 2012):

- 14 countries present extensive information on tax expenditures, including both a narrative discussion and quantitative estimates.
- 8 countries present information, highlighting key tax expenditures, but exclude some details.
- 19 countries present some information, but this information lacks important details.
- 59 countries do not present information on tax expenditures.

Kraan (2004), p. 123 noted:

> Tax expenditures do not necessarily create a problem for the proper functioning of the budget as long as the budget procedure provides for the opportunity to change the substantive laws creating the entitlements and tax expenditures in the course of the budget process.

However, this does not often seem to be the case. Furthermore, the status of the tax expenditure reports varies. In many countries, parliament does not have to vote on

[5]Section 12 of the *Gesetz zur Förderung der Stabilität und des Wachstums der Wirtschaft* of 8 June 1967.

these overviews or discuss it in connection with the direct expenditure budget (OECD 1984, pp. 7, 10).

Tax incentives are, therefore, still not accounted and budgeted for in the same way as direct subsidies in most countries. In the following paragraph, I will illustrate this with the example of the Netherlands.

Example: Evolution of the Netherlands Tax Expenditure Report

Since 1998, the Dutch Ministry of Finance publishes a yearly overview of tax incentives as an annex to the yearly budget (*Miljoenennota*). Originally, only provisions that met the Dutch definition of tax incentives were included in the tax expenditure report. Provisions that reduced the government income, but were deemed to be in accordance with the benchmark structure of the tax legislation, were not included in the report. These were politically sensitive provisions: the deduction of interest on loans relating to residential property (estimated revenue loss in 2016: €10.1 billion (Ministerie van Financiën 2014a) and the deductibility of pension premiums (estimated revenue loss in 2016: €13.3 billion (Ministerie van Financiën 2014a). As of 2008, the budgetary loss of these provisions is included in the tax expenditure report, not under the heading 'tax incentives,' but rather under the heading 'income-reducing measures'. Apart from the terminology, this is an important improvement to the tax expenditure report, as the total costs of these two measures amount to 3.43% of the Dutch GDP in 2016. In comparison: the costs of the 95 "regular" Dutch tax incentives amount to 2.70% of the Dutch GDP in 2016 (Ministerie van Financiën 2014a). Currently, the Dutch tax expenditure report gives the following information (Ministerie van Financiën 2014a):

- Overview of tax incentives and income-reducing measures that are introduced or amended in the budget, together with the estimated loss of revenue for the year of the budget.
- Overview of existing income reducing measures, together with the estimated loss of revenue for a number of years, that is, the years 2013–2019 are included in the 2014 report.
- Overview of existing tax incentives in taxes on (i) income, profits and assets and (ii) indirect taxes, together with the estimated loss of revenue for several years (the years 2013–2019 are included in the 2014 report).
- Short overview of evaluations of tax incentives in the previous year and the current year.

The Dutch tax expenditure overview, which is published on the Internet each year, provides for a clarification of all tax incentives. Similar provisions are not accounted for; only provisions that meet the definition of tax exemption are included in the overview. The following information is provided for each of the 95 tax incentives (Ministerie van Financiën 2014b):

1. short description of the provision;
2. object of the provision;

3. responsible ministry; and
4. evaluation: where available, either a reference to the most recent evaluation or the year in which the next evaluation is planned.

The tax expenditure report does not have to be (and is generally not) discussed in Parliament. This means that even though the Netherlands now has a well-established practice of tax expenditure reports with extensive information on these tax measures, they are not under the same scrutiny and control as direct subsidies. The problem is not so much the availability of the information, but the use Parliament makes of it.

5.7 Assessing Effectiveness and Efficiency: Evaluations

Evaluations of measures are an important part of a sound government policy. It is important to assess whether measures have been effective and efficient and whether changes are necessary. As the OECD (2010), p. 31 observed:

> This report will not presume that designation as a tax expenditure is an implied badge of demerit, but rather that every tax provision or practice, designated tax expenditure or not, should be evaluated individually, on its own merit - as should every spending program, in a world of scarce resources.

Tax incentives and direct subsidies should be evaluated in the same way. This is important for the allocative and administrative function of the budget (Kraan 2004, p. 136). Because of the relative invisibility of tax incentives due to not being included in the budget or being discussed by Parliament, not all tax incentives are evaluated on a regular basis. If tax incentives are not put under a systematic and critical review, they can grow over time and avoid reform, reduction or repeal (OECD 2010, p. 33). Not surprisingly, the OECD (2015), pp. 6, 9 has included as principles of good budgetary governance to

> Closely align budgets with the medium-term strategic priorities of government, by considering how to devise and implement regular processes for reviewing existing expenditure policies, including tax incentives, in a manner that helps budgetary expectations to be set in line with government-wide developments

and

> To ensure that performance, evaluation and value for money are integral to the budget process, amongst others by evaluating and reviewing expenditure program (including tax incentives) in a manner that is objective, routine and regular, to inform resource allocation and reprioritization both within line ministries and across government as a whole.

Some countries, such as Canada, the Netherlands, New Zealand and the United Kingdom, apply special evaluation procedures to their tax incentives (Kraan 2004, p. 136). However, a regular evaluation of tax incentives is not a guarantee that ineffective or inefficient tax incentives will not be abolished. In 2010, an evaluation of the Dutch evaluation procedure for tax incentives was carried out by the Ministry of Finance, reviewed by an independent, external individual and published (Ministerie van Financiën 2010). The report concluded that most tax incentives were evaluated and that this had been carried out in a proper manner. However, conclusions from evaluations are not always followed when a new policy is developed. The government replied that other considerations are also taken into account when developing a policy on tax incentives. One gets the impression that evaluations only seem to play a part if these fit the political objectives of the government and that evaluations are otherwise disregarded. It cannot be denied that decisions on tax incentives are often highly political and influenced by lobby groups. However, as long as tax incentives are visible and accounted for, there is no difference in this respect with direct subsidies.

5.7.1 Sunset Legislation

Inclusion of tax incentives and similar provisions in the tax expenditure report and evaluation reports does not always have an impact on the decision to maintain or abolish tax incentives. This might have the effect that existing tax incentives remain in place and might even result in increasing revenue losses. Even though this increase is accounted for in the tax expenditure report, this might not have an effect on the tax incentive.

An additional measure to have more effective evaluations of tax incentives could be sunset legislation. Sunset legislation is legislation that automatically expires after a certain period (for example, 5 years) unless it is explicitly renewed or extended. This is the reverse of the practice in which tax incentives exist indefinitely unless explicitly abolished. Sunset legislation is often applied in the US. In the Netherlands, sunset legislation is applied in incidental cases.

The idea that legislation should expire after a certain period of time can be traced back to Thomas Jefferson, who wrote a letter on the subject to James Madison on 6 September 1789. From the principle that the earth belongs to the living and not to the dead, he derived that no society can make a perpetual law. In his opinion, every generation should make its own legislation, and thus every law should expire after 19 years (obviously, the life expectancy was much less in those days). He noted that exercising the power to repeal legislation might seem the same as an automatic repeal after 19 years. However, he remarked (Jefferson 1789):

> It would be the same if every form of government were so perfectly contrived that the will of the majority could always be obtained fairly and without impediment. But this is true of no form. The people cannot assemble themselves; their representation is unequal and vicious. Various checks are opposed to every legislative proposition. Factions get possession of the public councils. Bribery corrupts them. Personal interests lead them astray from the general interests of their constituents; and other impediments arise so as to prove to every practical man that a law of limited duration is much more manageable than one which needs a repeal.

Similarly, its seems very difficult to abolish existing tax incentives, due to the lobbying forces of interested parties and the fact that the silent majority of taxpayers does not quickly raise its voice. Automatic repeal of tax incentives, for example after the term of a certain government has expired, forces a parliament to periodically discuss the desirability of certain tax incentives. Lowi (1969), p. 309 was even of the opinion that a limit of between 5 and 10 years might be the only effective way to get substantive evaluations.

However, also sunset clauses will not prevent the case where small groups will start to lobby strongly when an incentive expires. Again, the visibility and the accountability of the tax incentive are key. If this is similar to a direct subsidy, the discussion whether or not a tax incentive should be prolonged would not be different from a similar discussion regarding a direct subsidy.

6 OECD Conditions for Successful Tax Incentives: A Fiscal Policy Perspective

In the previous section it was established that tax incentives have several serious drawbacks. However, as the OECD (2010), p. 24 observed:

> Tax expenditures remain a feature of all tax systems, and many are widely believed to be effective and efficient as well as politically unassailable (...) Tax expenditures have a role to play; they are employed widely, and there are few, if any, suggestions that all tax expenditures should be repealed.

The OECD (2010), p. 25 identified several conditions under which tax incentives are most likely to be successful, or even the best, policy tools to achieve their objectives. This was under the assumption that there are valid reasons for government involvement (such as market failures or merit goods). Below, I will discuss these conditions, which are a good starting point for establishing the potential benefits of tax incentives from a fiscal policy point of view.

6.1 Administrative Economies of Scale and Scope

Tax incentives might lead to lower administrative costs than direct subsidies, both for the tax administration and the beneficiary. Depending on their design, tax incentives do not need a special agency managing the incentive program. Also, the relevant information on the characteristics of households and businesses, such as income, may already be available to the tax administration. A spending agency would otherwise have to obtain information from the program beneficiaries. Furthermore, there is no need to first transfer taxes to the government, which would then subsequently transfer the money back in the form of a subsidy. This reduces the marginal administrative costs for both parties. For example, given a cultural policy goal of private ownership of art, an exemption of privately owned art from a wealth tax is more cost-efficient than taxing (and assessing the value of) these objects on a yearly basis and providing a direct subsidy for private ownership of art. Furthermore, private collections may be very interesting for a broader audience, but for the private owner of art, giving a work on loan to a museum or making a collection accessible to the public has many disadvantages. It leads to additional costs, for example, for security, transport and insurance and risks, for example of damage and hassle. Countries can use tax incentives to stimulate private owners of art to open their collection or cultural heritage to the public notwithstanding these disadvantages. This may be efficient when the information necessary for the incentive is already available, for example, when a tax exemption is applied.

6.2 Limited Probability of Abuse or Fraud

Where detailed verification is not necessary, a tax benefit can be cost-effective, especially as information from third-party sources is available, which can be used to check the claim of the taxpayer. If the taxpayer is aware that the tax administration has third-party information, this can also deter false reporting. A direct spending agency would first have to obtain such information from the tax administration. An example is a special exemption for developers of video games that decreases when the profit increases. As these developers will have to file tax returns for corporate income tax, the tax administration can easily and correctly apply such a profit-based incentive. A spending agency would first have to verify that the information provided for by the taxpayer is correct.

6.3 A Properly Wide Range of Taxpayer Choices

In case of wide ranges of private preferences the distinctions among different activities that qualify for governmental support may not be considered important. In such case, a simpler reporting and verification process through the tax system than through a spending agency might be more efficient than a direct subsidy. An example can be an exemption of museums from gift and inheritance tax: it is not deemed relevant whether the institution in question is an art or a heritage museum, a private or public museum nor whether it is located in a city or in a rural area: all museums qualify.

6.4 Measurement of Taxpaying Capacity

Deductions or exclusions from income can be justified as proper measurements of the ability to pay tax, or as essential to measure income accurately. An example can be the deduction of maintenance costs for privately owned monuments. However, the OECD (2010), p. 25 acknowledges that this criterion might be problematic, as under many applications of the tax expenditure concept, such deductions or exclusions could be considered structural features of the tax system rather than tax incentives.

7 Benefits of Tax Incentives from the Point of View of Creative Industries Policy

In the previous section, the OECD conditions for successful tax incentives were discussed. However, these conditions seem to be primarily inspired by fiscal policy. More generally, in most tax discussions on tax incentives the focus is on tax policy. In my view this is too narrow-minded, as tax policy serves government policy as a whole: it is not a completely separated policy field, but is an inherent part of total government policy. Therefore, not just tax policy arguments but also the policy field and policy objectives for which the tax incentive is intended are of importance when making the decision on the most appropriate policy instrument. In this chapter I will therefore discuss arguments in favor of using tax incentives from a creative industries policy point of view.

7.1 Taking Public Preferences into Account: Aligning Those Who Care and Those Who Pay

From an economic point of view, four roles can be distinguished in an economical transfer: the payer, the beneficiary, the one caring for the product or service and the decision-maker. In a market transaction, these four roles are usually combined in one person. If I care about a particular piece of Dutch design and I decide I want to have it, I pay for it and I then benefit from obtaining it. In a pure market transaction, the consumer, the public, has the power to decide. The producer, such as an artist, designer or video game company takes into account the preferences of consumers and produces for them.

The drawback of the market model is that some products might not be produced at all or in low quantities as consumers might not (yet) be interested in those products or perceive them as being too expensive (for an elaborate discussion, refer to Chap. 3). Some examples are avant-garde forms of art, certain opera performances and arthouse films.

As was discussed in Chap. 3, because of the perceived underproduction of certain products and services of the creative industries as a result of market outcome, governments have decided to interfere in these markets. In Europe, cultural institutions and certain art forms are often mainly funded by direct subsidies of local or national governments. However, many national governments also fund cultural institutions indirectly, by granting tax incentives for cultural giving. An example is the deductibility of gifts to museums, theatres and other cultural institutions. These different forms of government grants have different effects from a policy point of view. These effects, and whether or not these effects are intended by the policy, must be taken into account when deciding on the instrument to give financial support to the creative industries.

To make this analysis, three parties must be distinguished. First, all taxpayers, as ultimately, taxpayers finance government grants. They have to pay taxes to enable the government to provide for a direct grant or to make up for the loss of government revenue because of tax incentives. Art enthusiasts are a subgroup of the group of all taxpayers. The second party is the government, which makes the rules both for direct and indirect incentives and selects the eligible cultural institutions. A subgroup might be advisory boards or special agencies of the government that decide, or advise the government on eligibility. The third party consists of the cultural institutions that the government wants to support.

In Fig. 1 these three parties are graphically represented in the context of a direct subsidy.

Where a direct subsidy is provided, the four roles are spread over different parties. All taxpayers pay for the product or service, but the decision is made by the government or a government agency. The art enthusiasts, who care about the product or service, are only a sub group of all taxpayers and the beneficiaries of the subsidy might be an even smaller group. In Fig. 1, there is no direct financial relation between cultural institutions and art enthusiastic, the public. The preferences of the public are not really of relevance for the funding. The government or a governmental agency decides which cultural institutions get what amount of money, and all taxpayers have to fund this. In Fig. 1: the government first decides to give a grant of 100 and all taxpayers have to fund this 100 by paying tax. Art enthusiasts are not given any responsibility for sustaining the arts. This might have the effect that cultural institutions focus on the government and their advisory bodies and forget about the preferences of their public. The result may be elite art that is only aimed at a small group of insiders. The former Dutch state secretary and professor of economics Van der Ploeg (2002), p. 349 called this "high culture for a small elite". Mourato and Mazzanti (2002), p. 63 stated:

> Relying only on experts' judgement may be dangerous, leading to improper allocation of resources, arbitrariness, lobbying pressures for funding, and paternalism.

The alternative for expert decisions, top-down decisions by politicians and bureaucrats, also has mayor drawbacks. The decision process may lack transparency, there is much room for lobbying and favoritism, prestige projects may stand a better chance and it may have the effect of encouraging "state art" where the state attempts to impose its taste on the creative industries and artists conform to the tastes of politicians to obtain funds (Van de Ploeg 2002, p. 355).

In both cases, decisions are made by experts and by politicians and bureaucrats; rather than being guided by the preferences of the public, the preferences of the decision-makers prevail. In the Netherlands, where decisions are made by experts,

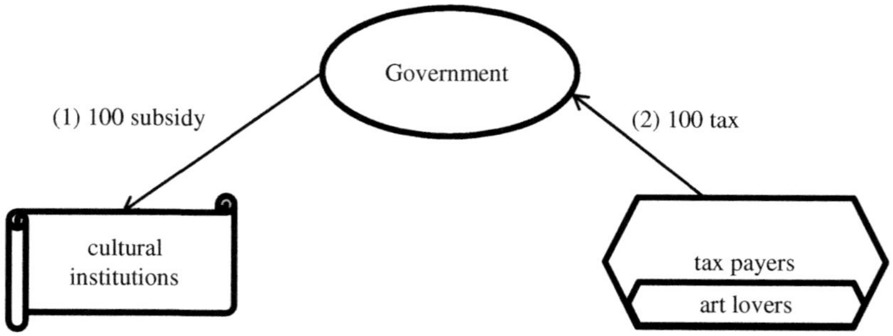

Fig. 1 Direct subsidy

this had the effect of populist parties claiming that the arts were merely 'hobbies of left-wing politicians' for which general taxpayers were no longer willing to pay, resulting in huge cuts on subsidies for the arts when the populist party became part of the government in 2010.

In the context of a tax incentive, the relation between the parties and the division of roles is different as is shown in Fig. 2.

The starting point with a tax incentive is the bottom-up decision of the art enthusiast to make a donation. In Fig. 2, this donation is 100 in order for the cultural institution to obtain the same amount as under the direct grant scheme of Fig. 1. Because of the incentive scheme, the art enthusiast gets a deduction for income tax purposes. As an example, I have chosen an income deduction against a tax rate of 50%, hence a tax deduction of 50, but a lower deduction, for example by using a fixed tax credit, is of course possible as well. Only this deduction, in the example of 50 rather than the whole gift, has to be funded by all taxpayers. Therefore, the role of payer is not fully imposed on all taxpayers; they have to fund only part of the incentive. The other part is paid for by the art enthusiasts: those who decide the funding and care about the product or service. Those who benefit are probably, but not necessarily, part of this group, but the beneficiaries can be a much broader group, for example students with low income who now can afford to attend a play for which the ticket price is below cost, because of private donations making up for the difference.

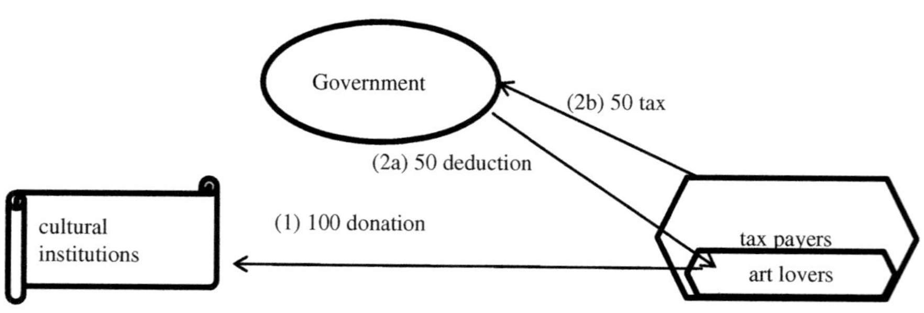

Fig. 2 Tax incentive

The effect of using a tax incentive instead of a direct subsidy is twofold. First, unlike the situation with a direct subsidy cultural institutions have to take into account the preferences of their public and create a bond with them to attract donations. Where the initiative for a direct subsidy lies with the government, with a tax incentive the public, the art enthusiasts, have the initiative in granting money. The second effect of using a tax incentive instead of a direct subsidy is that all taxpayers only have to pay part of the costs. The other part is financed by the art enthusiasts.

Private gifts are very important for cultural institutions for several reasons, as they have the following effects:

1. Broadening of the financial base of cultural and heritage institutions: an additional source of income next to government subsidies, leading to more funding.
2. Strengthening the financial base of cultural institutions: gifts from private individuals are less sensitive to political and economic changes, provided cultural institutions have created a bond with the art enthusiasts.
3. Strengthening the social base of cultural institutions: private gifts provide an opportunity to create and foster a bond with the public.

Therefore, if policy objects include that the creative industries take notice of the preferences of the public, create a bond between art enthusiasts and cultural institutions, broaden and strengthen the financial and social base of cultural institutions and/or reduce the costs of all taxpayers of the government support, a tax incentive such as a gift deduction is a more effective instrument than a direct subsidy. I do not claim that all direct subsidies for cultural institutions must be replaced by tax incentives. For certain costs, such as security, heating, accounts and other exploitation costs, it can be difficult to attract private funds. Such base costs could still be funded by direct subsidies. Furthermore, it might be deemed important to fund certain art forms that are recognized by experts, but not yet by the public. Therefore, my claim is not that either direct subsidies or tax incentives are the better instrument, but merely that these instruments can serve different policy objects. The applied instrument must fit this policy objective.

7.2 *Encourage Commercial Success*

Globerman (1980), p. 18 observed that if profitability is the criterion for efficiency of government aid, there is a strong case for providing private investors with tax incentives to invest in culture. The hypothesis behind this is that entrepreneurs are more likely to select projects that may be profitable than government bureaucrats. Using tax incentives enables the government to leave the initiative with the creative industry instead of making selections itself. If the policy is to encourage building up a national sustainable sector in certain creative industries, for example films, architecture or video games, tax incentives might therefore be a more effective instrument than direct grants. For less-commercial sectors of the creative industries, such as poetry and conceptual art, commercial success might not be the best benchmark, and not a reason to use a tax incentive.

7.3 Empowerment of Creative Industries

Creative industries might feel differently about direct subsidies and tax incentives. These feelings might influence their reactions to the policy instrument used and should therefore be taken into account when deciding on the most appropriate instrument for a certain policy. A government grant may create a feeling of dependency, which might stand in the way of developing entrepreneurship and a feeling of owned responsibility. Tax incentives that, for example, reduce corporate income tax burden for certain creative industries might, on the other hand, encourage an entrepreneurial spirit. These do not have the form of a direct money transfer and therefore maintain the feeling of independence. Tax incentives might therefore empower creative industries.

7.4 Raising Funds Quickly to Preserve Cultural Heritage

Not all cultural heritage that is regarded as having great importance for a country is owned by the government. Important cultural heritage, such as works of art, manuscripts, archives, heritage objects, monuments and historic documents can be privately owned in most countries. When the owner dies, their heirs will have to pay inheritance tax over the value of the cultural heritage. This might be an additional incentive for the heirs to sell the heritage, for example works of art, on a (foreign) auction. Museums or the government will not always be able to acquire the necessary funds in time to acquire the works of art. By the time they have gone through all the bureaucratic procedures to get a direct grant, the particular work may have been sold already. This means that after an auction the art may be lost to the public, or even to the country if the work is bought by a foreigner. In the case of heritage buildings, in some circumstances such a sale might lead to demolition.

To prevent this and to preserve important national heritage, many European countries have introduced the option of paying inheritance tax, and in some countries other taxes, by transferring such cultural heritage to the state. In England this tax incentive is referred to as "acceptance in lieu of tax" and in France as *dation* (for a more elaborate discussion of these specific tax incentives, refer to Sect. 6 of Chap. 7). The tax incentive has the advantage that the budget is already present, which enables the government to act quickly. In various countries this tax incentive has been important in acquiring major works of art now on public display. Such tax incentives can, therefore, be an effective and efficient way to achieve the cultural policy goal of preserving important cultural heritage for the nation.

8 How to Determine Whether to Introduce Tax Incentive or a Direct Subsidy

In the previous sections it became clear that tax incentives and direct subsidies each have their own benefits and drawbacks, both from the point of view of fiscal policy and creative industries policy. Which instrument is to be used to achieve a given policy goal, should, in my opinion, be based on the answers to the following questions:

1. Why is government interference necessary?
2. What is the policy objective?
3. What is the most effective and efficient instrument to reach this policy objective?

Only if these questions can be answered in a duly motivated way and only if the answers lead to the conclusion that tax incentives are the most effective and efficient instrument for a certain policy objective should such incentives be used. Furthermore, a prerequisite for the effective and efficient use of tax incentives is that these are accounted for, controlled and evaluated in the same way as direct subsidies (OECD 2010, p. 45).

In the past 20 years, the Netherlands has, for example, taken several measures to improve the accountability of tax incentives. One of the measures in the 2001 Budget was the introduction of a framework consisting of several questions that must be answered before a tax expenditure can be introduced. This Review Framework Tax Expenditures (*Toetsingskader Belastinguitgaven*) has been amended several times. The 2015 framework consists of the following questions (Ministerie van Financiën 2015 pp. 347–349, model 4.55):

1. Is the problem clear? Why does the government have to interfere and how does the problem relate to the policy field of the department proposing the tax incentive.
2. Is the objective stated clearly and unambiguously? The SMART requirements are leading: the objective of the proposed measure must be described in a way that is Specific, Measurable, Assignable, Realistic and Time-related.
3. Can it be proven why financial intervention is necessary? It must be argued why a financial instrument is chosen instead of other policy instruments.
4. Can it be proven why a subsidy is preferred over a levy? It must be proven why desired behavior can be incentivized more effectively by using a carrot rather than a stick.
5. Can it be proven why a tax incentive is preferred over a direct subsidy? Both for direct subsidies and for tax incentives the general budgeting rules must be applied, such as the expenditure cap in relation to direct subsidies and as regards tax incentives non-interference with automatic stabilizers. The weighing of a tax incentive against a direct subsidy must at least include target group reach, feasibility, accountability and enforceability, cost-effectiveness, simplicity, fit in tax structure and budgetary controllability.
6. Is an evaluation of the provision sufficiently safeguarded?

If the answer to one of the questions is negative, the tax incentive cannot be proposed. However, it is not clear whether this framework is always used when a new tax incentive is being proposed. It is not included in public documents regarding recently introduced Dutch tax incentives. Furthermore, if it is applied, this does not always seem to be done explicitly, as is illustrated by the answer, "the framework was applied implicitly" to Parliament regarding the application of the framework when a certain tax incentive was introduced.[6] It is questionable whether such an implicit application will lead to a thorough weighing of the alternatives.

However, if the choice for the instrument of a tax incentive is based on the three questions mentioned before, and if these are duly accounted for and evaluated, tax incentives can, in my view, be a valuable instrument to reach certain cultural policy objects in a more efficient and effective way than with the other policy instruments.

9 Conclusion

Tax incentives must be considered relative to alternative policy tools such as spending programs, regulations and information campaigns. As the OECD (2010), p. 24 rightly observed, these instruments all

> have their own process deficiencies in enactment and review, and introduce their own economic and political distortions.

Tax incentives are not necessarily a better or worse instrument than other policy instruments. Which instrument is best should be determined based on both the policy object and on fiscal policy considerations. Furthermore, it is important that tax incentives are controlled, accounted for and evaluated in the same way as direct subsidies. As this is currently not always the case, tax incentives are, in that respect, inferior to direct subsidies.

References

Anderson B (2008) PowerPoint presentation at the 5th annual meeting of OECD-Asia Senior Budget Officials, 10–11 January 2008, Bangkok. http://www.oecd.org/gov/budgeting/39944419.pdf. Accessed 8 July 2015

Christiaanse JH (1977) Tax expenditures. Weekblad fiscaal recht, pp 69–75

Department for Culture, Media and Sport (2015) Cultural gifts scheme guidance. http://www.artscouncil.org.uk/media/uploads/doc/CGSguidance27january2015.docx. Accessed 28 July 2015

European Commission (1997) Report from the commission to the council and to the European parliament in accordance with Article 12(4) of the sixth council directive of 17 May 1977 on

[6]Kamerstukken II, 2014–2015, 34200 XIII, nr. 7, answer to question 60.

the harmonisation of the laws of the Member States relating to turn-over taxes—Common system of value added tax: uniform basis of assessment COM(97) 559 final

Feldstein M (1980) A contribution to the theory of tax expenditures: the case of charitable giving. In: Araron HJ, Boskin MJ (eds) The economics of taxation. Brookings Institution, Washington, DC, pp 99–122

Grampp WD (1989) Pricing the priceless: art, artists, and economics. Basic Books, New York

Globerman S (1980) Direct versus indirect aid to the arts: a Canadian perspective. J Cult Econ 2:15–22

Heithuis E (2013) OverBelastingen 2.0. Inaugural lecture Open Universiteit Heerlen

IBP (2012) International budget survey. http://survey.internationalbudget.org/. Accessed 18 July 2015

IMF (2007) Code of good practices on fiscal transparency. http://www.imf.org/external/np/pp/2007/eng/051507c.pdf. Accessed 18 July 2015

Jefferson T (1789) Letter to James Madison Paris 6 September 1789. http://www.let.rug.nl/usa/P/tj3/writings/brf/jefl81.htm. Accessed 18 July 2015

Kavelaars P (2014) Giftenaftrek kan worden afgeschaft. Weekblad fiscaal recht, p 607

Kraan D-J (2004) Off-budget and tax expenditures. OECD J Budg 4(1):121–142. OECD, Paris. http://www.oecd.org/gov/budgeting/39515114.pdf. Accessed 8 July 2015

Lowi ThJ (1969) The end of liberalism: ideology, policy, and the crisis of public authority. Norton, New York

Mann FK (1947) The threefold economic function of taxation. Openbare Financiën (1/2):5–17

Manvel AD (1971) Opening comments. In: Surrey SS et al (eds) Tax incentives. Heath Lexington Books, Massachusetts 1

McDaniel PR (1976) The tax expenditure concept: theory and practical operation. Maandblad Belasting Beschouwingen, pp 245–256

Ministerie van Financiën (1987) Belastinguitgaven in de Nederlandse inkomstenbelasting en de loonbelasting. Staatsuitgeverij, 's-Gravenhage

Ministerie van Financiën (2010) Beleidsdoorlichting evaluaties belastinguitgaven. www.rijksbegroting.nl/binaries/pdfs/beleidsdoorlichtingen/beleidsdoorlichtingen-06-2010/fin-belastinguitgaven.pdf. Accessed 18 July 2015

Ministerie van Financiën (2014a) Inkomstenbeperkende regelingen en belastinguitgaven. In: Miljoenennota 2015. http://www.rijksbegroting.nl/2015/voorbereiding/miljoenennota,kst199383_6.html. Accessed 18 July 2015

Ministerie van Financiën (2014b) Toelichting op de belastinguitgaven. In: Miljoenennota 2015. http://www.rijksbegroting.nl/2015/kamerstukken,2014/9/19/kst812061_4.html. Accessed 18 July 2015

Ministerie van Financiën (2015) Rijksbegrotingsvoorschriften 2015. http://rbv.minfin.nl/2015. Accessed 21 July 2015

Mourato S, Mazzanti M (2002) Economic valuation of cultural heritage: evidence and prospects. In: De la Torre M (ed) Assessing the values of cultural heritage. The Getty Conservation Institute, Los Angeles, pp 51–73. http://www.getty.edu/conservation/publications_resources/pdf_publications/pdf/assessing.pdf. Accessed 21 July 2015

OECD (1984) Tax expenditures. A review of the issues and country practices. OECD, Paris

OECD (2010) Tax expenditures in OECD countries. OECD, Paris

OECD (2015) Recommendation of the council on budgetary governance. OECD, Paris

O'Hagan J (2011) Tax concessions. In: Towse R (ed) A handbook of cultural economics, 2nd edn. Edward Elgar, Cheltenham/Northampton, pp 408–412

Philipps L (2012) The globalization of tax expenditure reporting: transplanting transparency in india and the global south. Comparative Research in Law & Political Economy. Research Paper No. 43/2012. http://digitalcommons.osgoode.yorku.ca/cgi/viewcontent.cgi?article=1034&context=clpe. Accessed 18 July 2015

Schuster JMD (1979) Income taxes and the arts: tax expenditures as cultural policy. Massachusetts Institute of Technology, Massachusets. http://dspace.mit.edu/handle/1721.1/70147. Accessed 8 July 2015

Schuster JMD (1987) Issues in supporting the arts through tax incentives. J Arts Manag Law 16:31–50
Simon JG (1987) The tax treatment of nonprofit organizations: a review of federal and state policies. In: Powell WW (ed) The nonprofit sector. Yale University Press, New Haven/London
Stevers ThA (1978) Verslag van het debat. In: Grapperhaus, FHM, Een beschouwing over begrip en betekenis van belastinguitgaven in Nederland. Geschriften van de Vereniging voor Belastingwetenschap, nr. 147. Kluwer, Deventer 7–29
Surrey SS et al (1971) Tax incentives. Heath Lexington Books, Massachusetts
Surrey SS (1973) Pathways to tax reform. Harvard University Press, Cambridge
Surrey SS (1981) The concept of tax reliefs—Its relation to tax policy and budget policy. In: Häuser K (ed) Subventions, avantages fiscaux et prix/Subsidies, tax reliefs and prices. Éditions Cujas, Paris, pp 35–58
Surrey SS, McDaniel PR (1985) Tax expenditures. Harvard University Press, Cambridge
Surrey SS, Sunley EM Jr (1976) General Report. Cahiers de droit fiscal international, vol LXIa. Kluwer, Deventer, pp 15–63
Uemura T (2009) An estimation of tax expenditure in Japanese income tax from the viewpoint of the fiscal transparency. Govern Audit Rev 16(3):3–17. http://www.jbaudit.go.jp/english/exchange/pdf/e16d01.pdf. Accessed on 28 July 2015
Van der Ploeg R (2002) In art we trust. De Economist 150:333–362
Van Weeghel S (2015) Snoei in oerwoud aan aftrekpostjes. https://actueel.pwc.nl/diensten-en-sectoren/tax/fiscalist-stef-van-weeghel-snoei-oerwoud-aan-aftrekpostjes/. Accessed 8 July 2015
Wagner AHG (1880) Finanzwissenschaft. C.F. Winter'sche Verlagshandlung, Leipzig/Heidelberg
Willis JRM, Hardwick PJW (1978) Tax expenditures in the United Kingdom. Heinemann Educational Books, London
Whitehouse E (1999) The tax treatment of funded pensions. Social Protection Discussion Paper Series no. 9910. World Bank, Washington, DC. http://mpra.ub.uni-muenchen.de/14173/1/MPRA_paper_14173.pdf. Accessed 8 July 2015

Chapter 5
Tax Incentives, Harmful Tax Competition and State Aid Considerations in the EU

Raymond Luja

Abstract The creative sector is affected, like any other industry, by measures to avoid harmful tax competition when shifting taxable profits between countries. While those measures ought to be aimed at curtailing tax avoidance practices, they may also affect genuine business activities to some extent. Because research and development may play an important role in the creative process, special attention should be given to proposed OECD/G20 regulation concerning taxation of royalties. Within the European Union, state aid rules restrict the options of EU Member States with respect to providing aid to culture or to the creative industry at large. Certain incentives may require approval from the European Commission.

Keywords State aid · European Union · Intellectual property · Culture · Film

1 Introduction

In the next part of this book, several types of tax incentives for the creative industry are discussed. In this chapter, the question will be addressed to what extent individual states are free to design their tax incentives to their liking, with a particular focus on the Member States of the European Union.

Tax incentives for the creative industry in the EU are 'regulated' at different levels. At the OECD/G20 level, there have been recent proposals to curb tax avoidance. Those proposals have little to do with the creative sector as such, but they may have an impact on it, in particular in terms of providing tax incentives for

R. Luja (✉)
Department of Tax Law/Maastricht Centre for Taxation, Maastricht University, Maastricht, The Netherlands
e-mail: raymond.luja@maastrichtuniversity.nl

R. Luja
Loyens & Loeff N.V., Amsterdam, The Netherlands

© Springer Science+Business Media Singapore 2017

S. Hemels and K. Goto (eds.), *Tax Incentives for the Creative Industries*, Creative Economy, DOI 10.1007/978-981-287-832-8_5

royalties. These proposals will be briefly addressed in Sect. 2. Within the EU, it is mainly competition law that affects tax incentives. State aid rules impose the most obvious supra-national limits on tax incentives that can be granted by EU Member States.[1] In order to secure an EU-wide internal market with free and fair competition, EU Member States cannot grant tax incentives selectively, that is, to a particular company or sector of industry. These rules are discussed in more detail in Sect. 3. Exemptions to those rules that allow for the EU's approval of state aid in support of culture and creativity are addressed in Sect. 4. Some concluding remarks follow in Sect. 5.

2 Base Erosion and Profit Shifting

2.1 The OECD/G20 Initiatives

The creative industry might not have been at the center of attention in the international discussions on tax avoidance, but it may well be affected by it. Even before the 1997 OECD report on harmful tax competition, there had been efforts to restrict tax avoidance internationally. In 2015, the OECD/G20 (anti) Base Erosion and Profit Shifting efforts (the "BEPS project") promulgated a set of recommendations to adapt national tax systems so as to avoid double non-taxation and to ensure that profits are mostly taxed where activities take place. In 13 different reports, the OECD calls countries to action, a call endorsed by the G20 (2015, para. 15).

The creative sector is one of the sectors that may be affected by rules on transfer pricing intended to make sure that profits are allocated where value is created, especially when software (including games) or animated movies are produced in a joint cooperation between offices around the globe to ensure 24/7 progress.

These problems are normally not specifically related to tax incentives, which are the subject of this book, with one clear exception. The BEPS Action 5 report "Countering Harmful Tax Practices More Effectively, Taking into Account Transparency and Substance" puts particular emphasis on the taxation of intangibles, such as patents and copyrights.

2.2 When Is Tax Competition Deemed Harmful?

In determining whether something is harmful tax competition, a number of factors are considered by the OECD (2015):

[1]This chapter was last updated on 6 January 2016. National (and possibly constitutional) restraints on tax incentives are not addressed here, nor are restraints imposed by bilateral or multilateral trade agreements.

15. The four key factors are:

(a) The regime imposes no or low effective tax rates on income from geographically mobile financial and other service activities.
(b) The regime is ring-fenced from the domestic economy.
(c) The regime lacks transparency (for example, the details of the regime or its application are not apparent, or there is inadequate regulatory supervision or financial disclosure).
(d) There is no effective exchange of information with respect to the regime.

16. The eight other factors are:

(a) An artificial definition of the tax base.
(b) Failure to adhere to international transfer pricing principles.
(c) Foreign source income exempt from residence country taxation.
(d) Negotiable tax rate or tax base.
(e) Existence of secrecy provisions.
(f) Access to a wide network of tax treaties.
(g) The regime is promoted as a tax minimisation vehicle.
(h) The regime encourages operations or arrangements that are purely tax-driven and involve no substantial activities.

No or low effective taxation is the trigger in these discussions, as it is key to starting a harmful tax competition analysis in the OECD approach. It is the combination of some of these factors that might indicate harmfulness. Within the EU, the Code of Conduct Group, which examines harmful tax competition, uses a somewhat different starting point. There, the trigger is an effective tax that is lower than normal (EU Council 1997); low taxes across the board are not targeted as such.[2] Be this as it may, special treatment of intangibles is often perceived as involving a combination of low effective taxes and a lack of substance. This substance issue has been one of the central issues in BEPS Action 5 and is of direct relevance to applying tax incentives aimed at patents and copyrights.

2.3 *IP Boxes and Copyrights*

Special tax treatment of intellectual property presents a somewhat difficult environment (see Chap. 10 for examples). The OECD/G20—in an effort to curb international tax avoidance—agreed to a modified "nexus approach," which restricts special tax treatment of income from royalties. Such income may be treated favorably by means of output incentives, such as patent or royalty boxes. In this subsection, the focus will be on output incentives of this type, and not on input incentives, such as special tax treatment of labor, assets and other investments that go into the R&D process ("design").

[2]This code of conduct is more of a gentlemen's agreement amongst EU Member States and not an official legal instrument of the EU that can be enforced by its institutions.

On the one hand, the OECD does not want to hinder tax incentives for IP-intensive industries, as these industries may drive growth and employment. On the other hand, the OECD wants to make sure that IP regimes do not lead to a "beggar thy neighbor" policy in which passive IP income is attracted from other countries just to benefit from low effective taxation. The OECD does not take a position on whether countries should grant IP-related tax incentives; their effectiveness is often disputed as far as output-related tax benefits are concerned.

Without entering into the details of the OECD approach, the bottom line of the approach is that IP-income generated from only those activities carried out by the taxable entity itself may qualify for a special tax treatment (lower effective taxation), plus 30% of IP-income generated from activities that have been outsourced by that entity.

Qualifying IP is mainly IP in the form of (a) patents, broadly defined; (b) copyrighted software; and (c) certain other IP assets that are 'non-obvious, useful and novel' (OECD 2015, para. 34). Category (c) will be addressed later. Copyrighted assets other than software are not included in the definition of qualifying IP, with the rather simple excuse that "they do not arise out of the same type of R&D activities as software" (OECD 2015, para. 36). In addition, it is stated (OECD 2015, para. 36):

> Copyrighted software shares the fundamental characteristics of patents, since it is novel, non-obvious, and useful. It arises from the type of innovation and R&D that IP regimes are typically designed to encourage, and taxpayers in the software industry are unlikely to outsource the development of their core software to unrelated parties.

The latter may be true, but what, exactly, is this "type of innovation and R&D" that IP boxes are trying to target? Now, certain art forms require a lengthy process of experimenting with materials and, sometimes, even the development of new materials for the particular purpose of making art. Now, that process and those materials may be patented (or patentable, for smaller creative companies) by themselves. So, what is the difference? Software development often requires the involvement of a substantial team in order to be able to rationalize special tax treatment of any income flowing from copyrighted software, as a stimulus for a 'high-tech environment' some governments pursue, but that is not necessarily so. I cannot help but wonder whether, in some countries, constitutional law would allow the creative sector at large to apply for equal treatment, in case more individual or small-scale copyrighted creativity (like certain art, literature or photography) would be excluded.

As said above, some work done within the creative sector may clearly fall within the scope of IP boxes as intended by the OECD, particularly when patents are involved and for copyrighted software. For these situations, the OECD has called upon its members to limit any new and existing IP boxes (i.e., any tax incentives that lead to special treatment of IP income) to self-developed IP, causing substantial restrictions on outsourcing, as previously mentioned. This also means that in the case of joint projects, with teams working all over the globe in a 24/7 design/coding process, centralizing IP rights may become more troublesome when trying to make optimal use of the tax incentives on offer in the various jurisdictions.

At the same time, a side effect of BEPS Action 5 is that tax incentives that address copyrighted income from creative efforts that are not linked to software should come to an end. Given the particular nature of the art sector and the limited risk of tax avoidance if copyright income is retained by the producer/designer, there does not seem to be a convincing case for using a narrow definition of qualifying copyrighted assets. I am not arguing that output incentives will be effective enough in the long run to actually stimulate creative R&D, but, if they are, then why limit them to software?

As for category (c), the OECD also allows IP assets that share features of patents and that are similar to patents or copyrighted software to qualify, albeit this is limited to small- and medium-sized enterprises, who do not have to go through a costly patenting process. They should go through a national R&D certification process administered by the government (but not the tax authorities) instead. These SMEs must be taxpayers who have no more than €50 million in world-wide (group) turnover and who, by themselves, earn less than €7.5 million a year in gross revenue from all IP assets (OECD 2015, para. 37).[3] This may seem to open the way to get more assets covered for SMEs, but it raises new issues for EU countries since limiting tax benefits to SMEs may trigger the application of state aid rules. Those will be addressed next.

3 EU State Aid Rules

3.1 Background

Upon the establishment of the European Economic Community in 1958, one of its main objectives was to create a common market amongst its six founding members. In order to safeguard fair competition within that market, state aid rules were adopted that would prevent Member States from granting large subsidies to their domestic industries, which would then be able to compete within this new European market while enjoying more favorable conditions. Now, in 2016, the EU with its 28 Member States still uses the original 1958 definition. The European Court of Justice clarified in 1961 that any restriction on subsidies would be rather useless if other forms of financial benefits, such as tax incentives, were left unrestricted. It therefore pointed out that “aid” would cover such benefits as well, and not only classical (cash) subsidies.[4] For this reason, EU Member States may face supranational

[3]Amounts are based on a five-year average.

[4]Case 30/59, *De Gezamenlijke Steenkolenmijnen in Limburg v. High Authority of the European Coal and Steel Community* [1961] European Court Recordings, p. 3.

restrictions when granting tax incentives that are targeted at, for instance, culture or the creative industry at large.

3.2 *Definition of State Aid*

3.2.1 Cumulative Criteria

Article 107(1) of the Treaty on the Functioning of the European Union states that, unless otherwise provided, state aid is incompatible with the internal market and hence prohibited.[5]

In order for there to be state aid, a number of conditions must be fulfilled cumulatively:

1. There must be financial aid to an undertaking (i.e., either a company, incorporated or otherwise, or a self-employed person).
2. Such aid must be granted by a member state (or any lower level of government) or be financed out of state resources.
3. Such aid must threaten to distort EU competition and affect trade between EU Member States.
4. Any such aid must be selective, that is, targeted at the production of certain goods or at particular companies or industries.

So, how does this affect the creative sector?

3.2.2 Financial Aid to an Undertaking by a Member State

First, and more generally, tax incentives lead, by definition, to a financial benefit granted by a government. So conditions 1 and 2 will often be fulfilled rather easily unless Member States are obliged by EU directives or regulations to introduce special tax treatment.

In the context of the creative sector, an obligation to introduce special treatment seems to be relevant to only some special VAT rules related to the (re)sale of certain works of art (the margin scheme; see Chap. 9, Sect. 4) and VAT exemptions for certain services provided by authors, artists and performers (see Chap. 11).[6] Arguably, this falls outside of the scope of state aid, since it is the EU VAT Directive that provides an explicit basis for a lower rate or exemption.[7] According to state aid doctrine, a member state that merely complies with a clear and precise obligation from an EU directive or regulation cannot be held accountable for aid

[5]Similar provisions apply to the countries of the European Economic Area (EEA).

[6]Article 311, annex IX A and annex X B VAT Directive, OJ L 347/1 of 11 December 2006.

[7]Case C-460/07, *Puffer*, [2009] European Court Recordings I-3251, para. 70.

granted in this way. However, the relevant directive provides only the option to exempt authors, artists and artistic performance; thus, it is questionable whether the exercise of such an option constitutes an independent action that is attributable to a member state. That said, it is very unlikely that the application of such a rate will ever come into the scope of a state aid procedure, as the EU itself has allowed for it.

State aid must be granted to an undertaking to be considered as such; however, for state aid purposes, an undertaking does not have to have the objective of making a profit. Also, non-profit institutions may qualify as an undertaking if they engage in economic activities within the EU's internal market.

It is worth pointing out that there may be 'state' aid, even when there is no direct transfer of sums between the government and the company or artist. State aid rules also apply to indirect aid granted via third parties (see Chap. 7 for examples). Suppose, for example, that the government tries to stimulate its citizens to give money to museums or support funds for artists, by giving them a special tax deduction for gifts. This may qualify as an indirect benefit if this deduction leads to additional gifts. The same would apply if loans to museums—either in cash or by permanent loan of art—resulted in a special exemption of the value of those loans or works of art from wealth tax.

Now, take the following example. A world-renowned museum is planning on acquiring a Rembrandt painting. As explained above, museums that attract tourists from all over the world may be considered to be carrying out an economic activity under EU laws, since it is an activity that is likely to have an effect on cross-border services (some tourists fly to one city instead of another just because of the presence of a particular museum). Therefore, this museum is fully subject to state aid rules. In order to finance the acquisition, there is a proposal to engage in crowd-funding as part of a scheme in which several private investors will 'own' a small part of the picture that will be on permanent loan to the museum. So as to facilitate such crowd-funding, national tax rules prescribe that the (partial) ownership of/entitlement to any such painting on loan is to be exempted from income tax (as far as return on investment is concerned) and from wealth tax (as far as the value is concerned).

Here, indirect aid again plays an important part, since tax benefits to intermediaries resulted in a financial benefit for the museum. The rules will facilitate obtaining this painting because private investors have been given a financial incentive to provide a painting, via permanent loan, that the museum would have had to acquire and finance otherwise.

The point of all this is that exemptions such as the aforementioned income tax and wealth tax exemptions are often put in place as a small reward to the donor of a painting, whether it is one wealthy donor or a large group of smaller donors. For many of the donors, the act of donating may be rather unrelated to the tax benefit they gain, and the reasons may be primarily based on cultural, social or patriotic considerations. Even so, as the effect of the tax incentives has to be assessed at the level of the undertaking—the museum. There, it may have a considerable impact.

For those readers who now become worried when recognizing incentives like these in the national tax laws of EU Member States, be reminded that while these measures may meet the criterion for a transfer of a financial benefit, this does not mean that they will meet the other criteria. All criteria must be met, and in particular the element of selectivity must be met, and so the mere presence of indirect aid is not decisive. Even if there is state aid, there is room for approval as we will see in Sect. 4.

3.2.3 (Threat of) Distortion of Competition and Affecting Trade

As for the third criterion, a negative effect on trade and competition, we must look at the effects of a measure on third parties to judge applicability. Tax benefits for local artists with a highly local group of customers or benefits supporting local museums, rather than attracting out-of-region tourists, may be able to escape qualification as state aid if there is no measureable effect on competition. The emphasis here is on "may," because this threshold is normally met rather easily since it is the *potential* effect on competition that is relevant here (so also the crowding out of future competition, like the establishment of an auxiliary branch of a foreign museum or the establishment of new collections that will draw interest from other countries).

It should be mentioned that so-called *de minimis* aid is deemed not to have a noticeable effect on trade and competition within the EU, at least according to the European Commission (2013a). If, in total, an undertaking does not receive more than €200 000 in state aid from a government over a three (fiscal) year period, then the undertaking will be out of the scope of Article 107(1) TFEU[8] This could be helpful for giving small-scale support to local activities, but it is also rather tricky. The €200 000 limit applies to all aid—including tax benefits, cash subsidies and state guarantees—by any level of government (federal, state, municipal etc.) to an undertaking, directly or indirectly. Here, undertaking refers to the economic entity performing a particular activity, which can be a group of related legal entities that are each, by themselves, individual taxpayers. Last but not least, it should be clear in advance that the threshold will not be exceeded. If one ends up with a total of €200 001, then the entire amount would end up as state aid after all. This makes the *de minimis* aid exemption hard to administer and prone to errors in its application. Wage tax benefits, as well as classical corporate tax credits with fixed or capped amounts, would be better manageable in this respect. Yet, the *de minimis* exception may still be helpful to keep a local municipality from worrying too much about a local exemption of real estate tax or property occupation tax for smaller museums that receive little to no other government support.

So, a local effort might not have a noticeable effect on trade and competition, but how about the Uffizi, the Louvre or the Rijksmuseum? Obviously, with these kinds of museums, which attract tourists from all over the world, we may safely assume

[8]If an entity has been tasked with performing services of general economic interest (discussed later), then this limit will be €500 000 (European Commission 2012).

that any state aid will have an effect on trade and competition in the sectors of cultural and tourist-related services.

When we are talking of production within the creative industry, such as films, video games or even fine art, the very low threshold for testing a potential effect of aid will also not be that difficult to exceed. Even films that actually intend or claim to promote national or regional culture may have an impact on the international market. For instance, a (non-tax) Catalonian subsidy to promote subtitling or dubbing of films in Catalan, a language used in both the northeastern part of Spain and adjacent parts of France (as well as Andorra) was deemed to have a potential cross-border effect (albeit an acceptable one, as we will see next).[9] So, the bottom line is that it is safest to assume that the third criterion is fulfilled, except when limited to highly local efforts.

EU Member States could entrust certain entities with the carrying out of services of general (economic) interest (SGEI). To a large extent, defining SGEIs is at the discretion of Member States. In theory, it would be possible to consider granting free access to cultural exposure via museums for the elderly or the unemployed, discounted access to particular patriotic films or similar services as a potential SGEI. Compensation for SGEIs of up to €15 million per year does not require notifying the European Commission, provided that the aid has the effect of compensating for the costs of carrying out the public service being entrusted, taking into account any revenue from such service and a reasonable profit mark-up.[10] Normally, these services are to be entrusted contractually to a particular entity for a maximum of 10 years, subject to extension.[11]

3.2.4 Selectivity

The fourth criterion, selectivity, is by far the most difficult in addressing tax incentives. Benefits specifically targeted at particular sectors of industry, such as the creative sector at large or any particular branch thereof, will normally be deemed selective. Also, special tax arrangements that are put in place for individual taxpayers may qualify as selective if those arrangements diverge from normally applicable tax laws. Think of tax rulings that provide a favorable tax treatment to the digital industry, or even one-on-one deals made at some governmental level, for instance in an attempt to facilitate acquiring particular pieces of art or the establishment of a creative entertainment facility. Here, it should be pointed out that,

[9]Commission Decision C (2010) 1247 final of 24 March 2010, State Aid N 33/2010, para 22.

[10]Reasonable is defined as the normal return of capital pursued by a typical undertaking, taking the level of risk into account (which will depend on the sector of industry and the type of service, among other considerations; normally, the relevant swap rate + 100 basis points would be acceptable). Alternative profit level indicators may be acceptable as well. See European Commission (2012), Article 5.

[11]Also see European Commission (2011).

as an exception, state aid rules may allow for a special tax measure to address specific characteristics of the creative sector. But this is an argument that should be made in the process of having a proposed tax measure reviewed by the European Commission—as will be explained later—because this is really is the exception to the rule that beneficial sector-specific tax measures may be subject to scrutiny.

When it comes to indirect incentives, we have seen that allowing a deduction of gifts to museums could be problematic, as it might be perceived as indirect support triggered by state action. A more general provision allowing gifts to charities in general would not normally be considered selective. Museums, or at least special purpose vehicles set up as feeders for charitable donations to museums (not for day-to-day operations, but for the acquisition or preservation of a particular collection or education programs), might qualify for such a general charitable gift exemption without this leading to any selectivity.

3.3 State Aid Procedure[12]

3.3.1 Notification and Standstill

If a member state has the intention of granting state aid to the creative sector as a whole, or to a particular part thereof (like museums), Article 108(3) TFEU requires that member state to timely inform the European Commission of its intention. After such notification, a stand-still obligation will apply, which effectively prohibits the notified incentive from being introduced until such time as the Commission makes a final decision on the measure.

Normally, state aid is considered incompatible with the EU's internal market unless it has been approved by the European Commission as being for the greater good of the union and its Member States.

Upon notification, the Commission will open a confidential and preliminary investigation into the proposed measure—which could either be a tax scheme applicable to a group of undertakings or one-off aid for a particular undertaking—by starting to gather information from the member state. It will then try to decide within two months, which could lead to one of three outcomes: (i) no aid, so notification was not necessary; (ii) state aid, to which the Commission has no objections; or (iii) the Commission has doubts whether either there is such aid or, if so, whether it should be approved as other interests could be at stake. In this third situation, the Commission will open a full public investigation and invite interested parties (including the potential beneficiaries, their competitors and other Member States) to submit their comments. This may take up to another 18 months for a final decision, which could be (i) no aid; (ii) authorized aid; (iii) aid that will be approved if certain conditions are fulfilled, such as alterations or limitations to the initial

[12]For an overview of the entire procedure, see the procedural regulation (EU Council 2015).

proposal; or (iv) incompatible aid, which will not be authorized. The decision may be subject to appeal at the General Court as a court of first instance, and to further appeal to the Court of Justice of the EU.

3.3.2 Recovery of Unlawfully Granted Aid

The procedure above is a rather formal one, the duration of which can be an inconvenience to governments that are under public pressure or otherwise desire to act swiftly. For these and other reasons, notifications of potential aid measures are not always sent in time, or the measures are introduced after notification, in violation of the stand-still obligation. If a measure so introduced does indeed amount to aid, it may be unlawfully granted aid, which can be subject to recovery. Recovery means, in a nutshell, that taxpayers may be obliged to pay certain tax benefits (plus interest) back to the government over a period of up to 10 years, should the benefit indeed be found to have been unlawful.[13] So, a violation of EU rules may not just end up in a slap on the wrist for governments involved (who get their money back!), but it may also have direct financial consequences for the recipients of tax incentives.

4 Approval of Aid

As indicated above, the European Commission may consider approving of particular forms of aid.

4.1 Cultural Aid

4.1.1 Defining Culture

Article 167 TFEU states that the EU should contribute to the "flowering of the cultures" of EU Member States, particularly to promote cultural diversity. In the field of state aid, this has more or less translated into a pro-culture approach to aid in a number of areas, such as dissemination of European, national and/or regional culture and history; heritage conservation; non-commercial cultural exchanges; and artistic, audiovisual and/or literary creation.[14] Such aid to culture-promoting endeavors may be approved of where it does not affect trading conditions and EU competition to an extent contrary to the common interest of the EU and its

[13]The actual recovery period may be longer than 10 years as it may be interrupted or suspended.

[14]Article 167 TFEU.

Member States.[15] This provides the European Commission with a reasonable amount of leeway to design a policy as to which kinds and amounts of aid may deemed acceptable. Until 2014, such analysis was done mainly on a case-by-case basis, with the important exception of aiding the film sector at large.

Because EU Member States are confronted with a restrictive state aid regime, there is a tendency to get the most out of those exemptions that are awarded. In this context, it should be clarified that state aid to public broadcasting does not fall under the heading of cultural aid as such. Stimulus measures for TV or radio broadcasts aimed at spreading general news or supporting children's education is not treated as cultural aid, although at times some programs that directly and clearly relate to culture and cultural education could still be supported (European Commission 2009, paras. 33 and 34).

Aid for technical necessary works to secure monuments from decay or to renovate them has been approved in the past in the context of mining sites that would have been irredeemably destroyed otherwise. Here, however, it was clear that the museum's income, derived from providing access to these sites, would not have been close to sufficient to cover these costs.[16] When it comes to protecting the fine arts, the latter test would be relevant as well. If the government funds the restoration of art that is left in the hands of a museum able to garner profits from displaying the art afterwards, then it may be necessary to put a system in place to avoid compensating for such costs to the extent that museums can be expected to cover them by drawing on additional resources.[17]

4.1.2 Exemption from Notification: Rules

In the 2014 General Block Exemption Regulation (GBER, European Commission 2014), section 11 on aid for culture and heritage conservation was introduced. This section gives EU Member States more leeway in introducing tax incentives in the field of culture and heritage. Section 11 consists of two articles: article 53 on aid for culture and heritage conservation and article 54 on aid schemes for audiovisual works (this article will be discussed in Sect. 4.2). The categories of aid that fall under these articles are exempt from the notification requirement of 108(3) TFEU, which was discussed in Sect. 3.3.1. This exemption is based on article 109 TFEU, which allows the council to determine categories of aid that are exempted from the notification requirement and article 108(4) TFEU, allowing the European Commission to adopt regulations relating to those categories of state aid.

Preamble 72 of the GBER observes that cultural institutions and projects do not typically give rise to any significant distortion of competition, and that case practice has shown that such aid has limited effects on trade. It refers to article 167 TFEU,

---

[15]Article 107(3)(d) TFEU.

[16]Commission Decision C(2014) 3910 final of 24 March 2010, SA.38122(2014/N).

[17]This may be part of the compensation mechanism for SGEIs, addressed above in Sect. 3.2.3.

which recognizes the importance of promoting culture. The preamble states that because

> of the dual nature of culture, being on the one hand an economic good that offers important opportunities for the creation of wealth and employment, and, on the other, a vehicle of identities, values and meanings that mirror and shape our societies, State aid rules should acknowledge the specificities of culture and the economic activities related to it.

Article 53 GBER provides a list of eligible cultural purposes and activities and eligible costs. Aid that is exempt from the notification requirement includes aid granted for the following cultural purposes and activities:[18]

(a) museums, archives, libraries, artistic and cultural centers or spaces, theatres, opera houses, concert halls, other live performance organizations, film heritage institutions and other similar artistic and cultural infrastructures, organizations and institutions;
(b) tangible heritage including all forms of movable or immovable cultural heritage and archaeological sites, monuments, historical sites and buildings; natural heritage linked to cultural heritage or if formally recognized as cultural or natural heritage by the competent public authorities of a Member State;
(c) intangible heritage in any form, including folklorist customs and crafts;
(d) art or cultural events and performances, festivals, exhibitions and other similar cultural activities;
(e) cultural and artistic education activities as well as promotion of the understanding of the importance of protection and promotion of the diversity of cultural expressions through educational and greater public awareness programs, including with the use of new technologies;
(f) writing, editing, production, distribution, digitization and publishing of music and literature, including translations.

The GBER covers both investment and operating aid below determined thresholds. For investment aid, the eligible costs are the investment costs in tangible and intangible assets, including[19]

(a) costs for the construction, upgrade, acquisition, conservation or improvement of infrastructure, if at least 80% of either the time or the space capacity per year is used for cultural purposes;
(b) costs for the acquisition, including leasing, transfer of possession or physical relocation of cultural heritage;
(c) costs for safeguarding, preservation, restoration and rehabilitation of tangible and intangible cultural heritage, including extra costs for storage under appropriate conditions, special tools, materials and costs for documentation, research, digitalization and publication;
(d) costs for improving the accessibility of cultural heritage to the public, including costs for digitization and other new technologies, costs to improve accessibility for persons with special needs (in particular, ramps and lifts for disabled persons, braille indications and hands-on exhibits in museums) and for promoting cultural diversity with respect to presentations, programs and visitors;

---

[18] Article 53(2) GBER.

[19] Article 53(4) GBER.

(e) costs for cultural projects and activities, cooperation and exchange programs and grants including costs for selection procedures, costs for promotion and costs incurred directly as a result of the project.

For operating aid, the eligible costs are[20]

(a) the cultural institution's or heritage site's costs linked to continuous or periodic activities including exhibitions, performances and events and similar cultural activities that occur in the ordinary course of business;
(b) costs of cultural and artistic education activities as well as promotion of the understanding of the importance of protection and promotion of the diversity of cultural expressions through educational and greater public awareness programs, including with the use of new technologies;
(c) costs of the improvement of public access to the cultural institution or heritage sites and activities including costs of digitization and of use of new technologies as well as costs of improving accessibility for persons with disabilities;
(d) operating costs directly relating to the cultural project or activity, such as rent or lease of real estate and cultural venues, travel expenses, materials and supplies directly related to the cultural project or activity, architectural structures for exhibitions and stage sets, loan, lease and depreciation of tools, software and equipment, costs for access rights to copyright works and other related intellectual property rights protected contents, costs for promotion and costs incurred directly as a result of the project or activity; depreciation charges and the costs of financing are only eligible if they have not been covered by investment aid;
(e) costs for personnel working for the cultural institution or heritage site or for a project;
(f) costs for advisory and support services provided by outside consultants and service providers, incurred directly as a result of the project.

Overcompensation is excluded by using caps. The amount of investment aid may not exceed the difference between the eligible costs and the operating profit of the investment. The amount of operating aid may not exceed what is necessary to cover the operating losses and a reasonable profit over the relevant period. For operating or investment aid not exceeding €1 million, the maximum amount of aid may be set at 80% of eligible costs. For publishing of music and literature, the maximum aid amount may not exceed either the difference between the eligible costs and the project's discounted revenues or 70% of the eligible costs, whichever is smaller. The eligible costs are the costs for publishing music and literature, including the authors' fees (copyright costs), translators' fees, editors' fees, other editorial costs (proofreading, correcting, reviewing), layout and pre-press costs and printing or e-publication costs.[21]

Activities which, although they may present a cultural aspect under preamble 72, have a predominantly commercial character because of the higher potential for competition distortion, such as press and magazines (written or electronic), are not covered. Furthermore, the list of eligible cultural purposes and activities does not include activities deemed to be commercial, such as fashion, design or video games.

[20]Article 53(5) GBER.

[21]Article 53(9) GBER.

Any aid granted under the GBER will have to be publicized on a website. For tax advantages, amounts will be published in ranges only, so no exact number will be given.[22]

4.1.3 Exemption from Notification: Risks

The GBER provides for a number of general safeguards that make it rather hard to get tax schemes approved on the basis of this regulation. Tax benefits will have to be discounted in order to determine their gross cash-equivalent-needed to check whether the aid levels are tolerable.[23] Accumulation is the biggest concern, as cultural entities may try to get sponsorships and financial benefits from several levels of government. In such a case, all benefits granted by *any* level of government must be accumulated including cash grants, cheap loans, government guarantees and tax benefits. As it must be assured that no tax benefit will be given if the accumulated aid level would be too high, tax schemes may have to contain rather complex conditions that require considering a lot of non-tax data.[24] This is a major concern, because accumulation may result in the entire tax scheme not being exempt from notification and, hence, being qualified as unlawful aid and subject to (full or partial) recovery. It is also of particular importance to ensure that the tax scheme provides for a claw-back mechanism in case operating profits are higher than projected.[25] This is done to avoid overcompensating certain activities, although a "reasonable profit" may remain on balance. For this author, it is rather hard to imagine what should be considered "reasonable" in the context of largely subsidized cultural activities. This may be open to interpretation, which poses an inherent risk to any taxpayer involved should the GBER have been incorrectly applied by a member state.

However, for cultural aid, windfall benefits might be possible. There is no need to show that a tax scheme was already in place before any work on an aided project or activity started. It is simply assumed that any benefit to the cultural sector—within the limits discussed above—will act as an incentive; for many other categories of aid, an incentive effect must ordinarily be shown first in order to be able to avoid notification via the GBER.[26]

---

[22]Article 9 GBER; ranges will be in millions of EUR: 0.5-1, 1-2, 2-5, 5-10, 10-30, 30 and over.

[23]Article 7(2) GBER. For tax benefits that are granted on a periodic basis, such as annually, discount rates will have to be determined per year, in accordance with commission rules (Article 7 (4) GBER).

[24]Article 8 GBER.

[25]Reliable and reasonable projections of next year's profits may be used as an *ex ante* alternative for cultural aid, which is hard to put in a tax scheme.

[26]Article 6(5)(h) GBER in reference to Article 6(4) GBER.

4.2 The Film Industry

In the area of film support (see Chap. 8 for examples), the approval of state aid has been the subject of many cases. In the Second Cinema Communication of 2013 the Commission provides guidelines for the assessment of aid to the audiovisual sector, covering everything from concept-development to production to delivery to audiences (European Commission 2013b). According to European Commission figures, film support in the EU is estimated at €3 billion per year, of which €1 billion is provided via tax incentives (European Commission 2013b, footnote 1 to para. 6). Examples of these incentives include enhanced deductions, film tax credits and wage tax reductions.

As for supporting the delivery of films to audiences, the Second Cinema Communication gives more leeway than its predecessor from 2001. It allows aid to cinemas for distributing particular kinds of films as well as any transmedia or cross-media projects where film promotion is done through various means (films, related books or iPad apps, etc.). Member states should have a selection system in place with objective criteria in order to decide which films meet the threshold of contributing to culture. This is mainly left in the hands of the Member States to decide and may include the use of a particular language for eligibility, if needed. So, how culture is to be reflected in films is rather difficult and mainly up to the EU Member States. While conditions on the nationality of actors and producers and on the set's location in one member state may be at odds with primary EU law (the fundamental freedoms), requirements to show a level of creativity, diversity or heritage peculiar to a particular culture might do the trick. Either way, these may be relatively vague criteria used to define which films have a sufficient element of culture; these films may go beyond typical art house films in need of support.

The communication provides for tolerable aid limits. Aid to audiovisual production, distribution and promotion may cover up to 50% of the budget. As for production costs, 60% is allowed in case of a co-production between two or more EU Member States. Member States may set higher levels for "difficult" audiovisual works, such as short films, films by new, unknown directors (first or second film) and films with very low budgets as well as "otherwise commercially difficult works" (European Commission 2013b, para. 52 section 3).

Member States are allowed to introduce territorial spending conditions in order to maintain a critical mass of film infrastructure in a particular member state (or region of a member state). For instance, a member state may require that up to 50% of the production budget of any aided film is to be spent in its territory. In addition or as an alternative, a member state may require that up to 160% of the amount of aid granted is actually spent within its territory. Either way, territorial spending obligations cannot exceed 80% of the total production budget. These rules effectively apply to both subsidies (grants) as well as tax incentives.

The production of computer games is not covered by the aforementioned communication, as the Commission has too little experience with granting aid in this field. The European Commission (2013c) made a statement to the effect that not all games necessarily qualify as audiovisual works or cultural products. The production, distribution, marketing and consumption of games is different from that of films.

The European Commission seems particularly inclined to provide leverage to Member States competing for major international productions against sites such as Australia, Canada, New Zealand or the USA. The European Commission (2013c, paras. 39 and 40) reasons that attracting foreign productions may have a lasting impact because it may make use of local high-quality audiovisual infrastructure and of local cast members and help to transfer know-how and expertise. Experiences with this kind of aid will be closely monitored.

Preamble 73 of the GBER (European Commission, 2014) observes:

> Audiovisual works play an important role in shaping European identities and reflect the different traditions of Member States and regions. While there is strong competition between films produced outside the Union, there is limited circulation of European films outside their country of origin due to the fragmentation into national or regional markets. The sector is characterized by high investment costs, a perceived lack of profitability due to limited audiences and difficulties to generate additional private funding.

The criteria determined in the Second Cinema Communication (European Commission 2013b), mentioned before, are reflected in the block exemption rules for aid schemes for audiovisual works in article 54 of the GBER. In this article, aid schemes to support script-writing, development, production, distribution and promotion of audiovisual works is deemed compatible with the internal market pursuant to Article 107(3) TFEU and is exempt from the notification requirement of Article 108(3) TFEU.[27] However, the aid must support a cultural product. In order to safeguard this objective, each member state must establish an effective process, such as selection entrusted to a body of one or more persons, or verification against a list of predetermined cultural criteria.[28]

The aid that is to be exempt from notification may take the form of aid to the production or pre-production of audiovisual works or to their distribution. Member States may make the aid subject to territorial spending obligations, either requiring that up to 160% of the aid granted is spent in the territory of the member state granting the aid or by calculating the aid granted as a percentage of the expenditure on production activities in the granting member state. According to the GBER, the latter is typically suited to aid schemes in the form of tax incentives. In both cases, if a member state requires a minimum level of production activity in its territory for projects to be eligible for aid, that level may not exceed 50% of the overall production budget. In addition, the maximum expenditure subject to territorial spending obligations may not exceed 80% of that budget.[29] The eligible costs, for which the aid may be granted, are as follows:[30]

---

[27] Aid for film studio infrastructure is not covered (Article 54(9) GBER).

[28] Article 54(2) GBER.

[29] Article 54(4) GBER.

[30] Article 54(5) GBER.

(a) for production aid: the overall costs of production of audiovisual works including costs to improve accessibility for persons with disabilities.
(b) for pre-production aid: the costs of script-writing and the development of audiovisual works.
(c) for distribution aid: the costs of distribution and promotion of audiovisual works.[31]

The aid intensity for production may not exceed 50% of the eligible costs.[32] According to preamble 73, higher aid intensities are justified for cross-border productions and co-productions, which are more likely to be distributed in several Member States. For cross-border productions funded by more than one member state and involving producers from more than one member state, a maximum of 60% of eligible costs applies. For difficult audiovisual works and co-productions together with countries from the OECD's Development Assistance Committee List, the maximum is increased to 100%.[33] For all pre-production, the maximum is 100%. If the script or project so produced makes it into an actual work, such as a film, these pre-production costs need to be included in the overall budget for the calculations mentioned above. Moreover, the aid intensity (as a percentage) for production and distribution must be the same.[34] Member states may not require that any aid given may be used for only particular activities as part of the production process or for individual parts of the production value chain.[35]

Furthermore, aid may not be reserved exclusively for nationals or for undertakings established under national commercial law.[36] This means that the aid must be open to nationals and beneficiaries of other EU and EEA Member States. The GBER may not lead to the approval of aid that may violate primary EU law, which includes a non-discrimination provision, the freedom of establishment and the freedom to provide (cross-border) services within the EU's internal market. For that reason, tax incentives for the audiovisual industry implemented by EU Member States will, more so than what will be found in non-Member States, often have a broader scope than nationals or residents only.

As indicated in Sect. 4.1.3, a number of general safeguards that limit the usefulness of the GBER when granting aid via tax schemes exist. They apply here as well.

[31]See Chap. 8, Sect. 2.3 for a discussion of these various phases in the realization of a film.
[32]Article 54(6) GBER.
[33]Article 54(7) GBER.
[34]Article 54(8) GBER.
[35]Article 54(9) GBER.
[36]Article 54(10) GBER.

5 Concluding Remarks

OECD/G20 efforts to counter tax avoidance have an effect on a large range of tax incentives and special tax regimes. These rules, therefore, also affect the creative industry at large, even though, for the most part, that industry was never the intended target of any of those rules. They do not yet provide for explicit cultural carve-outs, although one may expect that tax incentives with a clearly cultural nature and objective will be scrutinized far less often than incentives that are more likely to lead to profit shifting between countries.

In order to counter the aforementioned effects within the EU's framework on state aid, there is a way out for cultural aid. This may offer relief to some parts of the creative sector. Even so, within the EU, Member States do face restrictions when providing tax benefits to the creative industry. For benefits targeted to the film industry, the European Commission offers reasonable leeway, even in situations where one may doubt whether a particular film does indeed have a particular signature linking it to national or regional culture. Here, lack of coordination offers room for traditional tax competition in favor of both foreign and domestic film producers.

Most EU Member States, when offering special tax incentives intended to trigger charitable gifts, crowd-funding or similar actions, have formulated such incentives in a way that they are sufficiently general in nature, so as to keep them out of the scope of state aid review. In theory, tax incentives targeted at nudging individual sponsors into financing particular creative industries would still be at risk should they be introduced in national law.

References

European Commission (2009) Communication from the Commission on the application of State aid rules to public service broadcasting, OJ C 257/1 of 27 October 2009

European Commission (2011) Commission Decision of 20 December 2011 on the application of Article 106(2) of the TFEU to State aid in the form of public service compensation granted to certain undertakings entrusted with the operation of services of general economic interest, OJ L7/3 of 11 January 2012

European Commission (2012) Commission Regulation (EU) 360/2012 of 25 April 2012 on the application of Articles 107 and 108 of the Treaty on the Functioning of the European Union to *de minimis* aid granted to undertakings providing services of general economic interest, OJ L114/8 of 26 April 2012

European Commission (2013a) Commission Regulation (EU) 1407/2013 of 18 December 2013 on the application of Articles 107 and 108 of the Treaty on the Functioning of the European Union to *de minimis* aid. OJ L 352/1 of 24 December 2013

European Commission (2013b) Communication from the Commission on State aid for films and other audiovisual works. OJ C 332/1 of 15 November 2013

European Commission (2013c) MEMO/13/993 of 14 November 2013, State aid: Commission adopts new film support rules—frequently asked questions

European Commission (2014) Commission Regulation (EU) No 651/2014 of 17 June 2014 declaring certain categories of aid compatible with the internal market in application of Articles 107 and 108 of the Treaty, OJ L 187/1 of 26 June 2014

EU Council (1997) Code of Conduct for Business Taxation of 1 December 1997. OJ C 2/1 of 6 January 1998

EU Council (2015) Council Regulation (EU) 2015/1589 of 13 July 2015 laying down detailed rules for the application of Article 108 TFEU, OJ C L248/9 of 24 September 2015

G20 (2015) Leader's Communiqué, Antalya Summit, 15–16 November 2015

OECD/G20 (2015) Base Erosion and Profit Shifting Project, Action 5—Final report: countering harmful tax practices more effectively, taking into account transparency and substance

Chapter 6
Tax Incentives Crossing Borders

Considering the Example of Tax Incentives for Charitable Giving

Renate Buijze

Abstract Many countries grant tax incentives for charitable gifts. These incentives, however, are not unambiguous in the case of cross-border gifts. Yet, potential donors to the creative industries have expanded across countries, providing fundraising opportunities outside the arts organization's country of residence. Although this provides opportunities for the creative industries, governments often have not anticipated this. In many countries, tax incentives for gifts to arts organizations remain a domestic issue. This creates tax barriers to raising funds abroad for arts organizations, as they face unequal competition with domestic arts organizations. Governments and private initiatives can overcome the tax barriers for cross-border charitable gifts. This chapter provides an overview of the current solutions that have been initiated by states and solutions initiated by private organizations in accordance with legislation. Furthermore, the crucial factors that influence the effectiveness of these solutions are indicated. The solutions are applicable to cross-border situations in general, but are illustrated through examples derived from the Netherlands.

Keywords Cross-border giving · Philanthropy · Tax treaties · EU law · Fundraising

1 Introduction

Globalization has a large influence on art and culture, including the creative industries. The content of creative products changes: the increased interaction between cultures influences the type of products produced. Furthermore, artists and arts organizations increasingly operate internationally, performing, selling, and exploiting their products across the globe. Audiences have easy access to these creative products from all over the world. Globalization thus changes many aspects

R. Buijze (✉)
Department of Tax Law, Erasmus School of Law,
Erasmus University Rotterdam, Rotterdam, The Netherlands
e-mail: buijze@law.eur.nl

© Springer Science+Business Media Singapore 2017

S. Hemels and K. Goto (eds.), *Tax Incentives for the Creative Industries*,
Creative Economy, DOI 10.1007/978-981-287-832-8_6

of the creative industries. Works of art are sold across borders, performing artists tour around the world, books are translated into multiple languages, and museum collections have been digitized and are accessible online. These are just a few examples of the influence of globalization on the creative industries. Due to globalization, people are no longer solely exposed to creative products in their own country, but have easy access to creative products in other countries as well. This influences the manner in which the creative industries are perceived (Throsby 2010, pp. 2, 3, 157–170).

The focus in this chapter is on the impact globalization has on private support for arts organizations. More specifically, focus lies on the use of tax incentives for private philanthropy to the creative industries. For the sake of this chapter, the term "philanthropy" follows the applicable definition that applies for tax purposes in the respective jurisdiction discussed. As Ostrower (1997), pp. 4–5 shows, this definition of philanthropy parallels the way that donors conceive and define their philanthropic activities. I follow the definition of creative industries provided in Chap. 2, to the extent that it concerns a philanthropic cause that is eligible to receive gifts with a tax benefit under the jurisdiction discussed. In most countries this will include only not-for-profit organizations in the creative industries. I refer to these players in the creative industries as "arts organizations."

In most Western countries arts organizations receive government support. For many years, the reasons for this support have been a topic of debate among scholars. Arguments have been put forward as to why governments should support arts organizations, but these arguments have also been countered. Dworkin (1985), pp. 226–227, DiMaggio (1987), pp 195–220, Klamer (1996), pp. 16–19, Heilbrun and Gray (2001), pp. 219–249, Throsby (2001), pp. 137–152, and Frey (2003), pp. 389–398, amongst others, provide insight in arguments used in this debate. Because most Western democratic countries grant direct or indirect governmental support to arts organizations, they subscribe to arguments that allow them to support arts organizations. Thus, according to the ethical convictions of most voters and sitting politicians in Western democratic countries, there seem to exist arguments that underpin the claim that arts organizations should be supported by the government.

Direct and indirect government support is historically only granted to resident arts organizations. This assumes that it is merely the taxpayers in the country that benefit from the supported arts organization. In a globalizing society, this argument no longer holds. People from abroad also benefit from the arts organization and these people may also desire to contribute to an arts organization they enjoy.

At this point in time, the private philanthropy for creative industries abroad is however, often hindered by the solely domestic application of tax incentives. Because gifts to domestic arts organizations are stimulated by tax benefits, foreign arts organizations are in a disadvantageous position when competing with domestic arts organizations when it comes to private funding. This disadvantage can be overcome by applying tax incentives in cross-border situations, which allows for a global approach towards indirect support for arts organizations. This chapter explores the manners in which tax incentives can be applied in cross-border situations as a method to provide indirect support to arts organizations in a globalizing society. This is done in a comprehensive overview of the current existing state solutions and private initiatives that allow for tax incentives on cross-border gifts. The Netherlands serves as an example to illustrate these different solutions, as all solutions described can be applied in cross-border situations in which the Netherlands is involved. Depending on the jurisdiction, a selection or all of these solutions also apply in cross-border situations involving other countries.

By granting tax incentives in cross-border situations, cross-border gifts are exempted from tax barriers. This allows arts organizations to compete with each other at an international level for private donors. Private donors can take over part of the support for arts organizations on an international level, with the governments contributing indirectly through the tax benefit they grant to donors.

The different forms of tax incentives to support arts organizations were previously discussed in Sect. 3 of Chap. 4. Specifically for charitable gifts, various schemes can be identified, mainly income deduction, tax credit, tax assignment, and refund to the charity. These schemes are described in Sect. 2.2 of Chap. 7. Regardless of the scheme used, the tax incentive decreases the relative cost of the gift and therefore stimulates charitable giving. The economic theory underlying this assumption is explained in Sect. 2 of Chap. 7.

In this chapter, I focus on the manners in which tax incentives on charitable gifts can be applied in a cross-border situation. Section 2 discusses the tax barriers that now exist on cross-border charitable giving to arts organizations. In Sect. 3 I discuss the factors affecting the availability of tax incentives in cross-border situations. Next, I provide an overview of state solutions (Sect. 4) and private initiatives (Sect. 5) that can overcome this problem. In Sect. 6, I summarize the different solutions and provide suggestions for further research to find the best solution in a specific context that allows for cross-border giving with tax incentives from a specific jurisdiction.

2 Tax Barriers to Cross-Border Gifts

Due to globalization, people do not only derive benefits from creative industries in their own country, they also benefit from creative industries in other countries. Therefore, philanthropists might want to contribute to arts organizations abroad. This occurrence provides an opportunity for arts organizations to raise funds outside their country of residence. Both arts organizations as well as their audiences are mobile, which expands the potential support base of the arts organizations. To finance their (international) activities, arts organizations can approach their new and potentially larger audience abroad to increase private and corporate donations.

Since arts organizations have easy access to their audience abroad due to globalization, this might seem like an interesting new alternative to complement income generated in the country of residence. From a tax point of view this is, however, less easy than it seems. The newly generated audience is located outside the country of residence of the arts organization. Indirect support is often granted on only those gifts made to resident charities. Therefore, tax incentives do not automatically apply to cross-border gifts, creating a tax barrier to contributing to a non-resident arts organization. This makes it more costly for a donor to contribute to a foreign charity than to a domestic charity. Thus, unequal competition arises between the two, where it is likely that the foreign charity will lose, especially since giving is shown to be price elastic (Peloza and Steel 2005).

The inapplicability of tax incentives to gifts in cross-border situations is an obstacle for arts organizations to raising funds abroad for their activities. The domestically oriented government support for arts organizations is outdated in comparison to the international performance of arts organizations. New opportunities that arise due to globalization are even hindered by the inapplicability of tax incentives on cross-border gifts. This might artificially restrain arts organizations from developing themselves into international organizations. The application of tax incentives to cross-border gifts to arts organizations could potentially remove this artificial barrier. This would allow arts organizations to benefit from the expansion of their outreach to audiences. Governments might want to encourage this to increase international social welfare and to create strategic cooperation with other countries. There are several possible solutions to enable the removal of tax barriers. Both states and private actors have undertaken action to create solutions.

In the next sections, I explore the manners in which tax incentives can be applied in cross-border situations as solutions to overcome the barriers to cross-border fundraising for arts organizations. There are several solutions; however, whether the tax barrier can be resolved depends on several factors.

3 Factors Affecting the Availability of Tax Incentives in Cross-Border Situations

Whether a solution can overcome the tax barrier on cross-border gifts depends on the interaction between:

(a) The availability of a tax incentive on gifts to charities and more specifically to arts organizations in the donor's tax jurisdiction;
(b) The requirements imposed on a qualifying gift in the donor's tax jurisdiction;
(c) The conditions imposed on the charity by both the donor's tax jurisdiction and the charity's country of residence; and
(d) The access to international tax treaties and supranational agreements.

The availability of a tax incentive in the donor's tax jurisdiction is crucial for tax incentives to apply. If there is no incentive available in the country where the donor pays its taxes, it cannot be applied in cross-border situations either. If, for example, fine art does not qualify as a charitable purpose in the donor's tax jurisdiction, nor in the charity's country of residence, the donor of the fine arts organization cannot get a tax break. In this case, however, this does not have to be problematic. There is no unequal competition between domestic charities and foreign charities, as gifts to domestic arts organizations would not qualify for a tax incentive either. Therefore the unequal competition between domestic and foreign arts organizations does not have to be resolved.

In the case that a tax incentive is available in the jurisdiction of the donor, the factors (b), (c), and (d) listed above all influence the effectiveness of a solution.

The requirements applicable on qualifying gifts decide under which circumstances a gift is rewarded with a tax incentive. If, for example, it is necessary for a gift to be spent within the donor's tax jurisdiction, it is close to impossible to receive a tax incentive on a gift that will be spent abroad. However, when for example a gift can only qualify for a tax incentive if it is made to a charity that is established under domestic law, but there are no geographical restrictions to the charity's spending of the gift, there are possibilities to receiving a tax incentive when the gift is ultimately spent abroad.

Second, the conditions regarding the control over the charity are of importance. A country that grants a tax incentive on a cross-border gift can require that the charity is subject to home country control, host country control, or both. In the case of home country control, the country where the charity resides decides whether the organization is a charity and therefore qualifies to receive tax rebate gifts. Host country control refers to control over the charity by the country that grants the tax incentive. Governments can also decide to use both home country control and host country control. In that case, the charity must meet both the requirements of the home country as well as the host country (Hemels 2009). If these countries use conflicting requirements, it is impossible to obtain a tax incentive on a cross-border gift.

Finally, the access to international tax treaties and supranational agreements determine in which cross–border situations a donor can rely on a tax incentive for a cross-border gift. If the donor's tax jurisdiction is part of an extensive network of tax treaties and supranational agreements, these can be utilized to receive a tax incentive on cross-border gifts to a wide range of countries.

Depending on these three main factors it might be more or less complicated, compared to a domestic gift, to receive a tax incentive on a cross-border gift. These factors also have a major influence on which of the solutions might work best under the available circumstances. The solutions are not solely applicable to arts organizations. They apply to charitable organizations in general, as long as the charitable organizations qualify as such in either its country of residence or in the donor's tax jurisdiction. Depending on the conditions imposed by the donor's tax jurisdiction and the charity's residence country, one solution might work better than the other.

In cross-border situations, the Netherlands is one of the few jurisdictions that allows for the application of all of the current existing solutions. Therefore the Netherlands is used as an example. The solutions can be divided into solutions initiated by states and solutions initiated by private parties, but facilitated by governments. In Sect. 4, solutions implemented by states are discussed.

In Sect. 5, solutions by private parties are mapped. All solutions discussed already exist in theory, and most of them are also applied in practice; however, they are not yet widespread across the globe. Therefore, it is worthwhile to outline the main solutions to enable cross-border philanthropy for arts organizations with the benefit of tax incentives.

4 State Solutions to Apply Tax Incentives in Cross-Border Situations

The application of tax incentives in cross-border situations can be regulated at different legal levels. At the national level, countries can grant tax incentives in cross-border situations under certain conditions. At the international level, countries can engage in bilateral solutions by concluding tax treaties in which they recognize each other's charities and mutually apply their tax incentives to cross-border gifts. On a supranational level, countries could overcome the inapplicability of tax incentives by agreeing not to discriminate against charities that are resident in other contracting countries or through the introduction of a common charity status that is granted the same tax preferences as a domestic charity. In the next subparagraphs, I exemplify the solutions that states can implement to enable cross-border charitable giving with the benefit of tax incentives.

4.1 Unilateral Solutions

A country can decide to open up its tax incentives on charitable gifts made to foreign charities. This can be done by removing geographical restrictions from the specific tax provision. By adding specific requirements to the provision, the government can target the tax incentives to a specific cause. In addition, conditions for control over the charity, such as host- or home country control, are important tools here for governments to determine where the supervision over the charities is situated.

The Netherlands does not place geographical restrictions on tax benefits for gifts. Dutch taxpayers can deduct their gift, whether it is a domestic gift or a cross-border gift, from personal income tax if the gift is made to an organization that is recognized as a 'Public Benefit Pursuing Entity' (PBE; *Algemeen Nut Beogende Instelling*) by the Dutch tax authorities. This holds for both domestic and foreign charities. Resident charities of the Kingdom of the Netherlands, another EU Member State or a state designated by the Ministry of Finance have to meet the same requirements to qualify as a PBE in the Netherlands.[1] States designated by the Ministry of Finance

[1] Article 5b(1)b AWR.

are states with which the Netherlands has an information-exchange agreement on personal income tax, corporate income tax, and gift- and inheritance tax. If a charity resides in a country that does not have such an agreement with the Netherlands, it can still meet the requirements of a PBE by accepting the obligation to provide additional information to the Dutch tax authorities.[2]

To obtain PBE status, an organization needs to meet certain requirements, of which the most important is that the organization pursues the public benefit exclusively or almost exclusively (at least 90%). The tax authorities provide a list with public benefit activities. Culture is included in this list.[3] PBEs that engage in cultural activities for at least 90% can request registration as a 'Cultural PBE'.[4] For Cultural PBEs, additional facilities exist. Both domestic and foreign PBEs that mainly focus on art and culture can obtain Cultural PBE status. By imposing its own requirements on foreign charities to be eligible to receive tax deductible gifts the Netherlands applies host country control. If the charity wants to raise funds in multiple countries this might complicate matters.

By consulting the PBE register at the Dutch tax authorities, donors can check which cultural organizations can receive gifts that qualify for a deduction from taxable income. Several arts organizations located outside the Netherlands have registered as a Cultural PBE. Not only arts organizations located in the border area with the Netherlands, such as the *Emsländisches Kammermusikensemble*—a chamber music ensemble in the German border town of Lingen—register as Cultural PBEs in the Netherlands. Also arts organizations located in different European cities register as such, for example the Tate Gallery in London, the Royal Museum for Fine Art and History in Brussels. Examples from outside Europe are the Museum of Modern Art in New York, the Museum of Contemporary Arts in San Diego, the San Diego Museum of Art in La Jolla and The Israel Philharmonic Orchestra in Tel-Aviv.[5]

4.2 *Bilateral Solutions: Tax Treaties*

Another way in which countries can overcome the tax barriers to cross-border charitable giving is to mutually agree on granting tax incentives to cross-border gifts. This can be done in bilateral tax treaties.

Most bilateral tax treaties are based on the model tax treaties by either the UN[6] or the OECD.[7] The model treaties both include a non-discrimination provision that

---

[2]Article 1c Uitvoeringsregeling AWR.

[3]Article 5b AWR.

[4]Article 5b(4) AWR.

[5]http://www.belastingdienst.nl/rekenhulpen/giften/anbi_zoeken/. Accessed 14 August 2015.

[6]UN—United Nations Model Double Taxation Convention between Developed and Developing Countries (2011).

[7]OECD Income and Capital Model Convention and Commentary (2010).

prevents nationals of a contracting state to be subject to taxation in the other contracting state other, or more burdensome, than the taxation of nationals in the other contracting state under the same circumstances.[8] Under the model tax treaties, however, the charities cannot turn to the tax authorities of the contracting state, since it does not recognize the arts organization in the other contracting state as a charity, nor is it obliged to do so under the model tax treaties. In the official commentary[9] of both the OECD Income and Capital Model Convention and the UN Model Double Taxation Convention it states that

> Neither are they [the contracting states] to be construed as obliging a State which accords special taxation privileges to private institutions not for profit whose activities are performed for purposes of public benefit, which are specific to that State, to extend the same privileges to similar institutions whose activities are not for its benefit.

Charities are thus excluded from the mutual recognition.

Furthermore, the cross-border application of personal allowances—which tax incentives on gifts to charities are classed as—is not taken into account in the OECD Income and Capital Convention and the UN Model Double Taxation Convention. It is assumed that the home state of the taxpayer takes this into account.

Because many tax treaties are based on these model tax treaties, countries explicitly have to agree on the inclusion of a provision on the mutual application of tax incentives for gifts to charitable organizations in the other contracting state. Although rare, this does happen. Again, as with the unilateral solution, countries have to decide whether they base control over recipient charities on host country control, home country control, or both. Because tax treaties decide which law is applicable, but do not shape laws, the requirements imposed on charitable gifts of either the home state, host state, or both apply. No additional requirements can be incorporated in the tax treaties.

Koele (2007), pp. 20–37 distinguishes four different categories of tax treaties in which the different types of control are reflected. First, there are conventions that regard charitable organizations explicitly as "resident" under a treaty, allowing these "resident" organizations to benefit from the same beneficial tax regulations as domestic organizations. Second, there are conventions that regard charities explicitly as a safe haven under the "limitation on benefits" concept included in the treaty. For these organizations to enjoy the tax benefits, they are seen as resident entities under the treaty. Third, there are conventions that regard exempt organizations as being exempt from taxes on income sourced in another state with respect to specific income items. Last, some conventions resolve the issues with regard to gifts or bequests to foreign charities.

---

[8]UN: article 24 Model Double Taxation Convention between Developed and Developing Countries and OECD: article 24 Income and Capital Model Convention.

[9]UN: commentary on article 24, paragraph 1, point 11 Model Double Taxation Convention between Developed and Developing Countries and OECD: commentary on article 24, paragraph 1, point 11 Income and Capital Model Convention.

An example of a tax treaty that includes a provision on charitable contributions is the income tax treaty between the Netherlands and Barbados.[10] The treaty states:[11]

> Contributions by a resident of a Contracting State to an organization constituting a charitable organization under the income tax laws of the other Contracting State shall be deductible for the purposes of computing the tax liability of that resident under the tax laws of the firstmentioned Contracting State under the same terms and conditions as are applicable to contributions to charitable organizations of the firstmentioned State where the competent authority of the first-mentioned State agrees that the organization qualifies as a charitable organization for the purposes of granting a deduction under its income tax laws.

The treaty requires both home- and host country control, as the charity has to be recognized as such by the tax laws in its place of residence and it also has to meet the requirements put upon charities in the country of the donor. Other examples of tax treaties that overcome the tax barrier to cross-border charitable giving are the tax treaties the United States has concluded with Canada, Israel, and Mexico.[12]

4.3 Supranational Solutions

A supranational legal authority can take measures to overcome the tax barriers to cross-border charitable giving amongst multiple countries. The EU is based on such supranational agreements that have the potential to overcome tax barriers to cross-border charitable giving. Supranational solutions can take multiple forms, of which two can be found in the EU. Although it is extremely difficult to unify taxes within the EU due to member countries refusing to give up their sovereignty over their tax systems, EU law does have the potential to overcome tax barriers to cross-border charitable giving. This potential lies in the four fundamental freedoms as stipulated in the TFEU and its enforcement by the ECJ. Furthermore, the Proposal for a Council Regulation on the Statute for a European Foundation[13] (hereinafter: the Proposal) was an initiative of the EC to overcome barriers that currently hinder the philanthropic sector in the EU through civil law. In the Proposal, specific provisions were included that were targeted at the taxation of charities and their beneficiaries. However, the Proposal has been withdrawn. Both EU law and the Proposal are discussed in the next two sub-paragraphs.

---

[10]Barbados—The Netherlands Income Tax Treaty (2006, as amended through 2009).

[11]Article 22 Barbados—The Netherlands Income Tax Treaty (2006, as amended through 2009).

[12]Canada—United States Income and Capital Tax Treaty (1980 as amended through 2007), Israel—United States Income Tax Treaty (1975) and Mexico—United States Income Tax Treaty (1992 as amended through 2002).

[13]COM(2012) 35 final, 2012/0022 (APP).

4.3.1 EU Law

The four fundamental freedoms in the TFEU have the potential to overcome the tax barriers involved in cross-border charitable giving within the EU. In four landmark cases, the ECJ ruled that if a country provides fiscal facilities for charities and charitable giving, these facilities should also apply in comparable situations within the EU. EU Member States retain the right to decide whether they want to provide these fiscal facilities and under what conditions. A residence requirement is prohibited, since this would infringe upon the four fundamental freedoms. The cases in which this was ruled are Stauffer,[14] Persche,[15] Missionwerk[16] and Commission v. Austria.[17] These landmark cases were again confirmed in the case Commission v. France.[18] The Persche case is most important in the light of this chapter, as it concerned the applicability of a tax incentive on a charitable gift to a charity in another EU Member State.

In the Persche Case,[19] the German resident Hein Persche claimed a tax deduction with regards to contributions in kind which he made to a Portuguese charity. The charity was recognized by the Portuguese tax authorities as a charitable body and was therefore eligible to receive tax deductible gifts under Portuguese tax law. The German tax authorities, however, did not grant the deduction since the recipient of the gift was not resident in Germany and the required gift certificate did not meet German standards. In line with the previous decision in the Stauffer case, the ECJ ruled that this decision was not in line with the free movement of capital. The German authorities tried to justify this by the need to safeguard the effectiveness of fiscal supervision, which was refused by the ECJ. This implies that tax laws which discriminate against gifts to charities based in other EU Member States, but equivalent to resident charities, are against the TFEU. It, however, does not require charities to mutually recognize each other's charities. The ECJ did highlight that the tax authorities can require the taxpayer to provide such proof as they may consider necessary to determine whether the conditions for deducting expenses provided for in the legislation at issue have been met and, consequently, whether to allow the deduction requested.[20]

The four fundamental freedoms decide in which manner existing law has to be applied. At this point, the most important question on the non-discrimination of charities in other EU Member States is whether the charity should comply with the national standards set out by the host state or with the standards of the state in

[14]Case C-386/04, *Centro di Musicologia Walter Stauffer v. Finanzamt München für Körperschaften* (2006).

[15]C-318/07, *Hein Persche v. Finanzamt Lüdenscheid (*2009).

[16]Case C-025/10, *Missionswerk Werner Heukelbach eV v. État Belge* (2011).

[17]Case C-10/10, *European Commission v. Republic of Austria* (2011).

[18]Case C-485/14, *European Commission v. French Republic (2015).*

[19]C-318/07, Hein *Persche v. Finanzamt Lüdenscheid (*2009).

[20]C-318/07, Hein *Persche v. Finanzamt Lüdenscheid (*2009).

which it is resident. The ECJ focuses on the requirements imposed by the country that has to grant the tax benefit, which leads to a host country control (Hemels 2009). Home country control would require countries to recognize each other's charities, which is not required by EU law.

For charity organizations that want to raise funds in multiple countries the host country control is burdensome. It entails that if they want to raise funds in several countries, they have to comply with the legislation of all these countries. This can make it impossible for donors from different countries to all receive the applicable tax incentive in their tax jurisdiction when they contribute to the same single foreign charity. A common charity status, imposed by a supranational legal institute, could overcome this problem. The European Foundation Proposal held this potential. Although the Proposal has been withdrawn, I will discuss it as an example to illustrate how a common charity status can overcome the tax barriers to cross-border charitable giving.

4.3.2 The Proposal for a Council Regulation on the Statute for a European Foundation

On February 8th, 2012 the EC presented a Proposal for a Council Regulation on the Statute for a European Foundation.[21] The Commission was of the opinion that part of the charity organization's funds was inefficiently spent due to juridical and administrative costs when working across borders within the EU. The aim of this new proposed European legal form was to overcome this inefficiency and make it easier for charitable organizations to conduct cross-border activities within the EU. The Commission explicitly mentioned:[22]

> It will allow foundations to more efficiently channel private funds to public benefit purposes on a cross-border basis in the EU.

As a result more funds had to end up at the public benefit purpose activities. On its turn, this had to benefit the public welfare and the economy of the EU.

The European Foundation or *Fundatio Europaea* was proposed as a separately constituted entity in private law for a public benefit purpose. This entity had to serve the public interest at large as defined by the Council Regulation via uniform and agreed-upon joint material and formal standards. Each Member State was supposed to appoint a supervisory body that monitored whether the FEs registered in that Member State met the requirements.[23]

One of the requirements was that the FE served the public interest at large. Arts, culture, and historical preservation were the first activities on the list of activities that serve the public interest at large.[24] Arts organizations could thus qualify as an

[21]COM(2012) 35 final, 2012/0022 (APP).

[22]COM(2012) 35 final, 2012/0022 (APP), p. 3.

[23]Article 47 FE Proposal.

[24]Article 5 FE Proposal.

FE. However, amongst others, the FE was also required to have assets equivalent to €25.000,[25] potentially limiting the ability of arts organizations with insufficient assets to registering. Another important requirement was that the FE should have activities, or aim to carry out activities, in at least two EU Member States.[26] The FE did not aim at replacing the foundation or other legal forms at the national level, but was proposed as an additional possibility.

Member States would have to regard the FE in the same way as domestic public benefit entities. This implied that its donors and beneficiaries would have received the same tax benefits as those of domestic charities. Chapter VIII of the Proposal on the fiscal treatment of FEs stated that all EU Member States had to treat FEs equally to public benefit entities under national legislation. Article 50 of the Proposal specifically monitored the equal treatment of beneficiaries of the FE to beneficiaries of public benefit entities within the country of residence of the beneficiary.[27] This provision thus had the potential to removing the tax barrier from cross-border charitable giving within the EU.

Research shows, though, that a European Foundation would have only been a partial solution (Hemels 2014, 2015). Although it seemed effective in removing tax barriers for cross-border charitable giving, this would have only been the case if the requirement that activities had to be undertaken in at least two Member States also included fundraising activities, and was not solely targeting the charitable projects themselves. The FE would not have been efficient for countries that had to establish a supervisory structure. For fundraising charities that would choose to obtain FE status, the solution would have been efficient, but for charities with a different legal status, the problem would remain unresolved. Besides, the Proposal did not address the risk of abuse of tax incentives. The biggest problem with the FE, however, was its feasibility, due to the fact that it required Member States to trust each other's supervising authorities.

Although the initial Proposal could have provided a partial solution to the inapplicability of tax incentives for cross-border gifts, agreement between Member States proved difficult to obtain. By November 2013, the tax provision was excluded in the discussion of the Proposal.[28] At the end of 2014, withdrawal of the Proposal was suggested due to a lack of prospects that an agreement could be reached.[29] In March 2015 it was withdrawn.[30]

---

[25] COM(2012) 35 final, 2012/0022 (APP).

[26] Article 6 FE Proposal.

[27] Article 50 FE Proposal.

[28] http://www.consilium.europa.eu/uedocs/cms_data/docs/pressdata/en/intm/141115.pdf Accessed 14 August 2015.

[29] http://ec.europa.eu/transparency/regdoc/rep/1/2014/EN/1-2014-910-EN-F1-1-ANNEX-4.Pdf Accessed 14 August 2015.

[30] http://eur-lex.europa.eu/legal-content/EN/TXT/?uri=uriserv:OJ.C_.2015.080.01.0017.01.ENG Accessed 14 August 2015.

5 Private Initiatives

Besides governments, private parties can also undertake initiatives to overcoming the tax barriers to cross-border charitable giving. They can do so by circumventing the cross-border situation, or by making strategic use of charities that function as an intermediary charity organization. The effectiveness of private initiatives, however, is dependent on the factors described in Sect. 3.

5.1 Circumventing the Cross-Border Situation

The tax barriers created by cross-border situations can be overcome by setting up a legal entity in the donor's country. This can be done either by establishing an entity in the donor's country with charitable activities or by establishing an entity in the donor's country solely for fundraising activities. The latter is also known as a 'friends of' organization.

5.1.1 Establishing a Legal Entity Abroad with Charitable Activities

When an arts organization establishes a legal entity abroad that conducts charitable activities that qualify as such under a foreign jurisdiction, it can receive a charitable status in that country, allowing the donors in that specific foreign jurisdiction to use the applicable tax incentive on their gifts to that organization. By doing so, the cross-border situation is circumvented.

Guggenheim Museums, for example, can be visited in New York, Venice, and Bilbao. Although affiliated with the USA-based Solomon R. Guggenheim Foundation, they are not all run by the same legal entity. The Solomon R. Guggenheim Museum in New York and the Peggy Guggenheim Collection in Venice are owned and operated by the Solomon R. Guggenheim Foundation.[31] The Museum in Bilbao, however, merely follows the guidelines and ethics code set by the Solomon R. Guggenheim Foundation, but remains a separate legal entity (the Guggenheim Museum Bilbao Foundation), with charity status in Spain.[32] Spanish donors can thus donate to the Guggenheim Museum Bilbao in their own country and benefit from the applicable tax incentive.

---

[31] According to the website of the Peggy Guggenheim Collection the Solomon R. Guggenheim Foundation is recognized by the Italian tax authorities as a charitable organization that can receive tax deductible gifts. http://www.guggenheim-venice.it/inglese/membership/tax_deduction.html. Accessed 14 August 2015. This is an example of a unilateral solution, where a foreign charity is recognized by the local tax authorities.

[32] http://www.guggenheim-bilbao-corp.es/en/guggenheim-network/. Accessed 14 August 2015.

However, as one can imagine when considering the Guggenheim Museums, this solution comes at a significant cost and it would be irrational to pursue this avenue solely for donors to receive a tax benefit on their gift. Besides, where fine arts and performing arts institutions are geographically mobile, to a certain extent, this is not the case for heritage sites and exhibition or performance spaces. Establishing a legal entity abroad with charitable activities can avoid a cross-border situation and thus are not encountered with the involved tax barriers, but for the majority of arts organizations this is nothing more than a theoretical solution to overcoming the tax barriers to cross-border charitable giving. For other charitable causes, such as disaster relief and development aid, this solution might well be practically feasible, since their activities consist of providing services, which are less attached to a physical location.

5.1.2 Establishing a 'Friends of' Organization

The cross-border situation that creates tax barriers is circumvented by setting up a legal entity for fundraising purposes in the donor's country, also called a 'friends of' organization. For this solution to be effective, the 'friends of' organization has to qualify as an organization that can receive gifts with a tax benefit. In this case, the donor can contribute to the 'friends of' organization and benefit from the applicable tax incentive in his own country. The 'friends of' organization can transfer the gift to the foreign organization which it raises funds for.

Whether the 'friends of' organization qualifies to receive gifts with a tax benefit depends on the requirements it has to meet. If there are high requirements regarding the capital the organization needs to have, this might make it difficult to establish a 'friends of' organization. Requirements applicable on qualifying gifts also influence the effectiveness of the solution. If the 'friends of' organization is not allowed to transfer the funds to an arts organization abroad, for example, this solution is not effective.

In the Netherlands organizations that provide financial support to public benefit pursuing entities or support them otherwise can qualify as a PBE.[33] The examples of two foreign charities that have established a 'friends of' charity in the Netherlands show that the final recipient of the gift in practice does not need to be a Dutch-registered PBE for the 'friends of' charity to be able to qualify as a PBE. The *Stichting Nederlandse Vrienden van het Israelisch Philharmonisch Orkest* (Foundation for the Dutch Friends of the Israeli Philharmonic Orchestra) and the *Stichting Nederlandse Vrienden van de Bibliotheca Alexandrina* (Foundation for the Dutch Friends of the Bibliotheca Alexandrina) both have cultural PBE status in the Netherlands.[34] Therefore, their Dutch donors can benefit from a tax incentive when making a gift.

[33]NL: article 5b AWR.

[34]http://www.belastingdienst.nl/rekenhulpen/giften/anbi_zoeken/. Accessed 14 August 2015.

Dutch arts organizations have also established 'friends of' organization abroad for fundraising purposes. In the United States, for example, organizations can set up a 'friends of' organization under the laws of the USA to raise funds in the USA for a specific foreign charitable organization.[35] The Mauritshuis, a fine art museum with a collection of paintings by Dutch and Flemish masters from the Golden Age, has such a 'friends of' organization in America, namely the American Friends of the Mauritshuis.[36] However, examples also exist in other countries: The Royal Concertgebouw Orchestra has 'friends of' organizations in Belgium, Switzerland, and France,[37] and in the United Kingdom, there is a support foundation named the Dutch Masters Foundation that raises funds for the Mauritshuis, the Royal Concertgebouw Orchestra, and the Nederlands Dans Theater.[38]

5.2 Intermediary Charity Organizations

Non-governmental organizations try to overcome the inapplicability of tax incentives for cross-border gifts by creating networks of organizations with charity status. Through this collaboration and the use of available fiscal facilities, donors can acquire the same tax benefit on cross-border gifts as on domestic gifts (Heidenbauer et al. 2013, p. 624; Hemels 2009; Von Hippel 2009, p. 291). In these networks, the donor gives to an intermediary organization with charity status in their own country and can therefore benefit from the tax incentive. The intermediary organization transfers this gift to the charity abroad. The intermediary organization usually charges a percentage fee of the gift for this service. The prerequisites for this structure to work are that the country where the donor pays its taxes (host country) must allow organizations with charity status to spend their gifts on activities abroad and that the mission of the final recipient organization is consistent with that of the intermediary charity organization. This is where the requirements imposed by the donor's tax jurisdiction are of importance.

The intermediary charity organizations regularly have multiple purposes and their core business is often to contribute to the public benefit by conducting charitable activities or to raise funds for these activities. Two examples of such intermediary charity organizations are the King Baudouin Foundation United States and Transnational Giving Europe. I have selected these two intermediary charity organizations as they, amongst others, perform their activities in the Netherlands, which is the country of focus regarding the solutions discussed in this article.

---

[35]US: IRC Section 170(f)(18).

[36]http://www.americanfriendsofthemauritshuis.org/. Accessed 14 August 2015.

[37]http://site.concertgebouworkest.nl/nl/steun/Internationaal/. Accessed 14 August 2015.

[38]http://www.dutchmasters.org.uk/. Accessed 14 August 2015.

5.2.1 King Baudouin Foundation United States

The KBFUS is a private initiative for American taxpayers who want to make a contribution to charities in Europe or Africa with the benefit of a tax incentive.[39] Over the period of 2003–2015, $96,328,965 was donated through the King Baudouin Foundation USA. Of this total amount, $13,499,693 was designated to charities working in arts and culture.[40]

In the USA, gifts can be deducted from taxes when they are made to an organization that meets the requirements under Section 501(c)(3) of the IRC, one of the requirements being that the organization is created in or under the laws of the USA (any state, the District of Columbia, or any possession of the USA including Puerto Rico). This puts territorial restrictions on the qualifying organizations, excluding all organizations that are not established under the laws of the USA. It does not, however, restrict qualifying organizations to spending their assets within the USA. This creates room for US charities to engage in activities abroad and for foreign charities to engage in the American fundraising market by establishing themselves under USA law. Foreign organizations can establish a 'friends of' organization in the USA, which is an example of a private initiative to circumvent a cross-border situation. Due to the administrative requirements under IRC 501(c)(3) this, however, is costly.

Another option for charities located outside the USA is to rely on the support of a qualifying organization under IRC 501(c)(3). This is exactly what KBFUS offers. KBFUS qualifies as a 501(c)(3) organization. European and African charities can register at KBFUS, or create a so-called 'American friends fund' at KBFUS. To do so, charities must fill out a due diligence form in which KBFUS, amongst others, validates whether the charity qualifies as such under its own tax law and whether it has a mission that is consistent with the mission of KBFUS. When the foreign charity meets the standards of KBFUS, an 'American friends fund' can be created at KBFUS holding the name of the organization. This is not a legal status, it only means that the foreign charity is supported by KBFUS and can benefit from KBFUS's 501(c)(3) status. This allows the American donors of the foreign charity to donate through KBFUS and deduct their gift from taxes. KBFUS takes care of all the administrative work involved. The American tax authorities require that organizations like KBFUS control the funds, and thus the foreign charity can only receive the gift made to KBFUS by handing in an application for financial support at KBFUS. KBFUS decides whether the gift is transferred. To cover the administrative costs involved with setting up an 'American friends fund,' KBFUS charges $1,500. In addition, a management fee of between 5% and 0.5% of the cumulative total of contributions within one calendar year is charged.[41]

---

[39]http://www.kbfus.org. Accessed 23 February 2016.

[40]http://kbfus.insight.foundationcenter.org/. Accessed 23 February 2016.

[41]http://www.kbfus.org/wp-content/uploads/2015/02/EUR-AFR_american-friends-funds.pdf. Accessed 23 February 2016.

Several Dutch cultural charity organizations have registered an American friends fund at KBFUS: de Kunsthal, Museum Boijmans van Beuningen, Prins Bernhard Cultuurfonds, Museum Catharijneconvent, the Netherlands Institute for Art History, the Dutch Language Fund, Rijksmuseum, and the Van Gogh Museum.[42]

5.2.2 Transnational Giving Europe

TGE is a network of European charities that help each other channel gifts between donors and charities resident in certain EU Member States and Switzerland. It is remarkable that, despite the judgments of the ECJ as discussed in Paragraph 4.3.1, there is an increasing demand for TGE, as their figures show. In 2009, at the start of TGE €2.946.708 was channeled through them. By 2013 this has almost tripled to 8.7 million euro.[43] This demonstrates that the supranational solution as currently applied in EU Member States is not sufficient yet to overcome the tax barrier. If the EU Member States adjust their legislation in line with the ECJ rulings, the situation might improve and TGE might become less essential.[44] Currently though, there is still a large demand for the services that TGE provides. TGE covers nineteen countries and serves more than 450 organizations.[45]

One of the beneficiaries of TGE is the Royal Concertgebouw Orchestra in the Netherlands.[46] If one of their donors resides in another country that is covered by TGE, the donor can make a gift to the Orchestra with a tax incentive. Let us assume their donor is resident for tax purposes in Spain.

In Spain a gift qualifies for a tax credit if the recipient meets the requirements under article 16 of Law 49/2002 of 24 November 2002 'law concerning the tax regime of non-profit entities and tax incentives for patronage'. Since it refers to the term foundation as a foundation created under Spanish foundation law, it entails that the Royal Concertgebouw Orchestra should establish itself as a Spanish foundation, to meet the requirements (Von Hippel 2014).

To prevent the Royal Concertgebouw Orchestra from having to establish itself in Spain to be eligible to receive gifts with a tax credit in Spain, the donor or the orchestra could approach TGE. The Dutch partner of TGE validates whether the orchestra is eligible for tax-deductible gifts under Dutch tax law. If the orchestra turns out to be eligible, which is the case, the Dutch TGE partner informs the Spanish TGE partner. The Spanish TGE partner checks whether the gift is in line with its statutes, as well as whether it meets the legal criteria under Spanish law.

---

[42] http://www.kbfus.org/our-services/services-for-nonprofits/list-of-american-friends-funds-at-kbfus. Accessed 23 February 2016.

[43] http://www.transnationalgiving.eu/tge/default.aspx?id=219948&langtype=1033. Accessed 14 August 2015.

[44] http://www.transnationalgiving.eu/tge/details.aspx?id=219940&LangType=1033. Accessed 14 August 2015.

[45] www.transnationalgiving.eu/en/beneficiary/. Accessed 23 November 2016.

[46] http://www.transnationalgiving.eu/en/beneficiary/nl/s. Accessed 23 February 2016.

If this is the case and the Spanish TGE partner is willing to receive the gift, the donor can make the gift to the Spanish TGE partner. Because the Spanish TGE partner holds PBE status under Spanish tax law, the donor can deduct the gift from his taxable income. The Spanish PBE partner then transfers the gift to the Royal Concertgebouw Orchestra. For this service, TGE charges a fee of 5% for gifts up to €50,000 and a 1% fee if the amount exceeds this number. The fee will, however, never be more than €6,500.[47]

By using TGE's services the donor knows beforehand that his gift is tax deductible. This would not be the case if the Royal Concertgebouw Orchestra relied on EU jurisprudence. Furthermore, for the Royal Concertgebouw Orchestra, the costs for the TGE service are transparent. This is not the case when the Royal Concertgebouw Orchestra solely relies on Spanish tax law, especially not since they might run the risk of having to overcome the tax barrier through actions taken in court.

6 Concluding Remarks

There is a discrepancy between the current domestic-oriented government policy to finance arts organizations and the global functioning creative industries. The widespread audience of arts organizations provides for a group of potential donors outside their country of residence, which arts organizations could benefit from. They are, however, hindered by unequal competition between domestic and foreign arts organizations due to tax barriers.

Granting tax incentives in cross-border situations could solve this unequal competition, but this is currently only exercised on a small scale. There are several state solutions available and also the charity sector and other private parties can make an effort to get access to solutions that allow donors to receive a tax incentive on their gift to an arts organization abroad. State solutions exist on different legal levels. On a unilateral level governments can remove residence requirements from their tax provisions. Tax treaties are bilateral solutions. Examples of supranational solutions are the enforcement of EU law and the withdrawn (for the time) proposal for a European Foundation. Private initiatives are solutions that make strategic use of existing tax legislation, namely: (1) establishing a charity in multiple countries; (2) 'friends of' organizations; and (3) networks of charity organizations in different countries that collaborate to allow donors to receive tax incentives in a cross-border situation.

Depending on the legal context of the countries where the cross-border transaction takes place, one solution might be effective in solving the tax barrier where another fails. Requirements imposed on qualifying gifts and the conditions imposed on charities as well as access to bilateral tax treaties and supranational agreements

---

[47]http://www.transnationalgiving.eu/tge/details.aspx?id=219956&LangType=1033. Accessed 14 August 2015.

are important. For the private initiatives to work, for example, it is necessary that charity organizations in the donor's tax jurisdiction are allowed to spend their funds abroad. For state solutions to work, the type of control required is of importance. From the perspective of charities, home country control would be most efficient, since meeting one set of requirements is sufficient in that case. Host country control would entail that if the charity wants to raise funds both in its residence country and abroad, it must meet multiple sets of requirements, which can put severe restrictions on the charity. This also holds true when a country requires both home country control and host country control. In theory, it could even be impossible to meet the requirements of both the home and host country if they use conflicting requirements. Therefore, the success of a solution largely depends on the kind of control that the legislator chooses. In any case, it is a prerequisite that a tax incentive is available in the donor's tax jurisdiction in the first place in order for a tax incentive to apply in a cross-border situation.

It would be valuable to know which solution is most successful in overcoming the tax barriers to cross-border charitable fundraising for arts organizations. This would provide arts organizations and their donors with the necessary information to lobby for a certain state solution, or to choose to invest in creating their own networks, to be able to benefit from the potential donors located abroad.

More factors have to be taken into account when evaluating the different solutions. For example the private initiatives initially seem to be more costly for the arts organizations in comparison to the state solutions, whereas the state solutions might require a large time investment to gain knowledge of a foreign tax system. Furthermore, the level of legal certainty provided by a solution beforehand is of importance. Some solutions do allow for tax incentives on cross-border charitable gifts, but one might first have to go to court for the tax incentive to be enforced, as is witnessed in the EU. This is costly and time consuming. Another factor is the level to which a solution prevents a crowd-out effect. If every single country were to remove geographical restrictions from their tax incentives on gifts to creative industries, all countries could benefit. However, if not all countries do so, the risk exists that a crowding-out effect will arise: countries can benefit from others granting tax incentives on gifts, but refrain from granting these tax incentives in cross-border situations themselves. The more countries to which a solution is applicable, the smaller the chance of crowding out, and the more successful the solution is in removing tax barriers. Further research is necessary to gain thorough insight in the solutions that allow for tax incentives on cross-border gifts, in order for arts organizations to benefit from the fundraising opportunities abroad which globalization offers.

References

DiMaggio P (1987) Nonprofit organizations in the production and distribution of culture. In: Powell WW (ed) The nonprofit sector. A research handbook. Yale University Press, New Haven, pp 195–220
Dworkin R (1985) A matter of principle. Harvard University Press, London
Frey BS (2003) Public support. In: Towse R (ed) A handbook of cultural economics. Edward Elgar Publishing, Cheltenham
Heidenbauer S, Hemels SJC, Muehlmann BW, Stewart M, Thommes O, Tukic T (2013) Cross-border charitable giving and its tax limitations. Bull Int Tax 67:611–25
Heilbrun J, Gray CM (2001) The economics of art and culture. Cambridge University Press, Cambridge
Hemels SJC (2014) The European Foundation proposal analysed from a tax point of view. Revista De Finanças Publicas e Direito Fiscal VI(3):253–286
Hemels SJC (2015) The European Foundation proposal: an effective, efficient and feasible solution for tax issues related to cross-border charitable giving and fundraising? In: Vanistendael F (ed) Taxation of charities, pp 143–174
Hemels SJC (2009) Are we in need of a European charity? How to remove fiscal barriers to cross-border charitable giving in Europe. Intertax 8: 424–434
Klamer A (1996) The value of culture: on the relationship between economics and arts. Amsterdam University Press, Amsterdam
Koele IA (2007) International taxation of philanthropy. IBFD Publications, Amsterdam
Peloza J, Steel P (2005) The price elasticities of charitable contributions: a meta-analysis. J Public Policy Mark 24(2):260–272
Ostrower F (1997) Why the Wealthy Give: The Culture of Elite Philanthropy. Princeton University Press, Princeton
Throsby D (2010) The economics of cultural policy. Cambridge University Press, Cambridge
Throsby D (2001) Economics and culture. Cambridge University Press, Cambridge
Von Hippel T (2014) Cross-border philanthropy in Europe after Persche and Stauffer: from landlock to non-discrimination?. European Foundation Centre and Transnational Giving Europe, Brussels
Von Hippel T (2009) Tax benefits for foreign-based charities: key challenges of the non-discrimination rule of the European court for justice. ERA Forum Springer 10:281–294

Part II
Cases: Focus on Specific Tax Incentives

Chapter 7
Tax Incentives for Museums and Cultural Heritage

Sigrid Hemels

Abstract Museums and cultural heritage are a specific sub-sector of creative industries. Usually, legal entities in this sector operate as an NPO or charity. Many countries apply tax incentives for charities, benefitting this sector. The best-known example of such incentives is probably tax incentives for donations. It is often stated that the USA's incentive is most generous in this regard; however, as this chapter will show, this assumption does not seem to be correct. Other incentives are tax exemptions for charities and tax incentives for volunteers. Important incentives for museums and archives are the ability to pay taxes with art and heritage objects as well as the wealth tax exemption of objects given on loan. A specific sub-sector of the cultural industries, businesses specialized in restoring and maintaining heritage, benefits from tax incentives that several countries provide to private owners of heritage buildings and objects.

Keywords Museum · Cultural heritage · Acceptance in lieu of tax · Gift deduction · Charity · Monument · Donation · Resale right · Volunteers

1 Introduction

Museums and cultural heritage are a specific sub-sector of the creative industries. Usually, legal entities in this sector operate as an NPO, PBE or charity. The terminology used differs between jurisdictions, but in this book, we use "NPO", "PBE" and "charity" synonymously. Terminology notwithstanding, what these entities have in common is that they pursue public benefit and not usually a profit.

S. Hemels (✉)
Department of Tax Law, Erasmus School of Law,
Erasmus University Rotterdam, Rotterdam, The Netherlands
e-mail: hemels@law.eur.nl

S. Hemels
Allen & Overy, Amsterdam, The Netherlands

© Springer Science+Business Media Singapore 2017

S. Hemels and K. Goto (eds.), *Tax Incentives for the Creative Industries*,
Creative Economy, DOI 10.1007/978-981-287-832-8_7

Many countries apply tax incentives for charities. A total of 87% of high-income countries, for example, provide tax incentives for charitable donations and even 44% of low-income countries provide such incentives (Quick et al. 2014, p. 35). Usually, the status of NPO, PBE or charity is necessary to obtain such tax incentives. For certain fields, the definition of a charity varies widely between countries. For example, in the UK the promotion of the efficiency of the Armed Forces of the Crown is specifically mentioned as being for the public benefit.[1] In the Netherlands, political parties are regarded to be for the public benefit,[2] where this is not the case in most other countries.[3] However, in the Netherlands, unlike other countries,[4] amateur sports and amateur performing arts such as choirs, orchestras and brass bands are not regarded as being in the public benefit.

However, in the field of museums and cultural heritage, there does not seem to be much divergence: most countries regard such activities as being charitable and for the public benefit. For example, in the UK the advancement of the arts, culture and heritage is explicitly mentioned as being charitable.[5] In Germany as well, *Förderung von Kunst und Kultur*; (advancement of the arts and culture) and *Förderung des Denkmalschutzes und der Denkmalpflege* (advancement of monument protection and monument care) is specifically included as a public benefit,[6] as is promotion of culture and the arts in Japan.[7] From the overview of EFC (2015), p. 58, it follows that arts, culture or historical preservation are accepted for public benefit tax status in most of the 40 countries in greater Europe, covered in this survey. Of these countries, only Sweden does not regard this as a public benefit.

However, not all tax incentives for museums and cultural heritage are related to charities. Several countries apply tax incentives to non-charitable owners of cultural heritage. For example, many countries allow taxes to be paid with art and cultural heritage and offer tax incentives for monuments. The latter incentives are, in fact, an indirect incentive for the restoration sector of the creative industries. In this chapter, only those tax incentives related to museums and cultural heritage are discussed. Tax incentives related to acquisition or ownership of works of art are instead discussed in Chap. 9, which focuses on tax incentives for the art market.

This chapter starts with an overview of tax incentives in relation to museums and heritage entities that are qualified as charities: tax incentives for donations to these entities (Sect. 2), tax exemptions for such entities (Sect. 3) and tax incentives for volunteers (Sect. 4). Subsequently, tax incentives for owners of cultural heritage are

---

[1]Article 3(1)(l) CA.

[2]Political parties are included under article 5b(3)(j) AWR, furtherance of the democratic legal order.

[3]For example, in the USA § 501(c)(3) IRC explicitly excludes intervening in any political campaign.

[4]For example, the UK explicitly mentions amateur sports in article 3(1)(g) CA as does the USA in § 501(c)(3) IRC and Japan in point 4 of the schedule attached to article 2 NPO Law.

[5]Article 3(1)(f) CA.

[6]§ 52(2)(5) and (6) AO.

[7]Point 4 of the schedule attached to article 2 NPO Law.

discussed: the exemption of works of art on loan from wealth tax (Sect. 5), acceptance of art in lieu of taxes (Sect. 6) and tax incentives for restoration and maintenance of cultural heritage, which double as indirect incentives for heritage restorers (Sect. 7). The chapter ends with a conclusion (Sect. 8).

2 Tax Incentives for Donations

In the USA, private and corporate donations are very important for museums and cultural heritage NPOs. Of total USA museum operating revenues, 38% comes from donors in the private sector (individuals, charities and corporations) and only 24% from direct government support (Bell 2012), p. 2. In Europe, cultural and heritage institutions are often funded mainly by direct subsidies from local or national governments; however, private donations, including corporate sponsorship have also become more important. For example, although 30% of the funding of the British Museum in London comes from government funding, 38% comes from fundraising (Rustin and Arnett 2015). The Dutch government imposes an own account income requirement, for example through fundraising, ticket sales and commercial activities, of at least 21.5% on museums.[8]

There are several reasons why European museums have intensified their fundraising efforts as well. Most museums do not receive enough government subsidies to pay the astronomical prices needed to purchase important works of art. Private donations of money and works of art as well as loans from private art collectors remain very important for museums. Furthermore, many European governments actively encourage museums to find private resources to fund part of their activities. The reason for this is not only because governments have tight budgets, but also because they want cultural institutions to be aware of their public. By having to attract additional funding from the public, cultural institutions must by necessity engage the public in their activities. In the Netherlands, this is referred to as 'cultural entrepreneurship'. The Dutch government has funded a Cultural Patronage Program with the intention of promoting cultural patronage by making cultural institutions aware of the various funding avenues and by increasing public awareness and willingness to give to cultural institutions. This is accomplished by, for example, expert workshops, a website[9] and publications. Part of this program involves raising awareness of tax incentives that can be used in promoting cultural patronage.

In many countries, the fundraising efforts of charities are supported by tax incentives for charitable donations. The idea behind this is that such tax incentives decrease the relative cost of giving compared to other forms of consumption and thus stimulate charitable giving. This assumption, however, is only valid if

[8]Tweede Kamer, vergaderjaar 2015–2016, 34 300 VIII, nr. 2, p. 23.

[9]http://www.daargeefjeom.nl/. Accessed 23 July 2015.

charitable giving is price-elastic. A good is price-elastic if—all else being equal—the quantity consumed of a good increases if its price decreases. If charitable gifts are price-elastic, the decrease in price due to the incentive would thus lead to an increase in charitable giving (Feld et al. 1983, pp. 26–27; Gruber 2011). Since the 1970s, the effects of tax incentives on charitable contributions have been studied extensively. A review of these studies conducted over time suggests that giving is price-elastic, at least among those with high income (List 2011, p. 172). The meta-study by Peloza and Steel (2005), p. 266 also demonstrates a price-elasticity of giving, with rates between −1.11 and −1.44. In the event that the price of giving is decreased with $1, charitable giving thus increases with amounts larger than $1. This research substantiates the assumption that tax incentives indeed encourage charitable giving.

It must be noted that tax incentives will almost never be the main reason for individuals to support the arts. Other motives will be dominant, as the tax incentive merely reduces the costs of giving. However, the incentive may be an additional reason to donate, or to donate a greater amount.

2.1 Tax Incentives for Donations in Numbers

Quick et al. (2014) pp. 10, 26, 34, 40 conclude that tax incentives for philanthropy are the norm rather than the exception. Overall, 77% of all 177 nations that were included in their research offer some form of incentive to corporate donors (89% of high-income countries, 65% of low-income countries) while 66% offer some form of incentive for giving by individual donors (86% of high-income countries, 44% of low-income countries). In 49% of those countries, the incentives differ for corporates and private individuals. However, this does not make a difference for the average participation rate in charitable giving (29%). It must be appreciated that not all of these countries necessarily provide tax incentives for donations to museums and heritage, as can be derived from Quick et al. (2014) p. 34.

A total of 80% of high-income countries offer incentives to both corporate and individual donors. Twenty-eight countries (16%) offer tax incentives to corporate donors but not to individual donors (Quick et al. 2014). Seven of these countries are former Soviet Union countries, 13 are located in Africa and 7 in Asia. Only one (Finland) is an EU Member state.

Furthermore, Quick et al. (2014), pp. 38–39 found that countries that offer tax incentives to individuals see higher rates of participation in giving money to charity. The proportion of people donating money to charity is 12% points higher in nations that offer some form of tax incentive to individuals (33%) than those that offer no incentives (21%). In high-income countries that offer tax incentives to individuals, on average 47% gave to charity, while this was 37% in countries without tax incentives for donors. These figures substantiate the importance of tax incentives for donations. Even though the figures are not specifically concerning museums and heritage, there is no indication that the conclusions would be different for that sector.

2.2 *Different Forms of Tax Incentives for Donations*

Tax incentives for donations come in different forms and often with thresholds and caps. In this section, four different designs of tax incentives for charitable donations are analyzed: income deduction (Sect. 2.2.1), tax credits (Sect. 2.2.2), tax assignments (Sect. 2.2.3) and tax refunds to charity (Sect. 2.2.4).

2.2.1 Deduction from Taxable Income

In many countries, tax incentives for donations take the form of a deduction from taxable income, for example, in the USA, Japan and Turkey. The benefit to taxpayers depends on the progressivity of the tax system, the applicable tax rate and applicable caps. For example, in the USA the cap is 50% of the contribution base for the taxable year,[10] which is rather high, but the maximum federal tax rate is 39.6%, a rate that a single person only reaches if he has a taxable income over €413,200 (Perez 2015). In Germany the cap is 20% of total income;[11] however, the tax rate in Germany is much higher at 45% (50.5% including solidarity surcharge) for an income over €250,730 in 2015. In the Netherlands, a cap of 10% applies for gifts that are not periodic gifts.[12] However, the maximum tax rate is 52% and is, in 2015, already reached at an income over €57,585.[13] Furthermore, a periodic gift, a gift of annuities that the donor has deeded to give for at least 5 years, is deductible up to 100% of the taxable income, and the remainder can be carried forward indefinitely to future tax years.[14] The common opinion that gift deduction is most generous in the USA and that the tax incentives for charitable contributions in Europe are much smaller than those in the USA (O'Hagan 2011, p. 408) is, therefore, not correct. Neither is the call for Europe to adopt a more US-type tax policy (as was, for example, identified by O'Hagan 2011, p. 408) founded on facts. Not only is the cap higher in the Netherlands, also because of the higher marginal tax rates, the benefit from gift deduction can in various cases be higher in Europe than in the USA, as the following examples will show.

Let us take as an example a single person with an income of 150,000 who gives 90,000 to a museum with charitable status. For simplicity, let us assume that one dollar equals one euro and abstract from other personal allowances and deductions. Table 1 summarizes the deductible gift taking into account the cap in the respective countries, the tax benefit and the net costs of the gift for this person in the three countries.

---

[10] § 170(b) IRC.

[11] § 10b(1) EStG.

[12] Article 6.39 IB.

[13] Article 2.10 IB.

[14] Article 6.34 and 6.38 IB.

Table 1. Effect of income deduction

Country	Deductible gift	Tax benefit	Net costs of gift
USA	75,000 (50% cap)	20,527 (28%/25%)[a]	69,473
Germany	30,000 (20% cap)	14,250 (42% + 5.5%)	75,750
Netherlands	15,000 (10% cap)	7,800 (52%)	82,200
Netherlands	90,000 (annuity)	46,800 (52%)	43,200

[a]Deduction partly at 28% and partly at 25%, the calculation is made using http://us.thetaxcalculator.net/. Accessed 22 July 2015

Table 2. Income deduction with lower income and smaller gift

Country	Deductible gift	Tax benefit	Net costs of gift
USA	1,000 (50% cap)	250 (25%)	750
Germany	1,000 (20% cap)	475 (42% + 5.5%)	525
Netherlands	500 (10% cap)	210 (42%)	790
Netherlands	1,000 (annuity)	420 (42%)	580

This example shows that with a large gift in the form of an annuity, the Netherlands rather than the USA is most generous. For gifts other than annuity gifts, the Netherlands, however, is least attractive, especially considering that the example did not take into account the threshold of 1% of taxable income, which is required for annuity gifts to become deductible.

What happens when a person has a lower income and gives a smaller donation to the museum? Let us assume a person with an income of 50,000 who gives 1,000 to a museum. Table 2 summarizes the effects.

In this case, Germany is the most generous. The reason for this is the relatively low tax rate in the USA, the relatively high rate in Germany and the fact that the gift is just under the German cap. When the gift has the form of an annuity, the tax benefit in the Netherlands is also larger than that in the USA.

To summarize: it is a misconception that the USA has the most generous tax incentive for charitable gifts, firstly, because the Netherlands is much more generous towards annuity gifts and it is relatively easy to design a gift as an annuity gift. But more importantly, the benefit does not depend on only the cap, but also on the marginal tax rate applicable to the donor. Furthermore, as was already discussed in Sect. 5.1 of Chap. 4, the examples show that high-income individuals benefit more from the tax incentives for charitable donations in an income deduction system than individuals with a lower income that is taxed at a lower rate: the “upside-down effect” of Stanley and McDaniel (1985), p. 87.

2.2.2 Tax Credit

The upside-down effect can easily be avoided by using a tax credit, a reduction of tax due, instead of an income deduction. In France, for example, 66% of the value

Table 3. French tax credit

Gift amount	Deductible gift	Tax benefit	Net costs of gift
90,000	30,000 (20% cap)	30,000	60,000
1,000	666	666	333

of gifts is deductible from tax, with a limitation at 20% of taxable income.[15] The examples would give the following results for France (Table 3).

In the first example the benefit is limited by the cap, in the second example it is fully deductible from taxes due. Even though the gift is capped in the first example, the tax credit is still very beneficial for the taxpayer. In comparison with Table 1, only the annuity gift in the Netherlands is more beneficial. The treatment of the gift that is not capped is more beneficial than all income deduction schemes that are included in Table 2.

Other countries also use a system of tax credits, for example, Canada. In Canada, gifts up to a limit of 75% of net income are eligible for a charitable tax credit. There are two charitable tax credits for both the federal government and the provinces and territories. The tax credit for the first $200 is the lowest personal tax rate (federal: 15% in 2015) except for Quebec, which uses the middle rate. The tax credit for the amount over $200 is at the highest tax rate federally (29% in 2015) and for all provinces and territories except Alberta, British Columbia, New Brunswick, Yukon and Ontario, which use a different rate, either higher or lower (Alberta only has one tax rate).[16] The tax credit is non-refundable and can be used only to reduce tax owed. The benefit from the tax incentive progressively increases with the amount given. In this respect, Canada differs from countries where the gift is deducted from income, such as the USA. If those countries have a progressive rate structure, the benefit from the incentive increases with the income. Canadian progressivity seems to be more in line with what is usually the object of the tax incentive: to encourage all individuals to give more to charity, not to encourage richer individuals disproportionally more than individuals with a lower income. Therefore, for these purposes the Canadian charitable tax credit is a more effective instrument than the US income deduction.

Table 4 visualizes the effect of the Canadian charitable tax credit for the person in our example, assuming this person lives in the largest province by population, Quebec (tax credit for the first $200 20%, for the amount over $200 24% in 2015).

The tax treatment of the large gift is most beneficial in Canada if compared with the examples included in Tables 1 and 3. For the smaller gift, France is more attractive, but Canada comes second.

The examples of the tax credits of France and Canada make it clear that it is possible to introduce a tax incentive for gifts that does not create upside-down effects. Furthermore, these examples underscore that the US tax incentive is not the

[15]Article 200(1) CGI.

[16]http://www.taxtips.ca/filing/donations/tax-credit-rates-2015.htm. Accessed 23 July 2015.

Table 4. Canadian tax credit

Gift amount	Deductible gift	Tax benefit	Net costs of gift
90,000	90,000	47,664	42,336
1,000	1,000	494	506

most generous in the world; Canada and France are more generous than the USA in both examples. But most importantly, the Canadian charitable tax credit in particular shows a much fairer and more efficient way to encourage higher gifts than the regular gift deduction from taxable income.

2.2.3 Tax Assignment

Another possibility to avoid the upside-down effect is to give taxpayers the possibility of assigning to a charity of their choice a certain proportion of their tax dues. This system could take inspiration from the *Kirchensteuer* (Church Tax), which exists in several German-speaking countries such as Germany, Switzerland and Austria. However, it must be noted that the church tax that the German State introduced after World War I is not a state tax where part is transferred to churches, but is rather a constitutional right of the churches to levy a tax that is then collected by the State on their behalf (Petersen 2015). In Austria and Switzerland, the national or lower government is also merely the collector of the tax levied by the churches.

However, it would be possible to enable taxpayers to decide that a certain proportion of their taxes due, for example 1%, is paid out to a charity or charities of their choice instead of to the state. This would make the decision-making on how to spend that portion of tax revenue for the public benefit more democratic.

Several countries, especially in Eastern Europe, apply this tax assignment system. Examples are Hungary, Lithuania, Poland, Romania and Slovakia (Nährlich 2013, p. 26). In 1997, Hungary was the first eastern European country to introduce this system. Individuals living in Hungary can designate 1% of their income taxes to specific NPOs, including museums, libraries and the National Opera, and another 1% to a registered Hungarian church denomination or an issue of national significance such as flood relief or emergency medical services.[17] In Lithuania, Romania and Slovakia, individuals can designate 2% of their income tax to NPOs, in Poland 1% (Nährlich 2013, p. 26). Usually, only one NPO can be chosen. If the designation option is not used, the tax will go to the state. According to Nährlich (2013), p. 26, 25% of Romanian taxpayers (2011), 40% of Polish taxpayers (2008), 46% of Hungarian taxpayers (2007) and 54% of Slovak taxpayers used this opportunity.

[17] Act CXXVI/1996 on the Use of Specified Amount of Personal Income Tax in Accordance with the Taxpayer's Instruction and Bullain (2006).

Italy has applied this system, commonly known under the name *cinque per mille*, since 2006, where 0.5% of tax due may be assigned to an NPO.[18] Since 1985 the *otto per mille* has also existed, where 0.8% of income tax can be designated to a church.[19] At first, designation to only the Catholic Church was possible, but gradually other churches were included as well. Nevertheless, the Catholic Church still benefits the most (Mastellone 2013, p. 387).

Whether such a system would be beneficial for museums and cultural heritage is questionable. For example, from surveys in the USA and the Netherlands it follows that religion is the most popular category for charitable donations and that culture comes in 5th in importance (of 9 categories) in the USA (Indiana University, Lilly Family School of Philantropy 2015) and 8th in the Netherlands (Bekkers et al. 2015).

2.2.4 Tax Refund to Charity

Another category of tax incentives for charitable giving that avoids the upside-down effect is providing a tax refund to charities instead of to donors. The UK gift aid scheme is a good example of this category of incentives.[20] Under the gift aid scheme, charities can claim 25% of every donation they receive from the UK tax administration. Hence, when a donor gives £100, the charity receives £125: £100 from the donor and £25 from the government. Donations qualify as long as they are not more than four times what the donor has paid in the tax year. Furthermore, the donor must have paid at least as much income tax and/or capital tax in the year of the donation as the basic rate the charity will reclaim, and the gift must exceed certain thresholds.[21] The UK has not fully erased the upside-down effect, as an additional scheme exists next to gift aid for taxpayers in higher tax brackets. Donors can claim the difference between the tax rate they pay and the basic rate of 20% on their donation plus gift aid. If the person in the previous example would pay taxes at a rate of 40%, in addition to the gift aid received by the charity, the individual can claim back the difference between 40 and 20% of the gross gift, including gift aid, received by the charity; hence, 20% of 125, £25.

What would be the effect of the UK gift aid in our example? Let us assume for reasons of simplicity that 1 dollar/euro equals 0.70 British pounds. Under that assumption, the income of the person in our example amounts to £105,000 (income tax abstracting from allowances £53,643) and £35,000 (tax: £7643) and the gifts to £63,000 and £700, respectively. Table 5 summarizes the consequences of the UK gift aid system for this person.

The outcome of the gift aid scheme is for the donor very similar to the outcome of the US gift deduction. However, gift aid is more beneficial for the charity. This

[18]Section 337–340 of the Law of 23 December 2005 n. 266 (Legge finanziaria l'anno 2006).

[19]Section 47 of law n.222 of 20 May 1985.

[20]Sections 413–430 ITA.

[21]Section 418 ITA.

Table 5. UK gift aid system

Gift	Gift aid	Charity receives	Tax credit	Tax expenditure	Net donor costs	Net donor costs
£63,000	£15,750	£78,750	£15,750	£31,500	£47,250	€67,500
£700	£175	£875	£175	£350	£525	€750

makes the gift aid scheme more generous than the US income deduction scheme. This example also shows that with various schemes, similar outcomes can be reached for donors. Which scheme is more beneficial mainly depends on percentages that are applied in calculation the deduction or tax credit.

2.3 *Donations in Kind*

In some countries, gifts that qualify for a tax incentive may be in cash or in kind. In other countries a special regime applies for gifts in kind. This is important for museums and heritage charities as donations in kind can be just as important for these institutions as donations in cash. For example, a collector may decide to donate an important painting instead of auction it if he knows that he will get a tax incentive. A specific problem that is related to donations in kind is the valuation of these donations, a problem that has been addressed in various ways, as the examples in this paragraph will show.

2.3.1 Same Rules for Gifts in Cash and Gifts in Kind

In both the Netherlands and the USA, the rules for gifts in cash are the same as the rules for gifts in kind. Many museums have benefited from the opportunity to receive tax-deductible gifts in kind. Often, the tax incentive seems to have been an encouragement to donate a work of art to a museum. In recent years, however, such donations of art have been brought into question in the United States, given doubts as to whether the valuation of works was correct. A high valuation of a work of art means a high deduction for the donor, and since the value of art is relatively subjective, it was feared that museums were pushed to overvalue the works. However, legislation limiting the option to deduct certain donations in kind has led to a dramatic decrease in the number of art donations (Spector 2008). In the Netherlands, such problems with the valuation of gifts in kind have not been reported.

2.3.2 Special Rules for Gifts in Kind

Australia and the UK apply special tax incentives for cultural gifts in kind. Donors and institutions must meet many additional requirements to make use of these tax incentives and strict rules apply for valuations.

Australia: Cultural Gifts Program

Since 1978, Australia has applied a Cultural Gifts Program to encourage Australians to donate items of cultural significance from private collections to public art galleries, museums, libraries and archives.[22] Since its start, over 680 million Australian dollars' worth of items have been donated through this program.[23] Gifts can range from paintings, books, sculptures, manuscripts and personal papers to jewelry, ceramics and entire technological, mechanical, scientific or social history collections. The receiving institution must determine that the gift confirms with its collection policy and must formally accept the gift into its permanent collection.

The market value of the gift is fully deductible for the donor. Some exceptions apply, for example if conditions are attached to the gift that prevent full custody, control and clear title of the receiving institution, if the donor receives any advantage of material nature or if the item was acquired for the purpose of making the donation (Attorney-General's Department 2013, p. 19). If an artist or dealer makes a gift that is part of their trading stock, the deduction is restricted to the cost of acquiring or producing the item(s). If it comes from the personal collection of an artist or art dealer, the donor must demonstrate that the item(s) were not held for commercial gain and must have been held in the personal collection for at least 12 months. The deduction can be spread over up to five income years. Furthermore, these gifts are exempt from capital gains tax.

The donor must obtain two valuations of the market value of the gift. The average of these valuations can be deducted. These valuations must be carried out by appraisers who are approved for the program.[24] Furthermore, the Attorney-General's Department (2013), pp. 31–67 gives detailed guidance to the appraisers on how to value the item(s). The donor can claim a tax deduction for the costs of these valuations if these are not paid for by the receiving institution. The receiving institution will arrange the valuations or assist the donor in finding these appraisers. The Ministry of Arts reviews the valuations. Both the donor and the receiving institution must file several forms, meet several requirements and have several obligations for the tax incentive to apply (Attorney-General's Department 2013).[25] Recipient institutions must acknowledge the Cultural Gifts Program when referring to donated works in display labels, publications and, where appropriate, promotional materials to help in promoting and ensuring ongoing support for the program (Attorney-General's Department 2013, p. 17). The donor must choose one of the acknowledgments included by the Attorney-General's Department (2013), p. 17.

[22]Subdivision 30-A ITAA.

[23]http://arts.gov.au/funding/tax/cgp/about. Accessed 28 July 2015.

[24]The list of approved valuers is posted on the internet and regularly updated: http://arts.gov.au/sites/default/files/funding/tax/cgp/List-of-approved-valuers-May-2015.pdf. Accessed 28 July 2015.

[25]All forms and certificates can be found on http://arts.gov.au/funding/tax/cgp/forms. Accessed 28 July 2015.

The standard acknowledgement is ‘Donated through the Australian Government’s Cultural Gifts Program’, but the donor may opt to add their name and/or the name of the person in whose memory the gift was donated.

UK: Cultural Gifts Scheme

Until 2013, it was not possible to give tax-deductible donations in kind in the UK. However as a part of the package to encourage charitable giving and philanthropy, the Cultural Gifts Scheme was introduced in March 2013. The scheme enables UK taxpayers—both individuals and companies—to donate pre-eminent works of art and other heritage objects to be held for the benefit of the public or the nation.[26] Artists may also use this scheme to donate their own work (Department for Culture, Media and Sport 2015).

In the financial year 2012–2013, only one donation was accepted under this scheme: lyrics and letters by John Lennon, leading to a tax reduction of £120,000 (Arts Council England 2013, p. 68). In the financial year 2013–2014 four items with a total tax reduction of £537,397 were accepted (Arts Council England 2014, p. 68), including Vincent van Gogh’s *Tête de Paysanne*, which accounted for a tax reduction of £495,000. The Arts Council England (2014), p. 5 expects that the scheme will become a major factor in enriching museum collections.

For this scheme “pre-eminent property” means:[27]

- any picture, print, book, manuscript, work of art, scientific object or other thing that the relevant Minister is satisfied is pre-eminent for its national, scientific, historic or artistic interest
- any collection or group of pictures, prints, books, manuscripts, works of art, scientific objects or other things if the relevant Minister is satisfied that the collection or group, taken as a whole, is pre-eminent for its national, scientific, historic or artistic interest, or
- any object that is or has been kept in a significant building if it appears to the relevant Minister desirable for the object to remain associated with the building.

The Acceptance in Lieu Panel assesses whether an object is to be considered pre-eminent and gives recommendations to the relevant Minister regarding the pre-eminence, valuation and (if applicable) the proposed allocation (Department for Culture, Media and Sport 2015). The relevant Minister depends upon the location of the object on the date of registration and whether the donor has expressed any wish about where the object is to be displayed. Depending on this interest of the item, the Secretary of State for Culture, Media and Sport, the Welsh Ministers, the Scottish Ministers or the Northern Ireland Department for Culture, Arts and Leisure is the relevant Minister.

---

[26] Schedule 14 FA12.

[27] Schedule 14 FA12, Section 22.

Objects may only be transferred to eligible institutions: institutions willing to accept an object being any museum, art gallery, library, archive or other similar institution having as its purpose or one of its purposes the preservation for the public benefit of a collection of historic, artistic or scientific interest; or any body having as its purpose or one of its purposes the provision, improvement or preservation of amenities enjoyed or to be enjoyed by the public.

Applications are assessed on a first-come first-served basis. Given the annual limitation of £40 million for the Cultural Gifts Scheme and Acceptance in Lieu of Tax Scheme, it can be considered not to make an offer at the end of the financial year, but instead, to postpone it to the beginning of the new year.

In determining whether an object or collection or group of objects is pre-eminent, any significant association of the object, collection or group with a particular place must be taken into account. The UK scheme is, therefore, more strict than the system in countries where gifts in kind are eligible for regular gift deduction schemes, such as in the USA and the Netherlands. In these countries, the museum or heritage charity that receives the gift makes the decision whether or not to accept the gift, not the government. In such countries, the gift does not necessarily need to be pre-eminent.

In the UK, individuals receive a tax reduction of 30% of the value of the object donated under the Cultural Gifts Scheme. Individuals may specify whether they want the tax reduction to be set off against income tax or the capital gains tax first. The tax reduction can be spread over 5 years beginning with the offer registration date.

Companies receive a reduction of their corporation tax liability amounting to 20% of the value of the donated work. Companies are not able to spread the tax reduction; it can be used only in the accounting period in which the offer was registered.

On completion of the gift and delivery to an eligible institution, an announcement is made with details on the gifted object and the amount of the tax reduction applied. The name of the donor remains confidential unless the donor gives specific written consent for their right of confidentiality to be waived. When an application is not successful or is withdrawn, no announcement is made. All donations under the scheme are accounted for in the yearly Acceptance in Lieu reports.

2.3.3 Comparison of Special Schemes and General Schemes

The Australian, and to an even greater extent, the UK tax incentive for gifts in kind are much better controlled and accounted for than, for example, the Dutch and US gift deductions in kind. However, this does come at the costs of less flexibility for the donor and a larger administrative burden for the government, donors and receiving institutions.

3 Tax Exemptions for Cultural and Heritage Charities

Next to providing for a tax incentive for donors of charities, many countries exempt charities from certain taxes. As Brody (1998), p. 586 stated:

> Caesar should not tax God (or the modern secular equivalent).

This view seems to be shared by most countries in the world. Quick et al. (2014), p. 26 found that 94% of the 177 countries that were reviewed have some kind of tax exemptions for NPOs. They found a strong relationship between the presence of incentives for both corporate and individual donors and tax exemptions for non-profits (Quick et al. 2014, p. 35). In this research, a country was considered to have tax exemptions for NPOs if exemptions of any size in any category of taxes existed, including but not limited to capital, corporate, import, income, payroll, property taxes and VAT. Only 9 countries did not provide for any tax exemption for NPOs (Quick et al. 2014, p. 30). No country in North America and South Asia is without tax exemptions for NPOs.

A very common exemption for charities is an exemption of corporate income tax. In the USA tax exemptions for charities have always been very important, not only the corporate income tax exemption, but also the property tax exemption. The first federal income tax statute, enacted to finance the Civil War, exempted trustees of charitable trusts. The income tax statute of 1894 exempted all charities as did the corporate excise tax statute of 1909 (Brody 1998, p. 605). However, in 1950, after the Mueller Macaroni Company case, where a company operated tax-free for the benefit of the New York University Law School, a tax was imposed on feeder organizations and an unrelated business income tax was adopted (Brody 1998, p. 606). Where charities compete with others who are regularly taxed, the effects of the exemption for a level playing field of different economic operators must be taken into account. For example, in the Netherlands, no specific corporate income tax exemption exists for charities. All foundations and associations, whether charitable or not, are taxable if and insofar as they operate an enterprise and for all such entities a small general exemption applies. In the EU, the state aid legislation must be taken into account when applying or introducing tax exemptions for charities, including museums and cultural heritage charities. Refer to Chap. 5 for an elaborate overview of these EU state aid rules.

Another common exemption for charities is an exemption from gift and inheritance tax. Quick et al. (2014), p. 41 found that 41% of countries reviewed imposed an inheritance tax (72 countries), and 58% of those countries provided for exemptions for charitable transfers (42 countries).

Furthermore, not only national tax legislation can provide for exemptions, but also lower levels of government, can provide for specific exemptions in their taxes.

3.1 No Resale Right for Museums Buying Contemporary Art

Upon the sale of contemporary art, in many countries the resale right (*droit de suite* in French) has to be taken into account. Although technically speaking this is not a tax, I will briefly discuss this levy and the exemption for museums as it is in many ways similar to a tax.

Since 1 January 2006, Member States of the European Union have had to comply with the Resale Rights Directive.[28] In broad terms, the resale right gives artists who are nationals of a Member State of the European Union or the European Economic Area and their heirs the inalienable right to receive a royalty based on the sale price obtained for any resale of an original work of art in which a professional art dealer is involved. The resale right runs for the life of the artist plus 70 years after their death. The resale right is calculated as a portion of the sale price of the work of art.

The resale right reduces the proceeds from the sale. Furthermore, if the artist is still alive, the fact that the buyer will probably have to pay a sum to the artist determined by the resale right upon future disposal of the artwork might lower the price that the buyer is currently willing to pay. However, the resale right does not apply if the work of art is sold to a museum that operates on a non-profit basis and is open to the public. This incentive might, therefore, slightly reduce the price museums have to pay for modern and contemporary art.

4 Tax Incentives for Volunteers

Gifts and loans are not the only important means of creating a bond between cultural institutions and the public. A donation of time, that is, volunteering, can achieve this objective as well (Bekkers et al. 2015, pp. 142–144). Furthermore, volunteers can reduce the costs of cultural institutions and enable activities that would not otherwise be possible. A donation of time is not limited to only the rich. In fact, volunteering enables lower income groups, such as unemployed and retired people, to become engaged in cultural institutions. Volunteers' activities can take many forms, for example, providing information at information desks, providing guided tours in a museum (this can be seen in many Japanese museums, for example, the Edo-Tokyo Museum in Tokyo,[29] where there is often two way volunteering: the overseas visitors who are guided by the volunteer also help the volunteer to practice a foreign language such as English) and helping with the indexing and maintenance of

[28]Directive 2001/84/EC of 27 September 2001.

[29]http://edo-tokyo-museum.or.jp/en/information/. Accessed 23 July 2015.

museum objects. For example, in the Amsterdam Museum volunteers help out with indexing and restoring the collection of costumes.[30]

According to Stratemeyer et al. (2010), p. 3, the Netherlands and Canada have the largest voluntary sectors in relation to the economic population. Bekkers et al. (2015), p. 137 estimated that in 2014, 37% of the Dutch population participated in volunteering; however, this was less than the 41% of 2010. For the art and culture sector, the percentages were 4% in 2010 and 3% in 2014. In any case, in many countries, volunteering is regarded to be an essential part of civil society.

It is debated whether tax incentives for volunteers are a good policy instrument. According to Spyker and Peloza (2009), p. 9 voluntarism has the potential to deliver a much higher egoistic benefit, such as networking opportunities and skill development, than monetary donations, for which reason they suggest that the tax deductibility of voluntarism may play less of a role, as self-serving benefits are offered through other means. Spyker and Peloza (2009), p. 12 fear that the attachment of economic and tax value to donations may reduce the motivations of volunteers to participate. Furthermore, Spyker and Peloza (2009), pp. 10, 13 observe from a literature review that cash and time donations are complimentary and that charities seem to prefer cash over time, as they can decide on how to spend it. They also mention that in times of financial crisis donors might be motivated to make less cash donations and more time donations, which could negatively impact the free spending possibilities of charities. This preference of charities could be a reason not to incentivize time donations. Finally, Spyker and Peloza (2009), p. 13 warn that the introduction of tax incentives may shape the attitudes of donors and the public at large to view NPOs as an extension of the consumer model and that moving volunteerism toward a classic market exchange may have adverse long-term effects on rates of participation and attitudes towards voluntarism.

However, Stratemeyer et al. (2010), p. 3 recommend acknowledging volunteer time utilizing the same mechanisms developed for donations to charitable organizations, in recognition of the important contributions of volunteers to society. These researchers expect that a tax incentive as a recognition tool will positively impact volunteer commitment and are of the opinion that volunteers have a right to proper recognition. Furthermore, they expect that non-traditional incentives will help to broaden the narrow demographic of the volunteer base.

In most countries, including the USA, Canada and Japan, volunteer time cannot be deducted as a gift in kind. Problems that are mentioned in this regard are the hourly wage that must be taken into account, whether there should be a limit of the number of volunteer hours that can be claimed and whether the incentive should be limited to certain types of volunteer activities. Spyker and Peloza (2009), p. 12 warn that donors would be motivated to overvalue their donated time, while NPOs may have conflicting objectives between satisfying donors and reporting high value time donations and the negative impact to direct cash donations. Furthermore, they

[30]http://hart.amsterdammuseum.nl/31611/nl/vrijwilligers. Accessed 23 July 2015.

fear that the tax administration would face excessive administrative costs with respect to compliance.

In the Netherlands, volunteer activities are stimulated by a tax incentive in the wage and income tax. A reimbursement for volunteers is not taxed if this does not exceed €1500 per year, €150 per month and €4.50 per hour.[31] Furthermore, if a volunteer has a right to receive such reimbursement and the cultural institution is able and willing to pay out this reimbursement, but the volunteer refuses the reimbursement, the volunteer can deduct the reimbursement that he did not want to receive as a gift for personal income tax purposes.[32] Next to these incentives for volunteers, charities, including cultural institutions, that are liable to pay corporate income tax (this is a minority, as most Dutch charities are exempt from this tax) with volunteers can get a special corporate income tax deduction.[33] These institutions can deduct the net costs that they would have had if they had paid the volunteers the minimum wage for their activities. Through these tax incentives, the Netherlands makes volunteering more attractive. This does not only serve cultural policy goals, but also social policy goals such as providing work experience for the unemployed and making sure that people without work (including housewifes and pensioners) feel part of the society.

5 Exemption of Works of Art on Loan from Wealth Tax

Owners of art are not always willing to donate their works of art or heritage objects to a museum, but many of them are willing to give works on loan to museums. However, if a loan to a museum would imply a higher wealth tax for the owner of the work of art this could be a disincentive to give the work on loan. On the other hand, it could be an incentive to give a work on loan to a museum if this would reduce the wealth tax that would have been levied had the work of art not been given on loan at all. In the Netherlands, the tax legislation explicitly states that a work of art or heritage on loan to a museum is exempt from wealth tax unless it is held as an investment. Because of this exemption, there is no disincentive to give the work of art on loan to a museum (in the Netherlands, movable property in private use, including works of art and heritage, are deemed not to be possessions, for which reason art that is held at home is not taxed with wealth tax). This is important as it encourages people to give their works of art on loan to a museum and allows museums to exhibit them either on a semi-permanent basis or in special exhibitions.

---

[31]Article 2(6) LB and article 3.96(c) IB.

[32]Article 6.36(1) IB.

[33]Article 9(1) (h) Vpb.

6 Acceptance in Lieu of Tax

European governments consider the preservation of cultural heritage such as paintings, historic buildings and archives to be an important task. As a number of major works of art are in the possession of individuals, the question is what happens when the owner of a work of art dies. In some cases, their heirs will decide to sell the work of art, if only to pay inheritance tax. However, museums will not always be able to acquire the necessary funds in time to buy them. This means that after an auction, the works may be lost to the public, or even to the country if they are bought by a foreigner. In the case of heritage buildings, in some circumstances such a sale might lead to their demolition.

To prevent this and to preserve important national heritage, many countries have introduced the option of paying inheritance tax, and in some countries other taxes, by transferring such cultural heritage to the state. The tax incentive has the advantage that the budget is already there, which enables the government to act quickly.

Examples of European countries with such tax incentive are the UK, France, the Netherlands, Ireland, Italy, Belgium and Spain. In Japan as well, it is possible to pay inheritance tax with land, buildings or art. In December 1998 the Law Concerning Public Display of Art Objects at Museums was enacted in Japan and established a system of enrolled art objects. Individual or corporate owners of art may apply to have their art object enrolled. Enrolment is decided based on the opinions of experts. The enrolled objects are systematically displayed and managed by museums for five or more years based on an agreement between the owner and the art museum. Art objects that are enrolled at the time of inheritance may be used as in-kind payment of inheritance tax (Ministry of Education, Culture, Sports, Science and Technology 2000). In Japan, inheritance tax first must be paid in cash, and payment of inheritance tax in kind is approved only when it is difficult for the taxpayer to pay in cash. An order of priority is used for payments in kind: first, payment in government bonds, land and ships, then in corporate bonds and stock and finally in movable goods including art works. The only benefit of having an enrolled art work is that the work of art gets a higher priority, at the same level of government bonds, land and ships. It is, therefore, a tax incentive with a rather limited scope; it makes payment in kind easier with an enrolled art work than with an art work that is not enrolled (Agency for Cultural Affairs 2014, pp. 11, 73). Furthermore, regarding land and buildings, the government must sell the property on auction and add the proceeds to the budget. This is, therefore, not an incentive for the preservation of historical or cultural heritage (Hemels and Shiba 2015, pp. 62–63). This Japanese incentive is rarely used. An example is the historic building where Empress Michiko was born. After her father died in 1999, it was offered to the Government in lieu of inheritance tax. Officials decided to demolish the house and auction off the land. In this case the incentive could have been used as an instrument to preserve important cultural heritage for the country and future generations, but unfortunately it had to be used to obtain budget for government expenditures in the current generation.

The European incentive differs from country to country. Its name, requirements, transparency regarding the results and taxes and the objects to which it applies also vary. In this paragraph I will discuss some examples.

6.1 The Early Adapters: UK and France

In the UK this tax incentive is referred to as "Acceptance in Lieu of Tax Scheme"[34] and in France as *dation en paiement*.[35] The UK and France have a relatively long and successful tradition of using this tax incentive. In the UK it was first introduced in 1910 for historic buildings. However, it was not until 1956 that offers of moveable property without a link to historic buildings were permitted. In France the *dation* was introduced by the law no. 68-1251 of 31 December 1968. It applies to works of art, books, collections and documents with a high artistic or historic value.[36] The UK and French government, and museums in these countries, give substantial publicity to the incentive and its successes. The French Centre Pompidou organized a special exhibition in 2003 called 'La dation Brancusi' following the *dation* of the artist's archives in 2001. The catalogue of this exhibition, Tabart (2003), is still for sale.

In the UK and France, the tax incentive has been important in acquiring major works of art that are now on public display. For example, in the fiscal year 2013–2014 the UK accepted 24 works of art and archives resulting in almost £30 million of taxes being satisfied. These represented a wide variety of items, including an 18th-century painting of Venice by Guardi, portraits by Lawrence, Van Dyck and Constable, a 17th-century buff coat, a collection of 20th-century graphic works by Richard Hamilton, the Chester of Chichely archives, Philip the Good's copy of a 15th-century illuminated manuscript, Mount Steward land in Northern Ireland, works by 20th-century painters Frank Auerbach from the estate of the painter Lucian Freud (the collection also included a Picasso and a Yeats, part of it was used to satisfy 2014–2015 tax, the total tax credit amounted to 16,252,425) and, spread over 2012–2013 and 2013–2014 a painting of John Ruskin by John Everett Millais (tax credit of in total £7 million). These items were distributed to a range of museums, galleries, national trusts and archives all over the UK.

The Musée Picasso in Paris is a good example of the success of the French incentive, as its existence is a direct result of the use of the *dation* after the death of Picasso and later of his wife, Jacqueline.[37] Through this incentive, France has

[34]Section 230 IHTA.

[35]Article 1716 bis CGI and article 384 of the annex of the CGI.

[36]Article 1716 bis CGI.

[37]http://www.museepicassoparis.fr/collections/presentation/. Accessed 28 July 2015.

obtained many works and manuscripts including those by Bacon, de Beauvoir and Sartre, Chagall, Courbet, Duchamp, Goya, Matisse, Monet, Montesquieu, Pollock, Proust, Rothko, Rousseau, Rubens and Vermeer (Commission interministérielle d'agrément pour la conservation du patrimoine artistique national 2008; Ministère de la Culture et de la Communication 2015).

6.2 Eligible Objects

Not every work of art can be used to pay taxes: the cultural heritage has to be of significant cultural or historical value to the country in question. For example, in the UK the item has to be pre-eminent for its national, scientific, historic or artistic interest, and in France the objects must have high artistic or historic value. Such cultural heritage might include works of art, manuscripts, archives, heritage objects and historic documents, but in some countries such as the UK and France, immovable property such as buildings and land is also acceptable. Unlike most other countries, Ireland has set a minimum value threshold: to be eligible for tax relief for donations of heritage items, a single item or a collection of items must have a minimum value of €75,000.[38]

Many countries have special committees that advise on the acceptance (or rejection) of cultural heritage. The size of these committees varies widely. For example, in the Netherlands the committee consists of only three people, of whom two (including the chairman) are not art experts but instead have a financial/tax background. In France, the committee has five members: three with an art/heritage background (including the chairman) and two with a financial/tax background. In the UK, the panel consists of 12 persons, all with an art or heritage background. In my view, the dominance of art and heritage experts is preferable to the situation where the Ministry of Finance has the dominant role in the advisory committee.

6.3 Value Taken into Account

In most countries, for example, France and Belgium, 100% of the value of the work of art is taken into account to establish the amount of tax that should be paid. 'Some countries give a bonus to encourage heirs not to auction the work of art, but make use of the tax incentive instead. In the Netherlands, 120% of the value is taken into account for that reason.[39] This means that for a work of art with a value of €100,000, an inheritance tax assessment of €120,000 may be paid.

[38]Section 176, paragraph 2(c)(i) FA95 and Section 1003 paragraph 2(c)(i) TCA.
[39]Article 67(3) SW.

In the UK the value used is net of capital gains tax and inheritance tax that would have been payable had the item be sold on the open market. To encourage heirs to use the scheme in preference to making a private sale, a so-called "douceur" of 25% of the tax payable on a private sale is added to the net value. Stanco (2014), p. 1610 gives the following example: if the item would be sold on the market for 100,000, inheritance tax amounting to 40,000 would be due, resulting in a net value of 60,000. This is the relevant value for purposes of the tax incentive; however, the douceur of 25% of the tax of 40,000 (10,000), which would have been due had the item be privately sold, is added to this value. This results in an amount of 60,000 + 10,000 = 70,000 being taken into account to reduce inheritance tax. In Ireland, 80% of the value has been taken into account since 2010; before, this was 100%.

6.4 Ownership

In many countries, the state becomes the owner of the object, which can subsequently be given on loan to a museum. This is the case in the Netherlands and France. In the UK, an object is allocated to a suitable institution. However, when an offer has been made with the condition that the work be allocated to a particular institution and the minister has agreed to the allocation, it is immediately transferred to that institution as soon as the offer is completed. In making a case for allocation, the institution must address how the public will be given access to the item, how it would fit in with the existing collection and the use in the educational program.

6.5 Eligible Taxes

Most countries only allow the paying of inheritance tax with art. However, some countries, such as Ireland, Spain and Italy also allow other taxes to be paid for through cultural heritage. These tax incentives may benefit companies and so offer governments other opportunities to retain important cultural heritage. In Ireland, for example, this can be used to deduct a tax credit from income tax, corporation tax, capital gains tax, gift tax or inheritance tax liabilities (including interest and penalties).[40] Through this tax incentive, the National Library of Ireland managed to acquire a previously unknown six-page James Joyce manuscript in spring 2006. The Allied Irish Bank bought this manuscript for €1.17 million at auction with the purpose of donating it to the National Library and crediting the value against its corporation tax liabilities. In 2004, it had not been possible for the National Library to buy this manuscript (Murphy 2012). The incentive made it possible to preserve the manuscript for Ireland and make it available to the public and researchers. Other

[40]Section 1003 TCA.

objects Irish museums, galleries and libraries have acquired through the incentive are the 1916 Proclamation, several paintings by Francis Bacon, the J.B. Yeats. archive and several of his paintings, the W.B. Yeats library and several other papers of James Joyce. Various companies, such as Guinness and the Bank of Ireland, have paid their taxes with (a part of) their collection. Therefore, the Irish incentive is also an effective and efficient way to preserve heritage artifacts owned or acquired by companies.

6.6 Accountability

The way information is provided varies widely over the different countries. In the Netherlands, information on the objects obtained is not systematically communicated. It depends on an individual museum to which the Dutch state has given the item on loan whether it is communicated how the item was obtained. For example, in 2009 the Rijksmuseum exhibited 16 drawings of a collection of 45 drawings from the collection Van Regteren Altena that it obtained through the tax incentive (Rijksmuseum 2009). The amount of the tax incentive is almost never made public in the Netherlands. Ireland is more open, as it publishes a list with the name of the donation, the value and the institution that received it (Department of Arts, Heritage and the Gaeltacht 2015). However, the UK is the best example of how to account for this tax incentive. Every year, an illustrated report is published (for example, Arts Council England 2013 and 2014) in which not only the objects, the value of the tax incentive and the receiving institution can be found, but also beautifully illustrated descriptions of the objects, the names of the members of the panel and the expert advisors, both with their affiliations.

6.7 Use

Stanco (2014), p. 1611 compared the use of the tax incentive in the Netherlands, the UK, France, Belgium and Ireland. He related the amount of accepted items to the inhabitants of these countries, resulting in the graph is reproduced in Fig. 1.

For the UK, Ireland and the Netherlands, Stanco (2014), p. 1612 made an overview of the amount of items/collections for which the tax incentive was used and the amount of tax paid (in euro) with the items. This overview is reproduced in Table 6.

From these figures, it becomes clear that the Dutch bonus does not have a significant effect on the use of the incentive. Stanco (2014), p. 1613 mentions a 2012 survey from which it followed that 86% of Dutch high net worth–individuals with an art collection did not know about this tax incentive. The lack of transparency regarding this tax incentive, therefore, seems to have an adverse effect: where the incentive is unknown it might thus not be used as often as it could be. Transparency seems to be much more important than simply providing for a bonus.

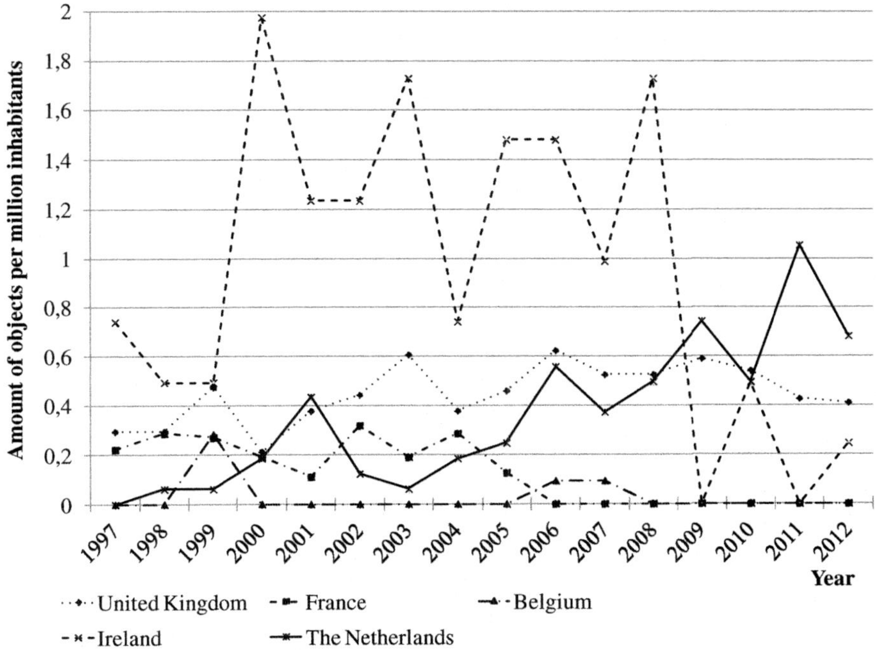

Fig. 1. Amount of objects per million inhabitants

Table 6. Overview of the use of the tax incentive in the UK, France, Ireland and the Netherlands

	UK	France	Ireland	Netherlands
2012	25: 36,621,00	?	1: 153,350	11: 1,400,000
2011	26: 9,711,000	?	0: 0	17: 4,000,000
2010	33: 18,369,000	?	2: 1,940,000	8: 9,000,000
2009	36: 23,166,000	?	0: 0	12: 15,000,000
2008	32: 17,784,000	?	7: 5,348,970	8: 2,500,000
2007	32: 29,601,000	?: 32,420,000	4: 5,273,320	6: 1,500,000
2006	38: 29,484,000	?: 4,610,000	6: 6,020,695	9: 1,300,000
2005	28: 15,210,000	8: 14,090,000	6: 5,492,171	4: 180,000
2004	23: 25,389,000	18: 24,410,000	3: 5,141,004	3: 1,000,000
2003	37: 46,683,000	12: 43,680,000	7: 5,568,988	1: 0
2002	27: 35,100,000	20: 55,310,000	5: 4,248,742	2: 275,000
2001	23: 24,600,000	7: 43,730,000	5: 2,711,119	7: 680,670

The most important effect on the use of the incentive seems to be the possibility to pay taxes other than only inheritance tax, given the high use of the incentive in Ireland. However, since 2010 the use of the incentive seems to be declining. In 2011, no item was accepted and in each of the years 2012–2015, only one item with a relatively low value under €200,000 (in 2013: €375,000) was accepted (Department of Arts, Heritage and the Gaeltacht 2015).

The tax incentive seems to be most successful in the UK. This can probably be explained in part by the fact that many UK taxpayers own valuable art works. However, part of the effect of the incentive can be expected to be due to the transparency of and publicity regarding the results of the tax incentive.

6.8 *Conclusion*

The examples used in this section show that the possibility to pay inheritance tax and other taxes with important works of art can be an effective and efficient way to achieve the cultural policy goal of preserving important cultural heritage for the nation. However, these examples also show that transparency is important. Countries such as the Netherlands should follow the example of the UK, not only because a democratic society demands that tax incentives are accounted for, but also to make the tax incentive more known to the public and thus enforce creative industries policy. The example of the UK shows that this is possible. Rather than giving an extra tax benefit as the Netherlands does, it seems to be more effective to greatly publicize the achievements of the tax incentive.

7 Tax Incentives for Restoration and Maintenance of Cultural Heritage: Indirect Incentives for Heritage Restorers

It is impossible for a government to own all monuments in a country and maintain them. An example is the 17th-century Canal Ring in Amsterdam, which was added to the UNESCO World Heritage List in 2010. The canal houses that line these canals are an important characteristic of the Canal Ring. Many canal houses are registered monuments. These houses were built by individuals and the majority of these houses are still privately owned both by individuals and companies. The maintenance of this important characteristic of the Canal Ring has, therefore, mainly been a private affair. The government wants to make sure that these monuments are preserved. A special tax incentive is one of the instruments governments apply to pursue this cultural policy goal.

The reason behind such tax incentives is that governments cannot afford to subsidize the maintenance of all the heritage in their territory, but by providing for a tax incentives, governments can reduce the maintenance and restoration costs for private owners. Furthermore, it is expected that private owners will take good care of the heritage they own. Therefore, society as a whole benefits from this private preservation as it is a way to maintain buildings of historical interest.

Heritage maintenance businesses, such as specialized carpenters and painters, indirectly benefit from this incentive. As private owners do not have to bear the full costs of the maintenance, this reduces their net maintenance costs and they might be more willing to engage this sector of the creative industries (heritage maintenance is in this view presumed to be price-elastic). An additional benefit is that the specific skills needed for heritage restoration will be in greater demand and will not become forgotten. This effect for the heritage restoration sector of the cultural industries is not always acknowledged, but undoubtedly an effect of such tax incentives aimed at the restoration of cultural heritage.

Countries apply various tax incentives for maintaining and restoring cultural heritage. The design of these incentives depends on the tax rules that would otherwise apply to this heritage. For example, where in the Netherlands, maintenance costs of houses are in general not deductible, individuals owning a registered building of historical interest could deduct 80% of certain maintenance and restoration costs from their taxable income.[41] While the Netherlands provides for a tax incentive for only the maintenance of buildings of historical interest, other European countries grant tax incentives for other forms of cultural heritage as well. For example, in Italy individuals can deduct 19% of voluntary expenses made for the maintenance, protection or restoration of registered cultural artifacts from their taxable income.[42] Companies can fully deduct such costs.[43]

In Germany, it is possible to deduct up to 9% of costs for the maintenance and restoration of protected monuments for a period of up to 8 years and up to 7% in the following 4 years from one's taxable income, provided that certain requirements are met.[44] If the cultural heritage is not used for income-raising purposes or as a private residence, up to 9% of the costs for maintenance and restoration can be deducted for a period of 10 years.[45] This incentive does not only apply to protected buildings, but also, for example, to protected gardens, city walls and archeological sites. Furthermore, this tax incentive also applies to furniture, works and collections of art, scientific collections, archives and libraries that have been owned by the taxpayer's family for at least 20 years or that are registered as artifacts of national heritage An important requirement for this German tax incentive is that it applies only if the heritage site or artifact is open for research or to the public, for example, by being loaned to a museum or open for viewing upon appointment. This makes it possible for taxpayers, who indirectly finance the incentive, to enjoy heritage, which is preserved thanks to the incentive. Furthermore, through this tax incentive

[41] Article 6.31 IB. The government has proposed to abolish this incentive for efficiency reasons.

[42] Article 15(1)(g) TUIR.

[43] Article 100(2)(e) TUIR.

[44] § 7i EStG.

[45] § 10g EStG.

the German government enables the public to enjoy privately owned cultural heritage that might otherwise not be open to the public. Exceptions to this requirement of public accessibility are only made if this is necessary to preserve an artifact (for example, a very fragile document that must not be exposed to light).

Spain provides for a similar tax incentive for companies that own cultural artifacts. Such companies may deduct from taxable income 15% of the costs of maintenance, restoration, transportation and exhibition of this heritage.[46] As in Germany, an important requirement to benefit from this tax incentive is that the heritage must be open to the public. Again, this tax incentive combines various benefits: cultural heritage will be maintained with a combination of public (the tax incentive) and private funds, restoration skills are preserved and the public will be able to enjoy privately owned heritage.

8 Conclusion

Many countries provide for tax incentives for museums and cultural heritage. A very important tax incentive that most countries provide for in some form is a tax incentive for donations. The deduction of gifts from income, such as is applied in the USA, is best known. However, as was discussed in this chapter, this might actually not be the optimal form of incentive. A tax credit that progressively depends on the donated amount, such as is applied in Canada, is probably more effective and efficient. Furthermore, from the examples in this chapter it became clear that the general presumption—that the USA tax incentive for donations is the most generous—is not correct.

Donations in kind are more problematic for tax purposes than donations in cash, as the former must be formally valued in order to calculate and grant the tax incentive. However, in general, it will be difficult to find an objective value. Australia and the UK have, therefore, introduced strict valuation rules. The advantage is that these donations are better controlled and accounted for. However, these schemes are less flexible and lead to administrative burden on museums, donors and governments.

Tax exemptions for museums and cultural heritage charities are common in most countries. Tax incentives for volunteers are, on the other hand, not without controversy. In most countries, volunteer time is not taken into account as a tax-relevant gift, mainly because of valuation difficulties. However, the Netherlands provides for several other tax incentives for volunteers, such as an income tax exemption, the deductibility as a gift of a volunteering reimbursement that is not received and a corporate income tax deduction for charities employing volunteers.

Several countries enable their taxpayers to pay tax with special cultural heritage and works of art (acceptance in lieu of tax). This has enabled these countries to

[46]Article 38(1)(b) LIS.

obtain formerly privately owned objects for public collections. The visibility and accountability of this tax incentive varies widely between countries. In my view, countries should follow the example of the UK, a country that is very transparent regarding this incentive. This transparency is not only required in a democratic society, but it also generates publicity for the tax incentive, possibly attracting taxpayers who might not have known about the incentive otherwise. For higher effectiveness, publicity seems to be more important than a numerically higher incentive.

Tax incentives for the maintenance and restoration of cultural heritage are an indirect incentive for the restoration sector of creative industries, even though the incentive is usually provided to the private owner of the cultural heritage. These tax incentives have several benefits: cultural heritage is maintained and under some incentives, is made public; furthermore, restoration skills are preserved.

It can, in short, be concluded that tax incentives are an important source of funds for the museum and cultural heritage sector of the creative industry.

References

Agency for Cultural Affairs (2014) Policy of cultural affairs in Japan. Fiscal 2014. http://www.bunka.go.jp/english/about_us/policy_of_cultural_affairs/pdf/2014_policy.pdf. Accessed 11 Dec 2014

Arts Council England (2013) Acceptance in Lieu report 2013. http://www.artscouncil.org.uk/media/uploads/Acceptance_in_Lieu_report_2013.pdf. Accessed 28 July 2015

Arts Council England (2014) Cultural gifts scheme and acceptance in Lieu report 2014. http://www.artscouncil.org.uk/media/uploads/Cultural_Gifts_Scheme_and_Acceptance_in_Lieu_publication_Nov14.pdf. Accessed 28 July 2015

Attorney-General's Department (2013) Cultural gifts program guide. Tax incentives for cultural gifts to Australia's public collections. http://arts.gov.au/sites/default/files/collections/cultural-gifts-progam-guide.pdf. Accessed 28 July 2015

Bekkers R, Schuyt T, Gouwenberg B (2015) Geven in Nederland 2015. Reed Business Information, Amsterdam

Bell FW (2012) How are museums supported financially in the U.S.? United States Department of Stae. Bureau of International Information Programs. http://photos.state.gov/libraries/amgov/133183/english/P_You_Asked_How_Are_Museums_Supported_Financially.pdf. Accessed 22 July 2015

Brody E (1998) Of sovereignty and subsidy: conceptualizing the charity tax exemption. J Corp Law 23: 585–629

Bullain N (2006) About miracles and misperceptions—lessons from the "percentage mechanism" in Hungary. http://www.icnl.org/research/library/files/Hungary/miracles.pdf. Accessed 21 Oct 2015

Commission interministérielle d'agrément pour la conservation du patrimoine artistique national (2008) La Dation en paiement. http://www.culture.gouv.fr/culture/actualites/communiq/albanel/Plaquedation.pdf. Accessed 28 July 2015

Department for Culture, Media and Sport (2015) Cultural gifts scheme guidance. http://www.artscouncil.org.uk/media/uploads/doc/CGSguidance27january2015.docx. Accessed 28 July 2015

Department of Arts, Heritage and the Gaeltacht (2015) Tax relief for donations of heritage items under Section 176 of finance act, 1995 and Section 1003 taxes consolidation act, 1997. http://www.ahg.gov.ie/app/uploads/2014/08/donations_1995_to_date.pdf. Accessed 11 Dec 2015
EFC (2015) Comparative highlights of foundation laws: the operating environment for foundations in Europe. EFC Brussels
Feld AL, O'Hare M, Schuster MDJ (1983) Patrons despite themselves: taxpayers and arts policy. New York University Press, New York
Gruber J (2011) Public finance and public policy. Worth Publishers, New York
Hemels SJC, Shiba Y (2015) Tax legislation as instrument to support private patronage of the arts and cultural heritage. Tokoha Law Rev 2(1):45–68
Indiana University, Lilly Family School of Philantropy (2015) Giving USA 2015. Annual report on philanthropy for the year 2014. Giving USA Foundation, Chicago
List JA (2011) The market for charitable giving. J Econ Perspect 25:157–180
Mastellone P (2013) Religion and taxation in Italy: the principle of laïcité and compliance with EU law. Eur Tax 53:378–391
Ministère de la Culture et de la Communication (2015) Dation en paiement. http://www.culture.gouv.fr/culture/infos-pratiques/fiscal/dation.htm. Accessed 28 July 2015
Ministry of Education, Culture, Sports, Science and Technology (2000) Japanese government policies in education, science, sports and culture 2000. http://www.mext.go.jp/b_menu/hakusho/html/hpae200001/hpae200001_2_137.html. Accessed 28 July 2015
Murphy SJ (2012) Irish historical mysteries: the trade in Joyce manuscripts. http://homepage.eircom.net/~seanjmurphy/irhismys/joyce.htm. Accessed 28 July 2015
Nährlich S (2013) Percentage philanthropy. Selbstbestimmte Steuerzuweisungen an Gemeinnützige. Stiftung Sponsoring 4:26–27
O'Hagan J (2011) Tax concessions. In: Towse R (ed) A handbook of cultural economics, 2nd edn. Edward Elgar, Cheltenham, pp 408–412
Spyker CL, Peloza, J (2009) The potential impact of Canadian federal and/or provincial tax credit incentives for volunteer participation. Volunteer Alberta, Edmonton. http://volunteer.ca/content/potential-impact-canadian-federal-andor-provincial-tax-credit-incentives-volunteer. Accessed 23 July 2015
Peloza J, Steel P (2005) The price elasticities of charitable contributions: a meta-analysis. J Public Policy Mark 24(2):260–272
Perez W (2015) Federal income tax rates for the year 2015. http://taxes.about.com/od/Federal-Income-Taxes/fl/Federal-Income-Tax-Rates-for-the-Year-2015.htm. Accessed 22 July 2015
Petersen J (2015) Kirchensteuer kompakt Strukturierte Darstellung mit Berechnungsbeispielen. Spinger Gabler, Wiesbaden
Quick E, Kruse TA, Pickering A (2014) Rules to Give By. A global philanthropy legal environment index. Nexus/McDermott Will & Emery/Charities Aid Foundation, Washington. http://www.nexusyouthsummit.org/wp-content/uploads/2014/12/RULES-TO-GIVE-BY-FINAL-Print.pdf. Accessed 22 July 2015
Rijksmuseum (2009) Grote schenking uit collectie Prof. Dr. I.Q. van Regteren Altena. http://62.212.91.193/collectie/aanwinsten2009/tekeningen-regteren-altena?lang=nl. Accessed 28 July 2015
Rustin S, Arnett G (2015) The sponsorship files: who funds our biggest arts institutions. The Guardian 2 March. http://www.theguardian.com/culture/2015/mar/02/arts-corporate-sponsorship-tate-british-museum. Accessed 22 July 2015
Spector M (2008) A portrait of art as a tax deduction. Wall Street J 22 July. http://www.wsj.com/articles/SB121667821980971651. Accessed 22 July 2015
Stanco GP (2014) Ruim vijftien jaar kwijtschelding van successierechten met kunst; een evaluatie. Weekblad fiscaal recht 7077:1604–1614

Stanley SS, McDaniel PR (1985) Tax expenditures. Harvard University Press, Cambridge Massachusetts/London

Stratemeyer G (ed) (2010) Tax credit incentives for volunteer participation. http://volunteer.ca/content/tax-credit-incentives-volunteer-participation-white-paper-supporting-policy. Accessed 22 July 2015

Tabart M (2003) La dation Brancusi. Designs et archives. Editions du Centre Pompidou, Paris

Vanistendael F (ed) (2015) Taxation of Charities. IBFD Amsterdam

Chapter 8
Tax Incentives for the Audio Visual Industry

Sigrid Hemels

Abstract In this chapter, various tax incentives for the audiovisual industry are discussed. Especially in the Americas and Europe, tax incentives for film and television production are the most prominent incentives. For that reason, these will be discussed extensively, using various examples and showing the incentives in relation to the specific features of this sector of the creative industry. Incentives aimed at producers, investors and consumers of these products are discussed separately. Notwithstanding the dominance of the incentives for film and television, tax incentives for developing video games, which are provided for by several countries, are discussed as well, as is a special French incentive for phonographic recordings and music videos.

Keywords Film · Video game · Television · Phonographic recording · Music video · Co-production · Tax competition · State aid

1 Introduction

The audiovisual industry, including film, television, Internet and video games, is probably the most commercial, international and powerful sector of the creative industry. According to InfoComm (2014), the audiovisual industry generated $91 billion. Furthermore, it is a labor-intensive sector providing jobs for a highly skilled workforce that is less vulnerable to competition from countries with low labor costs (Debande and Chetrit 2001, p. 8). Barnes (2015), p. 19 mentions that the James Bond film *Skyfall* had 1007 individuals involved in the production. Also, the AV industry can, as a side effect, increase tourism and merchandise sales as well as

---

S. Hemels (✉)
Department of Tax Law, Erasmus School of Law,
Erasmus University Rotterdam, Rotterdam, The Netherlands
e-mail: hemels@law.eur.nl

S. Hemels
Allen & Overy, Amsterdam, The Netherlands

© Springer Science+Business Media Singapore 2017
S. Hemels and K. Goto (eds.), *Tax Incentives for the Creative Industries*,
Creative Economy, DOI 10.1007/978-981-287-832-8_8

promote a country generally (Barnes 2015, p. 36). Furthermore, from an environmental point of view, it is a relatively clean and sustainable industry. Therefore, governments expect important economic benefits when attracting AV activity to their countries.

However, the audiovisual industries also have cultural aspects. Debande and Chetrit (2001), p. 8 qualify the role of media as being crucial in terms of making information available to citizens, shaping belief systems and forming cultural identity. The European Commission (2013), p. 1 states that AV works, and films particularly, play an important role in shaping European identities. Preamble 5 of the 2010 European AMS Directive states:

> Audiovisual media services are as much cultural services as they are economic services. Their growing importance for societies, democracy — in particular by ensuring freedom of information, diversity of opinion and media pluralism — education and culture justifies the application of specific rules to these services.

European Commission (2013), p.1 gives special attention to films

> because of their cost of production and cultural importance. Film production budgets are substantially higher than for other audiovisual content, they are more frequently the subject of international co-production, and the duration of their exploitation life is longer. Films in particular face strong competition from outside Europe. On the other hand, there is little circulation of European audiovisual works outside their country of origin.

This cultural aspect of the audiovisual industries has the effect that governments want to prevent dominance by one country (in particular, the USA), which results in less cultural diversity and diminished pluralism in AV products. InfoComm (2014) provided an overview of the market share of the various regions in 2014, based on end-user spending (Table 1).

This sector has, therefore, various dimensions that induce governments to include it in their cultural, social and industrial/economic policy objectives. The European Commission (2015a) described the importance of "content industries" (AV and other media content) as follows:

> Content industries play a key economic, social and cultural role in Europe. (…) Content industries are not only crucial to cultural diversity; they are also of paramount importance for the economy of the European Union. For instance, the audiovisual sector alone directly employs over one million people in the EU.

In his foreword to a report on the economic impact of UK tax incentives for the AV industries, George Osborne, UK Minister of Finance, argued that British films, videogames, animation and television enhance the UK's reputation and attract tourism from abroad (Barnes 2015, p. v):

Table 1 Market share based on end-user spending

North America	37.3%
Asia-Pacific	34.5%
Europe	19.1%
Latin America	5.2%
Middle East/Africa	3.9%

> In addition to its cultural value, the creative sector is delivering real benefits to our economy. It adds billions to UK GDP each year and supports jobs across the country. The growth of the creative sector also benefits other parts of the economy, as it empowers our workforce to develop new skills and provides the infrastructure for innovation.

For all of these reasons, countries want to attract investments by the AV industries. In this respect, countries sometimes work together to attract co-productions, such as by signing bi-lateral or multilateral co-production agreements with countries that provide state support systems for their own film industries, thereby giving access to support systems of both states. For example, Priot et al. (2015), p. 31 give an overview of the more than 40 countries with which France concluded such bilateral treaty. These include Australia, Canada, China, Hungary, India, New Zealand, South Africa and the UK, but not the USA and not Japan. In each treaty, the minority and majority contributions are stated, for example 20% against 80% in the treaty with Canada, China, Mexico, South Korea, Spain and the UK. Not all countries have as many bilateral treaties as France. For example, according to KFTV, Austria has co-production treaties with only seven countries (Canada, France, Germany, Italy, Switzerland, Luxembourg and Spain). The members of the European Council and some other European countries concluded the European Convention on Cinematographic Co-Production.[1] European cinematographic works made as multilateral co-productions and falling within the scope of the convention are entitled to the benefits granted to national films by the legislative and regulatory provisions in force in each of the signatory countries of the convention participating in the co-production concerned.[2] The preamble of this treaty states that the defense of cultural diversity of the various European countries is one of the aims of the European Cultural Convention and that cinematographic co-production is an instrument of creation and expression of cultural diversity on a European scale, which should be reinforced. This convention applies to co-productions between producers of three or more signatory countries.[3] For bilateral co-productions involving signatory countries with a bilateral treaty, the bilateral treaty applies. For multilateral co-productions, the provisions of the convention override those of the bilateral agreements to the extent that those conflict with the provisions of the convention.[4] The contribution may not be less than 10% nor more than 70% of the total production costs for a multilateral co-production (20–80% for a bi-lateral co-production).[5] In order for the convention to apply, a co-producer of a non-signatory country may not take part in more than 30% of the budget. Furthermore, the co-produced work must meet the definition of a European cinematographic work. To be European, the co-productions must at least score a minimum of 15 points out of 19 points regarding involvement of European

---

[1]CETS No. 147.

[2]Article 4(1) ECCC.

[3]Article 2(2) ECCC.

[4]Article 2(3) ECCC.

[5]Article 6 ECCC.

directors, authors, actors and crew.[6] Projects of a blatantly pornographic nature or those that advocate violence or openly offend human dignity are not eligible.[7]

Tax incentives are one of the means by which countries, and sometimes states or provinces within countries, compete for the favor of the AV sector. This competition can be quite aggressive. France, for example, has produced a full-color glossy marketing brochure in English (Priot et al. 2015) showcasing the benefits foreign producers can get if

> there is something French in the script…. In any case, you feel that you should partner with someone in France and figure out how to raise money from the French market.

The brochure includes several advertisements, not only for providers of film-related services, but also for various regions in France, which are competing with each other to earn the favor of foreign film producers ("Looking for film locations and free assistance? Welcome to Brittany"; "Be inspired by Guadeloupe"; "Corsica welcomes your shoot"). Olsberg SPI (2015), p. 15 mentions that 26 fiscal incentive schemes in 17 European countries in 2014.

In the EU, the design and implementation of tax incentives for the AV industry is bound by the EU state aid rules, as was described in Chap. 5. Furthermore, in order to understand these tax incentives, it is important to appreciate the specific economic characteristics of the market for AV products. Therefore, this chapter will start with a description of the economic characteristics of the market for AV products, in Sect. 2. Given these characteristics, three economic agents can be distinguished when analyzing the AV sector from an economic point of view: investors, producers (including distributors and the marketing function) and consumers. Any of these agents can be the target of tax incentives aimed at AV industries. They are the starting point for the discussion of the various tax incentives for films in this chapter. In Sect. 3, tax incentives aimed at producers and distributors will be discussed; in Sect. 4, the focus will be on investors; and in Sect. 5, tax incentives for consumers are discussed. Section 6 focuses on tax incentives for developers of videogames, which have been recently introduced by several countries, and Sect. 7 discusses a special French tax incentive for phonographic recordings and music videos. Copyrights are not addressed in this chapter (see Chap. 10).

---

[6]Appendix II of the ECCC.

[7]Article 5(3) ECCC.

2 Economic Characteristics of the Market for Audiovisual Products

2.1 US Dominance

Debande and Chetrit (2001), pp. 26–27 observe that the rationale for public support for the AV industry is based on the identification of various market failures associated with the functioning of the market, such as information deficiencies, technological bottlenecks and insufficient cultural diversity. As early as the 1920s, the UK and Italy had introduced legislation to protect their national film industries. Vogel (2011), p. 73 observes that, at that time, the USA had begun to dominate the world cinema, using its advantages over its rivals: the largest home market, a well-developed industrial organization and an ideology of optimism and happy endings. These advantages have only become stronger: Vogel (2011), p. 92–94 explains the dominance of the USA in export as being a function of historical happenstance, technological innovation, availability of capital, application of marketing prowess and culture. In his view, the following are essential elements from an economist's standpoint:

1. movies and television programs are non-rivalry (viewing by one consumer does not use up the product or detract other viewers from enjoyment; the same can be said for video games);
2. the USA has a relatively large home market in terms of population and penetration of cinema screens, television sets and other devices, thus providing a relatively greater opportunity for cost amortization in the home market; and, last but not least,
3. the fact that English, the USA's base language, is the second-most used language (after Mandarin Chinese) in the world, the speakers of which live in the wealthiest countries, resulting in a relatively small "cultural discount," defined as the reduction in value of an imported film or program due to cultural differences.

According to Vogel (2011), p. 94 these advantages make it unlikely that the export dominance of the USA in films will be greatly eroded soon, although he expects that, because of new technologies and the production of regional production skills, the US share in television will be gradually reduced.

The European Commission (2013), p. 2 observed that with the public support provided in the EU, the EU cinema produced 1299 feature films in 2012, compared with 817 in the US (2011) and 1255 in India (2011). However, one could question whether more is necessarily better. The European Commission does not give other quantitative or qualitative information on this comparison. The European Commission (2013), p. 7 endorsed global competition with the help of public financial support with locations and facilities elsewhere, such as in Australia, Canada, New Zealand or the United States. According to the Commission, foreign production may have a lasting impact because it makes wide use of local infrastructure and cast. This is primarily an economic argument. It seems that, especially outside the US, public support for the AV industry is a political topic, inspired by both cultural and economic motives.

Often, the AV industries are not bound to a specific location. Debande and Chetrit (2001), p. 23 noted the existence of economics of agglomeration: in this case, a geographical clustering of specialized labor force. However, it might be that clustering will decrease through globalization and technological developments. Furthermore, as Vogel (2011), p. 78 observes, the feature film business has a specific economic structure: large oligopolistic production/distribution/financing organizations regularly interfacing with and being highly dependent on a fragmented assortment of small, specialized service and production firms. The latter opens perspectives for smaller countries. The same applies for new sectors, such as design of video games.

2.2 *Cost Structure*

Debande and Chetrit (2001), pp. 8, 23, 72 mention high fixed[8] and sunk[9] costs and low marginal[10] costs as the economic characteristic of AV products on the production side. This is especially the case for AV products such as films. These require high investments, a large consumer base and a good system for distribution to benefit from economies of scale. Technological developments, for example, distribution of AV products through websites such as YouTube, definitely influence these characteristics. Vogel (2011), p. 47 mentions that the unregulated aspect of the Internet makes it a powerful agent of change that allows alternative forms of service distribution to circumvent traditionally structured segments. However, as long as the initial fixed costs of AV products remain relatively high, it will require efforts, such as marketing campaigns, to attract a large enough consumer base to recover the initial investment. Vogel (2011), p. 50 observes that even with the assistance of marketing and distribution platforms such as YouTube and Facebook, it is still difficult to monetize the accessibility and interest in niche products, the big hits and brands still generate most value and the mediocre content in the middle loses share. He mentions (p. 52) that advertising is important to media industries because the product has unique, time-perishable characteristics. Once the relatively large investment in the project's original development has been assimilated, each additional unit normally entails little extra marginal cost:

> At that point advertising often becomes the primary marketing tool and the dominant component of unit cost.

---

[8]Costs that must be incurred no matter how many units are produced.

[9]Costs that cannot be recovered if the production ceases.

[10]Cost to produce an additional unit.

In Vogel's (2011), p. 99 view, this will not change because of Internet-based technology:

> Marketing costs remain inorderly high as the old and the new compete for the attention of wide-ranging, yet fickle, audiences.

Also, the European Commission (2013), p. 4 appreciated the importance of distribution and promotion of films. It observed that:

> The objective of protecting and promoting Europe's cultural diversity through audiovisual works can only be achieved if these works are seen by audiences. Aid to production alone risks stimulating the supply of audiovisual content without ensuring that the resulting audiovisual work is properly distributed and promoted. It is therefore appropriate that aid may cover all aspects of film creation, from story concept to delivery to the audience.

Debande and Chetrit (2001), pp. 11–12 and Vogel (2011), p. 125 distinguish two basic costs components of a film. First, "above- the-line" costs, which are the costs of creative elements such as cast, directors, writers, producers and literary and music rights. Second, "below- the-line" costs, which comprise all other costs, charges and expenses for production and postproduction, such as crew, transport, locations and props as well as direct costs, including administration, insurances and publicity. They note that the smaller the budget, the higher the percentage of the budget spent on "below-the-line" costs, and vice versa. Debande and Chetrit (2001), p. 13 note that most costs are incurred early in the production cycle. Furthermore, they observe that nearly all revenues generated by a film are received within the first five years of its life cycle, with the majority received within 18 months of the start of distribution cycle.

The European Commission (2013), p. 1 observes that it is difficult for film producers to obtain a sufficient level of upfront commercial backing and that the high risk and perceived lack of profitability of the sector make it dependent on state aid. According to the European Commission, many European films would not be made if financing were left purely to the market, because of a combination of high investments and limited audiences for European AV works.

2.3 *Various Phases in the Realization of a Film*

Debande and Chetrit (2001), pp. 9–11 distinguish the following, interrelated stages of activity in the production and commercialization life cycle of film, broadcasting and multimedia markets.

- Development phase: the producer acquires the rights for an original screenplay, searches for artistic technical and financial partners, estimates the budget and makes a finance plan. The feasibility, commercial potential and cost and likely return on investment of the production are estimated and evaluated, resulting in a go/no-go decision.

- Production phase: three stages can be distinguished (1) pre-production, during which the producer gathers all human resources (production crew, casting), technical resources (shooting schedules, selections of locations) and financial resources (budget); (2) production (shooting of the film); and (3) post-production, covering the editing of the film, composing, recording and adding the soundtrack, special effects and other such tasks;
- Distribution phase: the distribution company promotes and sells the product to exhibitors;
- Exhibition and broadcasting phase: the film or television program is shown and consumed.

In these phases, the three economic agents that can be the target of a tax incentives can be distinguished: investors, producers (including distributors and the marketing function) and consumers. In order to be effective, these tax incentives must take into account the peculiarities of the AV sector that have been discussed in this section.

3 Tax Incentives for Producers and Distributors of Film and Television

Nowadays, many countries provide tax incentives for the production and distribution side of film and television and sometimes even for other AV products, such as videogames and music videos. Many tax incentives can be found in English-speaking countries such as the USA, Canada, Australia and the UK. However, other countries, especially countries in Europe, also provide these types of incentives. EU Member States must take into account the state aid rules that were described in Chap. 5. According to the overview provided by KFTV, only a few Asian countries provide tax incentives for film and television. China announced a reduced tax rate of 15% for film companies based in Shanghai and a tax exemption on income derived from the distribution of Chinese films to rural areas. Thailand is planning to introduce a tax rebate of 15% for every 30 million Thai Baht spent in Thailand in 2017. Direct subsidies in the form of cash rebates, which can be obtained in Singapore, Malaysia and Korea, for example, seem to be more common in Asia. Other countries, such as Japan, India and the Philippines do not provide any of these incentives.

In this section, I will discuss various examples of tax incentives for producers and distributors of films and television programs. Because there are so many incentives, I had to make a choice of focus. I give a very general overview of incentives in Canada and the USA, just to show the amount of incentives available in these countries, and then I go into more detail about Australia's incentives, as Australia is relatively new in the international film business. After that, I focus on incentives in the EU, discussing the details of French and UK incentives since these countries have introduced incentives for various parts of the AV industry and often had to pioneer within the boundaries of the EU state aid rules.

3.1 USA

In total, 39 of the 50 States of the USA and Puerto Rico have tax incentives of one kind or another aimed at the film and television industries, according to NCSL (2014), which gives an overview of all State Film Production Incentives or Programs. Typically, these incentives are in the form of a rebate on wages of residents of the state and other qualifying expenditures (e.g., production costs) in the specific state. The percentages vary: 40% of budget items paid to Puerto Rico entities or residents, 37% on Oklahoma expenditures, 35% for Alabama and Ohio wages, a 58% Alaska transferable tax credit, a 30–35% New York post-production tax credit, with a 30% fully refundable tax credit when filming in the State, a 14% refundable tax credit on Montana crew, and a 10–12% wage reimbursement in Maine. Most States provide rebates between 20 and 30% (in this range: Arkansas, California, Colorado, Florida, Georgia, Illinois, Kentucky, Louisiana, Maryland, Massachusetts, Michigan, Minnesota, Mississippi, New Jersey, New Mexico, North Carolina, Oregon, Pennsylvania, Rhode Island, South Carolina, Tennessee, Texas and Utah). In various states, a minimum expenditure and/or a cap apply. According to NCSL (2014), p. 1, the use of tax incentives and credits for film and television production is a relatively recent phenomenon; the number of states offering such incentives grew from just a handful at the beginning of this century to a majority of states by 2010.

Povich (2015) observes that some states, including Louisiana, which was the first state to adopt such incentives in 1992, are starting to question these incentives. NCSL (2014), p. 1, mentions that eight states have ended or suspended their programs, while other states, such as Hawaii, have increased their incentives or even started a program (Nevada is mentioned in this respect).

Povich (2015) claims that numerous studies show that states never recoup the tax revenue they give away with the credits. For example, Saas (2006) concluded that although film tax credits have succeeded in attracting large increases in film production in some instances, they have also cost sponsoring states a good deal in foregone revenue. His analysis shows that revenue losses are exacerbated by the tendency of these tax credits to subsidize activity not originally targeted and to provide more incentive than needed to induce the desired response. When film tax credits do hit their mark and induce more local film production, the resulting stimulus to overall economic activity appears to be rather modest. According to Povich (2015), studios shop for the best tax deals when choosing locations and frequently pit one state against another. She gives the example of Netflix's "House of Cards," which threatened to pull production out of Maryland in 2014 until the state extended its tax credit program, which gave out $62.5 million in credits between fiscal years 2012 and 2016, mostly to "House of Cards" and HBO's "Veep."

3.2 Canada

PwC (2015a) compiled an overview of all film and video incentives in Canada. At the federal level, the Canadian Film or Video Production Tax Credit provides for a rebate of 25% of qualified labor costs, up to a maximum of 15% of total production costs. Only Canadian-controlled taxable corporations whose primary business is production of Canadian films and/or videos through a permanent establishment in Canada are eligible. Furthermore, a minimum Canadian content is required, and the work must be broadcasted or distributed in Canada within two years of completion. Of the production costs, 75% must be paid to Canadian companies and individuals and 75% of post-production costs must be incurred in Canada. No Canadian content requirements apply for the Canadian Film or Video Production Services Tax Credit. However, this tax incentive is lower, at 16% of qualified Canadian labor (no maximum). Taxable corporations with a permanent establishment in Canada whose primary business is production of, or production services for, films and/or videos in Canada are eligible for this tax incentive. To obtain these incentives, a fee must be paid to the government.

In addition to these federal incentives, the provinces and territories of Alberta, British Columbia, Manitoba, New Brunswick, Newfoundland and Labrador, Northwest Territories, Nova Scotia, Nunavut, Ontario, Quebec, Saskatchewan and Yukon each have at least one tax incentive for film and/or television (PwC 2015a). Only the small province of Prince Edward Island does not have its own tax incentive for film and television. Furthermore, British Colombia, Ontario and Quebec also provide tax credits for digital animation, visual effects and post-production (PwC 2015b).

3.3 Australia

In Australia, a tax incentive called the Australian Screen Production Incentive is the primary mechanism of supporting film and television production (Australian Government 2015). It comprises three mutually exclusive offsets, which are credited against any existing Australian income tax liabilities of the producer.[11] If the offset exceeds the tax liabilities, the Australian Taxation Office refunds the remainder.[12] The incentives apply to Australian resident companies and foreign resident companies operating through an Australian permanent establishment.

According to the explanation regarding Sect. 376-1 ITAA, the offsets are designed to support and develop the Australian screen media industry by providing concessional tax treatment for Australian expenditure. The film must be a feature

[11] Division 376 ITAA.

[12] Section 367-23 ITAA.

film, mini-series of television drama or another eligible project.[13] Examples of projects that are not eligible include commercials, quizzes, training films, news programs and computer games.

The amount of the incentive provided is based on the so-called Qualifying Australian Production Expenditure (QAPE). This is the portion of the company's production expenditure on the film that is incurred for, or is reasonably attributable to, (1) goods and services provided in Australia for the making of the film (e.g. pre-production, production and post-production, but not, in general,[14] for financing, publicity and promotion, or copyright acquisition)[15]; (2) the use of land located in Australia for the making of the film; or (3) the use of goods that are located in Australia at the time they are used in the making of the film.[16]

These offsets are all related to the production and post-production phase.[17]

1. Producer Offset: this is a rebate for making an Australian film. The Producer Offset amounts to 40% of QAPE for feature films and 20% of QAPE for television and eligible projects other than feature films. A total and (in some cases) per-hour QAPE threshold must be met to qualify for the Producer Offset.[18] For example, feature films must meet a total QAPE threshold of AUD500,000.
2. Location Offset: a rebate of 16.5% of QAPE for any (not necessarily Australian) film and television project filmed in Australia with an Australian spend of over AUD 15 million.
3. Post, Digital and Visual Effects (PDV) Offset: a rebate of 30% of QAPE that relates to PDV work in Australia, regardless of where a project is shot.

These offsets are mutually exclusive.[19] It is not possible, for example, to claim both the Producer Offset and the Location Offset. Furthermore, films that benefit from Australia's direct subsidy program for producers of certain low-budget Australian documentaries, the Documentaries Producer Equity Program, are not eligible for the tax incentives. Other direct funding has no bearing on eligibility.

Because Australia is not an EU Member State, the design of the Australian tax incentives is not restricted by EU state aid rules. Australia is therefore not bound by cultural tests in designing its tax incentives and is free to restrict these to expenditures within Australia's territory. Nevertheless, in Australia the tax incentive is not motivated purely by economic policy considerations. An important requirement for the Producer Offset is that the film has Significant Australian Content (SAC) or

[13] Section 367-20(2).

[14] Section 376-135 ITAA.

[15] Section 376-125(1) ITAA and Screen Australia (2015), pp. 9–10.

[16] Section 376-145 and 376.150 ITAA.

[17] Section 376-2 ITAA.

[18] Section 376.65(6) ITAA.

[19] Section 376-2(2) ITAA.

is an official co-production.[20] The SAC test is regarded as a cultural test (Screen Australia, 2015, p. 6) and considers[21] the subject of the film (Australian 'look and feel,' significant creative connection with Australia), where it was made (taking into account all phases in the production cycle), nationalities and places of residence of its makers (producer, writer, director, lead cast, as well as supporting cast, below-the-line crew and other service providers), details of the production expenditure and any matter considered relevant (for example, copyright ownership, creative control, profit participation). According to Screen Australia (2015), p. 6 no single factor is determinative; the SAC test is a holistic test applied on a case-by-case basis. Films that do not meet the SAC test can be eligible for the Location Offset or the PDV Offset. Because these incentives do not include a cultural test, they would probably be regarded as prohibited state aid if an EU Member State were to introduce similar incentives. These incentives in combination with limitations on EU Member States imposed by EU state aid rules therefore, give Australia a competitive advantage over EU Member States.

3.4 European Union

Several EU Member States provide tax incentives for film and television productions. This includes Belgium, Czech Republic, Estonia, France, Hungary, Ireland, Italy, Lithuania, Malta, Spain and the UK. The tax incentives have to meet the requirements set by the European state aid regulations, which were discussed in Chap. 5. This means that these tax incentives cannot be designed as purely industrial incentives but have to include a cultural test. Below, I discuss some examples of EU tax incentives in various states: France, which has a long history of subsidizing films and the AV industry; the UK, which has recently been expanding its range of incentives for the creative industry; and Hungary, which has been very successful in attracting film activities.

3.4.1 France

When discussing tax incentives for the AV industry, France cannot be left out. Bermek (2007), p. 5 observes that

> The French State aid framework for the film and audiovisual industry is among the most comprehensive in Europe. It is also endowed with the highest financial resources in absolute terms. While direct aid distributed by the CNC (National Film Centre) and the French regions remains the most visible component of this scheme, this aid has been

[20] Section 376-65(2)(a)) and 376-70(1) ITAA.

[21] Section 376-70(1) and Screen Australia (2015), pp. 6–7.

increasingly complemented with more indirect financial mechanisms, and notably by tax incentives.

France does not only provide for an incentive for "French" films. It has also introduced a special incentive for foreign films.

French Films

Film and AV production companies subject to French corporation tax can benefit from a refundable tax rebate for production expenses related to the realization of feature films or approved AV works.[22] The tax rebate amounts to 20% of total qualifying costs spent in France. The percentage is increased to 30% if the production budget is less than €4 million. Qualifying costs include wages and compensation for French and EU and EEA authors, actors and crew members, all technical expenditures, transportation costs, and costs for accommodation and catering. The qualifying costs are capped at 80% of the production budget and in case of an international co-production at 80% of the part managed by the French co-producer.

The work must fall in either of the genres fiction, documentary or animation and meet the following requirements:

1. it must be made wholly or mainly in French or in a regional language in use in France;
2. it must be eligible for financial support for film and AV productions;
3. it must be carried out mainly on French territory.
4. It must contribute to the development of French and European film and AV creation as well as to its diversity.

Works that are pornographic, incite violence, are used for advertising purposes, or are quizzes, current affairs or sports programs are not eligible.

Special Incentive for Foreign Films

France competes for foreign productions by the refundable *crédit d'impôt en faveur de la production de films étrangers en France*[23] [Tax Rebate for International Production (TRIP)]. According to Priot et al. (2015), p. 22 TRIP was created because films and TV series situated in France or using French characters were frequently shot outside of France because of "the neighboring fiscal incentives." The main force behind this incentive, therefore, seems to be economic competition, rather than promotion of French culture. The films already promoted France and French culture, but were just not made in France.

[22] Article 220 sexies CGI.

[23] Article 220 quaterdecies CGI.

TRIP reimburses 30% of the eligible costs of foreign movies and TV productions shot in France as well as animation and visual effects projects made partly or completely by a French studio. Eligible costs include wages and compensation for French, EU and EEA authors, actors and crew members; all technical expenditures, transportation costs, location fees, costs for accommodation for cast and crew; and catering expenditures and expenditures relating to a shorter shoot outside France using the same crew and material. These costs are eligible only if paid through a French production services company, defined as companies that manage the physical production in France.

Companies that are liable for corporate income tax in France and that act as production services companies for the sequences filmed or produced in France and enter into a production services agreement with the foreign producer are eligible for TRIP. Even though the TRIP is a non-assignable debt of the French State to the French company, as soon as the provisional qualification letter is received, it is possible to discount the rebate at a bank. According to Priot et al. (2015), p. 29 the French banks that are used to discount tax rebates tend to advance a maximum of 80% of the prospective rebate amount.

The project must be a live action film, animated film of TV movie or series, but may not be pornographic or promote violence. The project must spend at least €1 million on eligible expenditures in France or 50% of the total budget on eligible expenditures in France (for television series, the costs of several episodes may be aggregated to reach either threshold). Documentaries, commercials and corporate films are not eligible. Live-action projects must shoot at least five days in France and obtain at least 18 points on the rating scale of the cultural test, including 7 points in the dramatic content block. Animated projects must score at least 36 points on the rating scale of the cultural test, including 9 points in the dramatic content block (elements related to French culture, heritage or territory). The animation cultural test applies if at least 15% of all shots or on average one and a half shots per minute are digitally processed. The focus is more on using French crew. According to Priot et al. (2015), p. 27,

> As a rule of thumb, a non-European film or series will more easily qualify when allocating VFX shots to a French vendor if at least one fourth of the shots are done in France.

According to Priot et al. (2015), pp. 22, 27, 80–87 TRIP funds were granted to over 81 productions from 18 different countries between 2009 and 2015, including films of Clint Eastwood, Woody Allen, Lasse Hallström, Martin Scorsese and Jackie Chan; the Hollywood movies *Sherlock Holmes: A Game of Shadows*, *Rosemary's Baby*, *Minions* and *The Hunger Games*; the television series *Gossip Girl* (USA) and Merlin (UK); the Chinese blockbusters *Black and White 2* and *Wong Kar-wai's The Grandmaster*; and the Japanese films *Foujita* and *Ouhi no Yakata*. Notwithstanding the limitations of state aid rules, it is clear that EU Member States still try to compete with countries, such as Australia, not bound by such ties.

3.4.2 Hungary

Hungary has been very successful in attracting international film producers since it introduced its tax incentive for film producers in 2003. According to Holdsworth (2014), Hungary's tax incentive is one of the most generous in Europe next to that of the UK. Hungarian production companies registered with the Hungarian Film Office and producing films, both for cinema and television, are eligible for a 25% refundable rebate on their qualifying expenditures in Hungary. Furthermore, 20% of the budget may be spent outside Hungary without suffering a reduction in the amount of the incentive. This increases the rebate even further, as the example in Table 2 shows.

International films can thus make use of tax incentives of several countries, obtaining both a Hungarian and a foreign tax incentive on the maximum of 20% expenses outside of Hungary. For example, Goodfellow (2015) quotes Cristina Giubbetti, sales manager international productions of the Cinecitta studios in Italy as saying

> The great thing about the tax credit is that it is easy to combine with other incentives. Ron Howard's *Inferno*, for example, has combined our incentive with a Hungarian incentive.

Through a co-production system, the money can flow back to the foreign co-producer. Qualifying Hungarian expenses include direct pre- or post-production expenses; wages; above- and below-the-line financing, administration and insurance costs; completion bonds; and accommodation costs, among other items. Indirect costs in excess of 2% of overall spend, distribution costs, royalties exceeding 4% of the Hungarian budget of the film and producers' fees above 4% of the Hungarian budget of the film are excluded.

Total state subsidies may not exceed 50% of the production budget. In case of co-production, this is 50% of Hungarian budget; in case of co-production with participation of another EEA's registered film production company, this is 60%. If another OECD Member State's registered film production company participates in the co-production, this becomes 100%. In the case of low-budget films and films produced in the Hungarian language, it is 100%, as it is in the case of documentaries, animation and experimental films.

Examples of Hollywood movies shot in Hungary are Die Hard 5 (Moscow scenes are shot in Budapest), *Munich* (Budapest doubles as Munich, Paris and

Table 2 Hungarian tax rebate with foreign expenses (based on data from Filming in Hungary)

Total budget	100
Expenses paid to service providers in Hungary	80
Expenses paid to service providers outside Hungary	20
Basis of 25% tax rebate	100
Tax savings	25
% of savings based on Hungarian expenses: 25/80=	31.25%

Rome) and *47 Ronin* (an eighteenth-century Japanese Samurai story). Additionally, international TV series, such as *The Borgias*, were shot in Hungary, which the writer-director-producer Jordan according to Filming in Hungary (2013)

> also didn't find a perfect choice, but here at least the summers are nice and long, and due to the co-production, it was financially reasonable to shoot here.

Italy, which would have been the logical choice, was out of the question for this Canadian–Irish–Hungarian co-production because it had no co-production agreements with these countries and thus no film incentives could be used. Holdsworth (2014) quotes the chief executive of the Hungarian National Film Fund, who said that the tax incentive is also increasingly attracting "top drawer European projects, including a raft of Scandinavian films." Also, many Dutch films that have 100% Dutch themes and a Dutch cast are made in Hungary. Examples are *Het Bombardement* (2012), about the German bombing of the city of Rotterdam; *Kenau* (2014), which is set in the Dutch city of Haarlem during the war for independence from Spain; and *Publieke Werken* (2015), which is set in Amsterdam and the north of the Netherlands at the end of the nineteenth century. Given these examples, one wonders how Hungary meets the cultural criterion required by the European state aid regulations.

Mayaluna films (2015), pp. 6–8 gives an English translation of the cultural criteria films have to meet in Hungary. The films have to pass a cultural test using a point system in which 16 out of 32 points must be obtained. Even though the test is called a "cultural test," it is, in fact, a combination of cultural criteria for which only 8 out of the 32 points can be obtained and of so-called "industrial criteria," for which 24 out of the 32 points can be obtained. Of the 8 points from the cultural criteria, 2 points are sufficient; the remainder may be scored on industrial criteria. Cultural criteria include an event or character which is part of Hungarian or European culture, history, mythology or religion; a setting in Europe; focusing on Hungarian or European traditions or reflecting important European values; or reflecting Hungarian a European culture and identity. The apparently much more important industrial criteria include whether the character of the film creates value as a result of its genre (4 points), whether creators include Hungarian or EEA citizens (with 1 point for every two scores for a maximum of 6 points), release of a final version in an official EEA language (4 points), using a shooting location in Hungary; and pre- or post-production in Hungary (this is listed as making use of Hungary's cultural resources). One gets the strong impression that the Hungarian film incentive is not really a cultural incentive, but is truly an industrial incentive. Holdsworth (2014) quoted the chief executive of the Hungarian National Film Fund:

> "It's great news for the Hungarian economy, the film industry, studios, service companies, crews, hotels and restaurants," she told The Hollywood Reporter. "For every forint (the local currency spent), the government gets 1.34 back in tax take," she added.

Furthermore, one might wonder whether the Hungarian approach fits the EU values with respect to fair competition and social values, especially when one views the first five reasons Mayaluna films (2015), p. 19 gives to film in Hungary:

- 25–30% tax rebate.
- No fringes. All Hungarian film crew are independent contractors and submit invoices for payment of services.
- 12-hour working days.
- Six-day work week, with no overtime penalties.
- Overtime pay for shooting crew only.

3.4.3 UK

Until 2007, the UK did not provide tax incentives for the AV industry. However, since 2007, the UK has been quickly catching up on countries such as France and Hungary. The UK now applies a whole set of tax incentives for various parts of the AV industry. These incentives are part of the Creative Industry Tax Reliefs (CITR). These incentives deserve some attention as an example of a comprehensive package of tax incentives for the AV industry. The UK tax authority even has a Creative Industry Unit that deals with these tax incentives (HMRC 2015). Additionally, the incentives are a good example of how the EU state aid rules, which were discussed in Chap. 5 (and more specifically, Sect. 4 of that chapter), can be incorporated in tax incentives for the AV industry. All tax incentives were approved by the European Commission before they entered into force. Last, but not least, the economic impact of these incentives has been recently analyzed in Barnes (2015). This makes it possible to get an idea of the results of these tax incentives.

The CITR consist of six corporation tax reliefs that provide for an additional deduction or, in case of a loss making company, a payable tax credit for qualifying companies:

1. Film Tax Relief (FTR),[24] which was introduced April 2007;
2. Animation Tax Relief (ATR),[25] introduced April 2013;
3. High-end Television Tax Relief (HTR),[26] introduced April 2013, extended to children's television on 1 April 2015;
4. Video Games Tax Relief (VGTR),[27] introduced April 2014;
5. Theatre Tax Relief (TTR),[28] introduced September 2014; and
6. Orchestra Tax Relief (OTR), introduced April 2016.

[24]Part 15 CTA.

[25]Part 15A CTA.

[26]Part 15A CTA.

[27]Part 15B CTA.

[28]Part 15C CTA.

Originally, only the AV industries were included in the CITR. The two most recent incentives are aimed at theatres and orchestras. These will be discussed in Chap. 11, Sect. 4. The rules and requirements are similar to those of the other four reliefs, which are discussed in this chapter. The payable tax credit included in the CITR for companies in a loss-making situation comes very close to a direct subsidy, the main difference being the source from which it is funded.

The UK applies special corporation tax rules for film production companies[29]; television production companies producing qualifying animation or high-end television programs[30]; and video game development companies.[31] Under these rules, activities in relation to film or television are treated as a separate trade for which special rules apply when calculating profits and losses. These companies can opt out of these rules, but then they are not eligible for CITR. Therefore, these CITR cannot be applied by every kind of company, only by specific companies that are liable to specific corporation tax rules.

In line with the EU state aid rules, all films, television programs, animations and videogames to which the CITR are applied have to pass a so-called "cultural test" or qualify through a UK bilateral co-production treaty or the European Convention on Cinematic Co-production and obtain a certificate from the UK Secretary of State for Culture, Media and Sport that the production is a "British film," "British programme" or "British video game." To pass the cultural test, the production must reach a threshold value of points on aspects such as cultural content (set in the UK/EEA, UK/EEA lead characters, based on UK/EEA subject matter, recorded in English or another UK indigenous language); cultural contribution (the product reflects British creativity, heritage or diversity); use of cultural hubs (at least 50% of production or post production takes place in the UK) and cultural practitioners (leading creative talents are British or EEA residents). For film, a minimum of 8 out of 35 points is required, and for the other sectors, 16 out of 31 points are required (Barnes 2015, p. 14).

Furthermore, the ATR and HTR do not apply to several types of programs, such as promotional programs, news or discussion programs, entertainment, competitions, live performances or training programs.[32] However, children's programs that include an element of competition can qualify if the prize total does not exceed £1000.

The enhanced deduction or payable credit is for all tax reliefs based on the so-called "core expenditure" and "UK expenditure'. In this context, "core expenditure" is defined as expenditure on pre-production, principal photography and

[29]Part 15, Chapter 4 CTA.
[30]Part 15A, Chapter 2 CTA.
[31]Part 15B, Chapter 2 CTA.
[32]Section 1216 AD CTA.

post-production for the FTR, ATR and HTR.[33] For the VGTR, this means expenditure on designing, producing and testing the video game.[34] UK or EEA expenditure means expenditure on goods or services that are used or consumed in the UK or the EEA.[35]

Below, I summarize the most important requirements for each incentive.

Film Tax Relief

The FTR applies if at least 10% of the total production costs relate to activities in the UK[36] and if the film is intended for theatrical release.[37] The cultural test for films is that these have to meet the requirements of the definition of a "British film" as included in Schedule 1 of the Films Act 1985.[38]

The FTR can take the form of a deduction of 100% of the so-called enhanceable expenditure.[39] This is defined as the lesser of UK expenditure or 80% of total core expenditure. For example, if the core expenditure for a film is 4 million, of which 2.5 million is spent in the UK, the enhanceable expenditure is 2.5 million, since the UK expenditure is less than 80% of the total expenditure of 4 million (3.2 million). This film production company can, therefore, deduct 6.5 million (4 million plus 2.5 million) from its taxable income instead of only 4 million. The calculations of the other types of CITR follow the same method.

If a loss is surrendered, the tax credit amounts to 25% of the loss, up to the amount of the enhanceable expenditure.[40] The maximum amount that can be claimed is the lower of the enhanceable expenditure in the accounting period or the amount of loss. This could, for example, be claimed if the core expenditure is 10 million (100% UK expenditure) and the income is 9 million. The loss before FTR application would then be 1 million (9 million − 10 million). The enhanceable expenditure in this example is 80% of 10 million (8 million), since that is less than the UK expenditure of 10 million. The post FTR loss would, therefore, be 9 million (1 million + 8 million). The loss that can be surrendered is 8 million, the enhanceable expenditure, because that amount is less than the post FTR loss of 9 million. The tax credit that the film production company would receive from the UK tax authorities would then be 2 million (25% of 8 million). Because of the tax incentive, the company would not have a financial loss of 1 million; in fact, it even makes a financial profit of 1 million. The film, which would be loss-making without

[33] Section 1184(1) and 1216AG(3) CTA.

[34] Section 1217AD(1) CTA.

[35] Section 1185(1), 1216AH(1) and 1217AE(1) CTA.

[36] Section 1198(1) CTA.

[37] Section 1196 CTA.

[38] Section 1197 CTA.

[39] Section 1200 CTA.

[40] Section 1202 CTA.

the tax incentive and might, therefore, not be produced, is now profit-making because of the tax incentive.

It is important to note that both the deduction and credit are made only in calculating the profit or loss of the separate film trade.[41] It is not possible to mix film losses with other profits.

Animation Tax Relief

The ATR applies if the program is intended for broadcast,[42] at least 51% of the total core expenditure is on animation and at least 10% of the total production costs relate to goods or services used or consumed in the UK.[43] Animations commissioned together are treated as one program for the ATR. The cultural test for this tax incentive is that the program must meet the conditions for being a "British programme."[44] The ATR amounts to 100% of enhanceable expenditure in case of a deduction[45] or 25% of the loss, up to the amount of the enhanceable expenditure, in case of a payable tax credit.[46] The relief is not available in combination with certain R&D-related relief.[47]

High-End Television Tax Relief

HTR applies if the program is intended for broadcast,[48] is made in the EEA, has a slot length longer than 30 min, meets the requirements of a "British programme" and is a drama, comedy or documentary. The average qualifying production costs may not be less than £1 million per hour of production length. As of 1 April 2015, children's programs, defined as programs for which the primary audience is expected to be under the age of 15,[49] can qualify as well. For these programs, the £1 million threshold and 30-minute slot length requirements do not apply. At least 10% of the total production costs must relate to activities in the UK. As is the case for the ATR, for the HTR, programs commissioned together are treated as one program. Also, just as for the ATR, the HTR amounts to 100% of enhanceable

[41]Section 1199(2) CTA.
[42]Section 1216CA CTA.
[43]Section 1216CE(1) CTA.
[44]Section 1216CB CTA.
[45]Section 1216CH CTA.
[46]Section 1216CI CTA.
[47]Section 1216C(4) CTA.
[48]Section 1216CA CTA.
[49]Section 1216AC(2A) CTA.

expenditure in case of a deduction[50] or 25% of the loss, up to the amount of the enhanceable expenditure, in case of a payable tax credit.[51] The relief is not available in combination with certain R&D-related relief.[52]

Results

According to HMRC (2014) the FTR was introduced in January 2007 to promote the sustainable production of British films. It seems that this objective has been met. In 2015, an economic impact report was published, which estimated the economic contribution of the UK FTR, ATR, HTR and VGTR (Barnes 2015). According to this report (pp. 34–36), for each pound of FTR granted across the period 2006/7 to 2013/4 (on average, FTR claims amounted to £164 million per year), £12.49 in additional GVA was created through direct and multiplier effects, resulting in additional tax returns of £3.74 for each pound of relief granted after deducting the estimated level of film production without the FTR. For the HTR, Barnes (2015), pp. 48–50 estimated the additional GVA during the first year of operation as £8.31 (the estimated relief claimed was £79 million), equating to additional tax revenue of £2.48 for each pound of relief granted. For the ATR, Barnes (2015), pp. 68–69 mentions that for each £1 granted in the first year of operation of the tax incentive (the tax relief claimed is estimated at £10.3 million), £1.06 additional GVA was created, resulting in £0.32 additional tax revenues for each pound of relief granted. The UK film industry is still growing, both in terms of contribution to GDP (£1400 million in 2013), employment (39,800 people in 2013, an increase of 22% since 2009) and trade surplus (£916 million in 2012), according to Barnes (2015), p. 4. More than £425 million has been invested in film infrastructure in the UK since 2007 (Barnes 2015, pp. 5, 32). According to Barnes (2015), p. 5 of the £21 million of tourism spending by overseas visitors in 2013, £840 million can be attributed to film-induced tourism. Barnes (2015), p. 5 states:

> The economic contribution generates a strong ROI to the Treasury from a fiscal perspective, before the major cultural benefits are taken into account.

According to HMRC (2014), in the years 2006/7 to 2013/4, 1240 film productions made 2290 claims, for a total of £1320 million. Of these claims, 250 (11%) were made by films with a budget over £20 million, and the total amount of these claims was £890 million. The 89% smaller budget films accounted for the remaining £420 million. Some films funded through the FTR are, according to BBC (2015), *Gravity* (starring Sandra Bullock), the Disney film *Maleficent* (starring Angelina Jolie) and the *Harry Potter* films. Examples of television programs that have benefitted from the HTR are *Game of Thrones*, *Outlander* and *Downton*

---

[50]Section 1216CH CTA.

[51]Section 1216CI CTA.

[52]Section 1216C(4) CTA.

Abbey, reports Kemp (2015). However, programs such as *Da Vinci's Demons*, *Downton Abbey* and *Game of Thrones* were already made in the UK before the HTR was introduced (Barnes 2015, p. 7). Furthermore, Barnes (2015), p. 43 has observed that 57% of high-end television production expenditures were made from outside the UK, implying that the distribution rights for these programs will typically held by non-UK companies.

These figures all look very attractive. However, it is not clear whether these investments would not have been made at all or would have been made in another country without the incentive, maybe at less cost. The European Commission (2013), p. 3 observed that competition occurs between EU Member States to attract investments from large-scale film production companies of non-member countries. Kemp (2015) observes that one of the aims of the HTR was to prevent big-budget television productions from being induced to go outside the UK, since in the recent past several UK television series were being produced in continental Europe instead of in the UK. Countries, therefore, use tax incentives to compete with each other. This might, in some cases, result in a "beggar thy neighbor" effect: the increase of the film industry in one country might lead to worse effects in other countries and to inefficiencies, leaving all countries worse off in the end. Furthermore, it is not a given that these incentives, which seem to work well in the UK, would also work in non-English speaking countries, as the UK has the same language benefit that the USA does. Merely copying the UK film incentives to, for example, Japan, would probably not duplicate the economic effects experienced in the UK. Furthermore, the tax incentives may have an upward effect on prices for film production in the UK. The European Commission (2013), p. 6 observed that the costs of film production seem to be higher in countries that apply film incentives with territorial conditions, and that such conditions may make them less efficient.

4 Tax Incentives for Investors in Film and Television

4.1 Risky Investments

Usually, high uncertainty is attached to investments in the AV sector. Vogel (2011), p. 71 observes:

> Ego gratification rather than money may often be the only return on an investment in film.

Debande and Chetrit (2001), pp. 8, 72 note that each individual AV work is a unique product characterized by important demand and cost uncertainty. Debande and Chetrit (2001), pp. 8, 72 and Vogel (2011), p. 71 illustrate this with an industry rule of thumb: from a portfolio of ten major theatrical films produced, six or seven will be unprofitable, two to three will break-even and one will perform very well. This uncertainty makes it difficult to attract commercial funding for films. This is a problem as, in the word of Vogel (2011), p. 84:

> The crucial initial element is capital.

4.2 Sources for Funding

Debande and Chetrit (2001), p. 74 and Vogel (2011), p. 116 distinguish three sources for funding of films (and this would also apply to other parts of the AV industry also):

1. Industry sources, including studio development and in-house production financing by independent distributors and end-users such as television networks;
2. Lenders, including banks, insurance companies and distributors;
3. Investors, including public and private funding pools.

Vogel (2011), p. 71 mentions that the success ratio for studios/distributors is considerably better than that for individual participants. He observes (p. 117) that common stock-based offerings are not a successful method to raise funds, because the return is highly uncertain and the underlying assets have little or no worth. Vogel (2011), p. 121 observes that established studios will typically be able to raise capital through debt or equity financings, but that it is much more difficult for an independent producer to get a production loan since the producer will have little to no collateral backing. According to Debande and Chetrit (2001), p. 8 the lending capacity of the AV market is relatively limited in Europe, and only a few banks are active on the market due to its specialized nature and to deterrence from past mistakes. These characteristics have induced governments to broaden the investment base and reduce risks for private investors, by direct subsidies (usually from a cultural policy point of view), guarantees or tax incentives.

4.3 Incentives for Private Investors: France

Most countries seem to focus AV industry tax incentives on companies. However, France still provides, until at earliest 31 December 2017, an incentive for private individuals (and companies) who invest in films through so-called Sociétés pour le Financement du Cinéma et de l'Audiovisuel (SOFICAs) [English: companies for the financing of films and AV works].[53] These investors are granted a tax reduction of 30% on their investment, capped at the lower of 25% of the total net income and €18,000. If the SOFICA uses at least 10% of its capital to acquire shares of production companies, the tax reduction is increased to 36%. A person may not hold more than 25% of a SOFICA.[54]

SOFICAs are public limited companies subject to corporation tax. A SOFICA's exclusive activity must be the funding of cinematographic productions and AV

[53]Article 199 unvicies CGI.

[54]Article 238 bis HH CGI.

works meeting the requirements for French qualified films.[55] Qualifying films must be in the French language, must have the nationality of an EU Member State and must have been accredited by the Director General of the CNC (the French National Centre for Cinema). However, SOFICAs may invest 20% of their annual funding into co-productions filmed in a language of an EU Member State where the majority co-producer is established.[56] In order to qualify, a film first has to obtain a minimum of 14 out of 18 points (television: 13 out of 18; documentary: 9 out of 14; animation: 14 out of 21) on a European scale. Points are obtained by authors (including composers), actors and crew having French nationality or coming from an EU Member State or from a country with which France has a co-production treaty (if created within the framework of such treaty). Points depend on importance: for example, for a director of a film 3 points can be awarded, for a composer, only 1 can. If the European scale is met, at least 25 out of 100 points of a French scale must be obtained as a minimum of French or EU elements, and persons in the artistic and technical aspects of a film are required. In order to accumulate points, lead and supporting actors as well as crew members must be of French nationality, come from an EU State or come from a European Council signatory state. Another requirement for qualification is that the movie must be produced or co-produced by a French movie company incorporated in France and not owned or controlled by non-European stockholders. Priot et al. (2015), p. 21 note that "qualifying French film" is not a very strict concept:

> What you may not know is that every year, one-third of all French-qualified movies (around 250 per year) are actually foreign-initiated projects co-produced by French companies. And obviously, many of these international ventures are not shot in French.

According to Priot et al. (2015), p. 44, SOFICAs mostly provide gap funding, providing producers with the last and most expensive money. Sometimes there is a guarantor who will repay the investors if needed. Each SOFICA can invest 20% of its money in foreign-language (i.e., non-French) qualified co-productions as long as the film's language matches the language of the foreign co-producer's country. According to Priot et al. (2015), p. 44, SOFICAs invested €33.99 million in 103 movies in 2014. Fourteen of these were majority foreign co-productions, mostly from British or Belgian producers.

4.4 *LP Incentives for Individuals: USA, Germany and the Netherlands*

Tax incentives used to attract private funding for films are not always deliberately aimed at supporting films. In fact, in the USA, Germany and the Netherlands, for

---

[55]Article 238 bis HE CGI.

[56]Article 238 bis HF.

example, the regular tax legislation on limited partnerships was used to mitigate the risks of private investors. These structures used the special legal and tax characteristics that LPs had in those jurisdictions.

From a legal point of view, a limited partner in an LP can, in general, not be held liable for more than the capital invested by that partner. This reduces the legal risk of a private investor in a film LP. However, from a tax point of view, LPs are usually regarded to be transparent. This enabled investors in a film LP to make use of special investment tax credits and to use the share in the LP losses (which share could, from a tax perspective, be much higher than actual losses) to reduce other income, such as wages, which are taxed the most heavily. This type of scheme was used in the USA before 1976. Between 1976 and 1986, the tax law changed. After the change, only the amount legally at risk could be written off, and the use of investment tax credits was limited. Eventually, these rules were repealed completely in the Tax Reform Act 1986, and passive losses became deductible against passive income only. Vogel (2011), p. 119 notes that since 1986 fewer and differently structured movie partnerships have been offered to the public.

However, the US concept of using an LP to fund a film crossed the ocean. In Germany, film investment funds (*Medienfonds*) made use of the German LP form (GmbH & Co. KG) and the German rule that intangibles, such as films, must be directly fully depreciated since these may not be included as an asset on the balance sheet.[57] Private investors could immediately deduct the loss from their other taxable income, such as business income or wages. Given the German tax rates, this meant that the tax office returned up to 50% of the investment. Kurp (2004) observes that in the years 1997–2003 German investors invested over €10 billion in 120 film investment funds. Of this amount, at least 70% went abroad, mostly to the USA. Examples of films that were funded with German tax money are the *Lord of the Rings*, *Chicago*, *Terminator* and *Mission: Impossible*. Because this was costing the German government too much money, the tax law was changed in 2005, with the effect that investment losses on so-called tax deferral programs (*Steuerstundungsmodells*) were no longer deductible from other income.[58] Germany still funds foreign films, but is now using direct subsidies.

4.4.1 The Netherlands

In 1995, the big surprise at the Dutch film festival was *Zusje* [Little Sister]. The first film of the young (31 years old) director Robert Jan Westdijk with an even younger (29 years old) lead actress, Kim van Kooten,[59] who made her first appearance on the screen, won the most important Dutch film prize, the Golden Calf. Many things

---

[57] §5(2) EStG.

[58] §15b EStG.

[59] Now a famous actress, author and screenwriter in the Netherlands but at that time known only as the daughter of a famous Dutch author/comedian.

about this film were creative and novel, including the way the film was financed: without government grants (which is rare for independent Dutch films) and with sponsoring and the use of the Dutch equivalent of the US LP: a *commanditaire vennootschap* (hereinafter referred to as an LP). Westdijk was the general partner and 39 private individuals were limited partners of *Grote Broer Filmwerken* [Big Brother Filmworks] LP (Mooij 1996; Doppert 1997). Crew and actors worked for no or low pay: 50% of the profits went to the investors and 50% to the crew and actors (Doppert 1997).

According to Doppert (1997), Westdijk was inspired by the book *Spike Lee's Gotta Have It: Inside Guerrilla Filmmaking*. Spike Lee (then 29) shot his first feature-length, independent film *She's Gotta Have It* (a hit in 1986), in 1985, making use of an LP and tax credits. In the Netherlands, just as in the USA, a limited partner of an LP can lose only the invested amount, and the LP is tax transparent. Furthermore, until 2001, limited partners in an LP with an enterprise were regarded as entrepreneurs in the Netherlands and could deduct LP losses from taxable income coming from other sources and make use of various tax incentives for entrepreneurs. At that time, the top marginal tax rate in the Netherlands was 60%, a rate which was reached at a relatively low level of income of approximately 90,000 guilders (about €40,000).

It seems that this novel way of film financing inspired the Dutch government to introduce special tax incentives for private investment in films in 1998. As of 1998, a limited partner in a film LP could not only make use of general tax incentives for entrepreneurs, but could also apply a depreciation at will and deduct the costs of film investment in the year of investment. This tax incentive was part of a package to support the Dutch film industry and was intended to be in place for five years. The idea was that after five years the additional support would not be necessary anymore and the Netherlands would have a healthy film industry. The incentivized film LP became a big hit as an investment product, and many additional funds became available for films. However, there was criticism as well: of the 40 films produced with funding from film LPs in 1999 and 2000, only 27 had a Dutch signature (Crum and Wils 2001). For example, 80% of the budget of the first film financed under the new tax rules, *Little Vampire*, seemed to have been spent in Germany and the film *Enigma*, which was produced by Mick Jagger, was for the greater part shot in England and had an English cast (Blokker 2000). The Dutch tax payers started to wonder why they had to finance these international films, which did not really seem to benefit the Dutch film sector. Of the 540 million guilders (about €250 million) spent by film LPs in 1999 and 2000, only 200 million guilders (about €90 million) were spent in the Netherlands.

In 2001, the Dutch Income Tax Act was reformed. Limited partners in an LP no longer had access to all tax credits for entrepreneurs. However, new tax incentives for private investors in films through an LP were introduced. In order to qualify for these tax incentives, at least half of the film budget had to be spent in the Netherlands. In 2002, the European Commission approved these tax incentives under the cultural exception for state aid (see Sect. 3.3.3 of Chap. 5). These new incentives, were, however, not as successful as the old ones. This was due to uncertainty regarding the new tax incentives and some scandals and a bankruptcy of the film LP *Soldaat van Oranje*, which got a lot of publicity. Furthermore, evaluations of the effectiveness of the incentives were not very positive (Drenth et al. 2003). In 2004, the Dutch Ministry of Finance concluded that a temporary measure could not ensure a healthy Dutch film industry. It was concluded that the Dutch home market was too small to generate a positive return, even in case of a blockbuster, for which reason tax incentives would have to give investors a return. As of 2006, the tax incentives were extended: investors in film LPs were given increased tax credits and could deduct 130% of their investment from their taxable income. An investor in the highest marginal tax bracket (at that time 52%, paid on an income of over €52,228) would, therefore, have a guaranteed return of 52% of 130% (i.e., 67.6%). The return of the investor did not depend on the success of the film. This was especially the case for failures. Table 3 illustrates this.

Table 3 Expected and realized returns of the film LPs in which the broker WVGH was involved (Hemels 2010, p. 138)

	Year	*Film*	No. of viewers	Expected minimum return (IRR) (%)	Realised (IRR) (%)	Capital for which WVGH intermediated
1	2000	*Magonia*	16,000	6.1	6.1	828,149
2	2000	*Zus & Zo*	41,868	8.5	8.5	2,096,465
3	2000	*Minoes*	837,372	13.4	25	1,134,450
4	2001	*Soldaat van Oranje*	0	4.1	−9	3,970,576
5	2001	*Pietje Bell 1*	820,760	4.5	2	1,730,037
6	2001	*De oesters van Nam Kee*	143,624	6	6	887,367
7	2001	*Ja zuster nee zuster*	460,544	3.8	3.1	2,032,935
8	2002	*Volle maan*	454,672	3.7	14	1,781,598
9	2002	*Phileine zegt sorry*	296,766	5.5	5.5	3,110,000
10	2003	*Kees de jongen*	60,637	5	5	445,000
11	2003	*Amazones*	26,563	6.2	6.2	1,040,000
12	2003	*Erik of het klein insectenboek*	112,369	6.2	6.2	1,410,000
13	2004	*Leef*	100,000	5.7	5.7	400,000
14	2004	*Johan*	31,000	6	6	2,285,000
15	2005	*Herman Brood*	27,000	8.6	8.2	1,655,500
16	2006	*Alles is liefde*	1,133,605	8.2	25.1	2,535,000

The Dutch experience seems to endorse the warning of Vogel (2011), p. 84:

> The number of projects will always expand to fully absorb the capital available, regardless of quality, and without regard to the quantity of other films scheduled for completion and release at around the same time.

As of 1 July 2007, the tax incentives for investors in film LPs were abolished and replaced by a direct subsidy for filmmakers. This was deemed to be more effective and efficient: according to the Ministry of Finance, the costs for implementing and maintaining a film LP were over 10% and the administrative burden and costs associated with that burden were high for the government also (Drenth et al. 2003). Drenth et al. (2003), p. 47 estimated that the film LP tax incentives had cost the Dutch government €170 million in foregone taxes in the years 1999–2003.

Since the tax incentives have been abolished, there have been offers to private investors to invest in a film, but because the tax schemes used for these investments are rather complicated and risky, this is no longer an easy way to fund a film in the Netherlands. At the moment, the Netherlands does not provide specific tax incentives for the film sector.

4.5 *Incentives for Corporate Investors*

Several countries try to increase private investments in films by offering tax incentives aimed at corporate tax payers. Because corporate tax rates are usually lower than personal income tax rates, such incentives are usually less expensive for governments.

An example of a country with such an incentive is Spain. Financial co-producers participating in a Spanish film production are entitled to a deduction of 5% of the investment, up to a limit of 5% of the income from the investment in the same period.[60] In order to qualify for the incentive, the entity must participate in the film production solely through the provision of financial resources. It has to be a serious investment, amounting to least 10% but no more than 25% of the total cost of the production in exchange for a share in the revenue derived from the exploitation of the film. The co-production contract must be filed with the Ministry of Education, Culture and Sport. The deduction may be taken into account only after the film has been completed.

This incentive is much more restrictive and is aimed at a much smaller group of investors than the LP tax incentives discussed in the previous section.

[60] Art. 38 LIS.

5 Tax Incentives for Consumers of AV Products

A price reduction of products from the AV industry is an easy way to provide an incentive to consumers to buy these products. Several Indian states apply a reduced entertainment tax on films either produced in their state or considered as having the nationality of their state. For example: in Andhra Pradesh, the rate is reduced from 21 to 8% for low-budget films and to 16% for big-budget films produced in the state; in Maharashtra Marathi, films are exempt from the 45% tax; Tamil Nadu exempts Tamil films from the 15% tax; and West Bengal applies an entertainment tax rate of 10% instead of 30% on Bengali and Nepali films (Film Federation of India).

EU Member States are allowed to apply a reduced VAT rate to admission to cinemas and reception of radio and television broadcasting services.[61] Not all Member States have exercised this possibility, but the European Commission (2015b), p. 4 shows that, for example, in Italy, the Netherlands, Croatia, Luxembourg, Malta, Finland, Sweden and Finland admission to a cinema is taxed at a reduced rate. In several countries, such as the Czech Republic, Greece, Croatia, Hungary, Slovakia and Slovenia, public radio and TV broadcasting are exempt (European Commission 2015b, p. 5, 7). France and Austria apply a reduced rate for pay television and cable television (European Commission 2015b, p. 5). However, hi-fi video, compact discs (European Commission 2015b, p. 15) and videogames are taxed at the regular rate in the EU.

In order for a tax incentive that reduces the consumer price to be efficient and effective, the product has to be price elastic. If the product is price inelastic, then the reduction in price because of a tax incentive, will not substantially increase the demand. In fact, a government is, in such cases, incentivizing consumers who would have bought the product anyway. Vogel (2011), p. 83 observes that ticket sales for new film releases are relatively insensitive to box-office prices per se: the demand for major-event movies, backed by strong word-of-mouth advertising and viewing is essentially price-inelastic. However, he suggests that sales may be more responsive to the total cost of going to the movie, which can include fees for complementary goods and services, such as babysitters, restaurant meals and parking. In that case, the price reduction of the cinema ticket because of a tax incentive would not have an effect on the demand since the price of the complementary goods would remain the same. Furthermore, he notes that for some groups, such as housewives and retired or unemployed people, lower prices can stimulate admissions at off-peak times and to somewhat older features. A reduced VAT rate for all consumers of all cinema tickets would then lead to overstimulation: a discount card financed by a direct subsidy for these specific groups and times would be much more effective.

---

[61]Art. 98 VAT Directive and Annex III, Sects. 7 and 8 of the VAT Directive.

6 Tax Incentives for Video Games

Film and TV are not the only AV sectors supported by tax incentives. Another important sector of the creative industry that is gaining attention in tax legislation is production of video games. This is a relatively new sector and provides interesting jobs for a highly skilled labor force.

In Europe, it has not been obvious that video games can be supported without infringing state aid rules. The 2014 EU General Block Exemption Regulation[62] does not include video games in the section on aid for culture and heritage conservation since these were deemed to be commercial in preamble 72 of the Regulation. However, France and the UK have implemented tax incentives for this sector of the creative industry. These incentives have been approved by the European Commission. It seems that competition with non-EU Member States was an important factor in this approval.

In the decision regarding the French incentive, the European Commission noted that UNESCO recognizes the video game industry as a cultural industry and the role it plays in the field of cultural diversity.[63] Furthermore, the Commission took notice of the argument of France and several third parties, that video games can act as a vehicle for images, values and themes that reflect the cultural environment in which they are created and may act on the ways of thinking and the cultural references of users, especially among young people. The Commission concluded that certain video games can have a cultural dimension and thus may constitute cultural products.[64]

From the European Commission decision on the UK incentive, it becomes clear that, at first, the Commission doubted that aid to games would be necessary, because they constitute a fast-growing market.[65] Furthermore, the Commission was concerned that the incentive could fuel a subsidy race within the EU and doubted that the potential distortions of competition would be balanced by any positive effects.[66] However, France and game developers from the UK, France, Germany and Finland have commented that they did not see a danger of a subsidy race among Member States and third parties, pointing out that the market was dominated by North America and Asia and that there was a staff drain to Canada, which does subsidize games.[67] According to the UK Independent Game Developers Association, between 2008 and 2010, Canada's employment in the sector grew by

[62]Commission Regulation (EU) No 651/2014 of 17 June 2014 declaring certain categories of aid compatible with the internal market in application of Articles 107 and 108 of the Treaty, OJ 26 June 2014, L 187/1. I refer to Chap. 5, Sects. 4.1 and 4.2 for a discussion of this Regulation.

[63]Commission Decision of 11.12.2007 C(2007) 6070 final, para. 63.

[64]Commission Decision of 11.12.2007 C(2007) 6070 final, para. 64.

[65]Commission Decision of 27.03.2014, C(2014) 1786 final, para. 11.

[66]Commission Decision of 27.03.2014, C(2014) 1786 final, para. 13.

[67]Commission Decision of 27.03.2014, C(2014) 1786 final, paras. 14, 15.

33%, during which time it declined in the UK by 9%.[68] According to the UK, the aid was mainly an answer to tax relief offered by Canada, the USA, and South Korea.[69] After some amendments in line with the French tax incentive for video games, the European Commission gave its approval. It held that a subsidy race among Member States would be rather unlikely since the competition comes mainly from North America and East Asia.[70] Below, by way of example, I will discuss Canadian, French and UK incentives. All incentives are aimed at reducing costs at the production side.

6.1 Canada

Sinclair (2013) and PwC (2015b) listed seven Canadian provinces that provided for a tax incentive for videogames. These are listed in Table 4.

All programs give an incentive for labor costs, making it attractive to conduct these labor intensive activities in one of these Canadian provinces. This was one of the reasons that the UK wanted to introduce a tax incentive as well.

The Ontario Interactive Digital Media Tax Credit (OIDMTC)[71] is the most generous. It was introduced in 1998 with broad eligibility criteria to support the growth of Ontario's emerging digital media industry and the creation of highly skilled jobs (Ontario Ministry of Finance 2015, p. 1). The Ontario Ministry of Finance (2015), p. 1 estimates that the OIDMTC has grown by over 40% annually between 2003/4 and 2014/15. Now that interactive digital media products have become mainstream, the tax credit is limited to target innovative products. The OIDMTC is available only for products with a primary purpose to entertain the user or to educate users under the age of 12. This refundable tax credit provides, amongst other things, a 40% tax credit on eligible Ontario labor expenditures and eligible marketing and distribution expenses incurred by qualifying Canadian corporations that develop and market their own products at a permanent establishment in Ontario. Eligible products include eligible digital games developed by a qualifying digital game corporation, and eligible digital games developed by a specialized digital game corporation.

More generally, it can be concluded that Ontario provides many tax incentives for the AV industry in its Taxation Act, 2007, as this excerpt from the contents of the act shows:

Section 90. Ontario computer animation and special effects tax credit
Section 91. Ontario film and television tax credit
Section 92. Ontario production services tax credit

[68]Commission Decision of 27.03.2014, C(2014) 1786 final, para. 16.

[69]Commission Decision of 27.03.2014, C(2014) 1786 final, para. 32.

[70]Commission Decision of 27.03.2014, C(2014) 1786 final, para. 52.

[71]Section 93 Taxation Act, 2007.

Table 4 Canadian provinces that provide for a tax incentive for video games (Sinclair 2013; PwC 2015b)

Province	Program	Incentive	Notes
British Columbia	BC Interactive Digital Media Tax Credit	17.5% of qualified British Columbia labor	Minimum cost restrictions apply
Manitoba	Manitoba Interactive Digital Media Tax Credit	40% of eligible labor	Max credit of CAD 500,000 per project
Newfoundland and Labrador	N and L Interactive Digital Media Tax Credit	40% of Newfoundland and Labrador eligible labor	Max rebate of CAD 15,000 per employee and CAD 500,000 per year
Nova Scotia	Nova Scotia Computer-assisted Labour Incentives	Lesser of 50% of NS eligible labor or 25% of total NS expenditures (bonuses for development outside Halifax)	Also credit on marketing and distribution expenditure to a maximum of CAD 100,000 per product.
Ontario	Ontario Interactive Digital Media Tax Credit	40% of eligible labor and eligible, marketing/distribution costs	Max marketing/distribution credit of CAD 100,000 per project
Prince Edward Island	PEI Innovation and Development Labor Rebate	25% of eligible PEI labor	For corporations that carry on a business within a strategic economic sector and undertake to develop new or innovative products (e.g., information and communication technologies)
Quebec	Quebec Production of Multimedia Titles Tax Credit	Up to 37.5% of eligible labor (including 7.5% premium for French-language versions)	Credits can be used for individual titles or overall activity

Section 93. Ontario interactive digital media tax credit
Section 93.1 Qualifying digital game corporation's tax credit
Section 93.2 Specialized digital game corporation's credit
Section 94. Ontario sound recording tax credit

6.2 France

France was the first EU Member State to introduce a tax incentive for video games,[72] which received approval of the European Commission on 11 December 2007.[73] The current incentive received approval from the European Commission in 2012.[74] Video game development companies (*entreprises de création de jeux video*) can benefit from a tax credit for expenses they incur during the creation of approved video games. The tax credit equals 20% of the qualifying expenses relating to activities carried out in France or another EU or EEA Member State. Qualifying expenses include staff costs, depreciation costs for fixed assets (not buildings) assigned directly to the creation of a video game and other operating expenditures. The annual tax credit is capped at €3 million per company.

The video game must meet the following requirements to be eligible for the tax credit:[75]

1. the development costs must be at least €100,000;
2. it must be designed to be marketed to the public;
3. it must be made mainly with authors and creative collaborators who are either French nationals or nationals of another EU or EEA Member State;
4. it must contribute to the development of French and European creation of video games and to its diversity, in particular as distinguished by the quality, originality and innovativeness of the concept and the level of artistic expenditure.

Similar to the French film incentives (see Sect. 3.4.1), requirements 3 and 4 are established by a point system.

6.3 UK

The UK Video Games Tax Relief (VGTR)was introduced in April 2014. On 27 March 2014, the European Commission decided that the incentive is compatible with the internal market on the basis of article 107(3)(d) TFEU, aid to promote culture and heritage conservation.[76]

In order to qualify for VGTR, the video game must be intended for supply, and at least 25% of the core expenditure must be incurred for goods or services that are provided from within the EEA.[77] Where the other CITR impose requirements for expenditures in the UK only, EU rules, which are stricter for video games than for

---

[72] Crédit d'impôt en faveur de la création de jeux vidéo, article 220 terdecies CGI.

[73] Commission Decision of 11.12.2007 C(2007) 6070 final.

[74] Commission Decision of 25.04.2012, C(2012) 2558 final.

[75] Article 220(III) terdecies CGI.

[76] Commission Decision of 27.03.2014, C(2014) 1786 final.

[77] Section 1217CE CTA.

film and television, made it necessary to expand the spending requirement of the VGTR to the EEA. The video game must be certified as a British video game.[78] Anything that is produced for advertising or promotional purposes or for gambling is not regarded a video game for the VGTR.[79]

The VGTR is modeled on the FTR (see Section "Film Tax Relief"). A company that qualifies for VGTR is entitled to an additional deduction of 100% of the EEA core expenditure, up to a maximum of 80% of the total core expenditure.[80] If the additional deduction results in a loss, the losses may be surrendered for a payable tax credit of 25% of the losses, up to the amount of the expenditure on goods and services provided from within the EEA.[81]

In order to comply with state aid rules, SMEs that have claimed R&D Relief on a project, cannot claim VGTR on the same project.

7 France: Phonographic Works

Since 2006, France has provided a tax incentive for production expenses related to phonographic works (*crédit d'impôt pour dépenses de production d'oeuvres phonographiques*).[82] This tax incentive has been changed several times, probably because of state aid considerations. The tax incentive was authorized by the European Commission on the basis of Article 107, para. 3 of the TFEU, promotion of culture. The European Commission has given its approval to the current tax incentive until 31 December 2018.[83] The European Commission confirmed that the current tax incentive falls under Article 53 of the General Block Exemption Regulation,[84] which was discussed in Chap. 5.

Phonographic production enterprises subject to corporate income tax are eligible for a tax rebate for expenditures on production, development and digitization of phonographic or videographic music registrations if the registration meets the following requirements:

1. it is made by companies established in France or an EU or EEA Member State that perform services related to the realization of phonographic registrations, music videos and post production;

[78] Section 1217CB CTA.

[79] Section 1217AA(2) CTA.

[80] Section 1217CG CTA.

[81] Section 1217CI CTA.

[82] Article 220 octies CGI.

[83] Decret no. 2015-704 du 19 Juin 2015, NOR MCCE1506434D.

[84] Commission Regulation (EU) No 651/2014 of 17 June 2014 declaring certain categories of aid compatible with the internal market in application of Articles 107 and 108 of the Treaty, OJ 26 June 2014, L 187/1.

2. it is of new artists, groups or composers who have not sold more than 100,000 albums of the two albums before this registration and who are at least half French-speaking or use a regional language of France.

Furthermore, approval of the French Minister of Culture is necessary. The tax incentive entails an additional deduction of 15% of the total qualifying expenses for the operations in France or an EU or EEA Member State. For micro, small and medium enterprises,[85] the deduction increases to 30%. Qualifying expenses include remuneration of performers, the producer, engineers and technicians; expenses related to the use of recording studios and rental and transportation of equipment and instruments; post-production expenses (editing, mixing, encoding, mastering and visual creation costs); expenses related to the cost of digitizing and encoding of production; and expenses related to the promotion of the artist (concerts, TV programs, website). Remunerations are capped at €50,000 per year and the qualified expenditure to which the tax incentive applies is limited to €350,000 per phonographic recording or music video and to €2.3 million per company per year. Furthermore, public subsidies must be deducted from the qualifying expenses. The tax offset may not exceed €1.1 million per year per company.

8 Conclusion

Competition between countries for the favor of the AV industry is fierce. All instruments are used, including tax incentives. As the competition intensifies, countries seem to increase their incentives as well. For example, in 2016, France increased its TRIP from 20 to 30% of eligible costs and its maximum from €20 million to €30 million, and the UK has been expanding its CITR. One wonders whether this competition is not leading to a race to the bottom, increased prices and an incentive for inefficiencies. In this respect, the AV industry is beginning to resemble the agricultural industry, which is also surviving only due to state support in certain parts of the world. The European Commission had no fear of a within-EU subsidy race for video games tax incentives because, currently, only France and the UK provide these in the EU. However, even in such sectors a subsidy race might start if more European countries start introducing incentives, as happened with film incentives.

The cultural component of these incentives seems to become thinner at the same time. The Hungarian incentive is a clear example of an incentive in which the cultural component seems negligible, but the UK incentives, too, seem to be more industry incentives than cultural incentives.

---

[85]As defined in article 2 of Annex II to Commission Regulation (EC) No 800/2008 of 6 August 2008 (General block exemption Regulation): enterprises that employ fewer than 250 persons and have an annual turnover not exceeding €50 million, and/or an annual balance sheet total not exceeding €43 million.

It seems that countries without a big home market (which China, India and the USA have) can no longer support a film industry without offering tax incentives. This can come at great cost, as the Dutch example showed. How much money does a country want to spend on this specific industry? How much money are the other tax payers prepared to spend on creating jobs in the AV industry? Is it worthwhile to engage in this fierce competition? One might even question whether these incentives are not interfering with creative freedom: what if a writer has set his story in Japan, but the producer prefers to transfer it to France because of the tax incentives in that country? What does this do to a story? Was the James Bond film *Spectre* partly situated in Italy because of Italy's tax incentive? According to Bardwell (2015), the president of MGM's motion picture group asked the creative team of this film to consider moving some scenes to London to make better use of the UK FTR. Sony even made changes in the script of *Spectre*, portraying Mexico in a more positive way, not making the villain Mexican and adding a Mexican actress as a "Bond girl" in order to obtain incentives worth USD 20 million from Mexico. CBS News (2015) quotes *Hollywood Reporter* executive editor Matt Belloni as saying:

> Movie studios make concessions to different countries and even different states in order to get tax incentives all the time. What is interesting here are the creative demands that the country was supposedly making on the studio and their willingness to play ball there.

It is questionable whether these tax incentives can attract sustainable activities to a country or whether the tax incentives merely result in a sector that is constantly on the move to countries with even better tax incentives, leaving behind yesterday's favorites. Some countries, such as the Netherlands and Luxembourg and states within federal-system countries, such as the USA, have already concluded that this is not the case and have withdrawn their costly tax incentive programs. In some cases, these have been replaced by a direct subsidy program.

References

Australian Government, Department of Communications and the Arts (2015) Australian screen production incentive. http://arts.gov.au/film-tv/australian-screen-production-incentive. Accessed 28 Dec 2015

Bardwell B (2015) From Mexico with love: how Sony got millions in incentives to rewrite 007 Film. http://www.taxanalysts.com/www/features.nsf/Features/D0DB13181492C8E285257DFD0048BA22?OpenDocument. Accessed 30 Dec 2015

Barnes A (2015) Economic contribution of the UK's Film, High-End TV, Video game, and Animation programming sectors. Report presented to the BFI, Pinewood Shepperton plc, Ukie, the British Film Commission and Pact. Olsberg.Spi and Nordicity, London. http://www.bfi.org.uk/sites/bfi.org.uk/files/downloads/economic-contribution-of-the-uks-film-high-end-tv-video-game-and-animation-programming-sectors-report-2015-02-23.pdf. Accessed 8 Dec 2015

BBC (2015) British film industry tax breaks approved by EU. http://www.bbc.com/news/entertainment-arts-34013145. Accessed 8 Dec 2015

Bermek H (2007) Tax incentives for films and audiovisual works in france. European Audiovisual Observatory. http://www.obs.coe.int/documents/205595/2408826/HBermek_Tax_incentives_films_france_en.pdf Accessed 28 Dec 2015

Blokker B (2000) Beleggen in Nederlandse speelfilms. Durfkapitaal zonder risico. NRC 29 September 2000. http://retro.nrc.nl/W2/Nieuws/2000/09/29/Vp/cs.html. Accessed 4 Dec 2015

CBS News (2015) Did Sony score $20 M from Mexico for new Bond film? http://www.cbsnews.com/news/mexico-asks-sony-script-changes-james-bond-film-spectre-tax-incentives/. Accessed 30 Dec 2015

Crum B, Wils J (2001) Stimuleringsmaatregelen filmindustrie, tussentijdse evaluatie – Eindrapport Research voor beleid, Leiden

Debande O, Chetrit G (2001) The European audiovisual industry: an overview. European investment bank (EIB) sector papers. http://www.eib.org/attachments/pj/pjaudio_en.pdf. Accessed 3 Dec 2015

Doppert M (1997) Organisatorisch brein achter Zusje. Folia 2. http://ww.doppert.nl/site2001/folia2.html. Accessed 4 Dec 2015

Drenth B, Den Boer-Drinkenburg B, Pen M, Gelevert J, Doornbos F (2003) Evaluatie van de stimuleringsmaatregelen voor de Nederlandse film 1999/2003. Berenschot, Utrecht

European Commission (2013) Communication from the commission on state aid for films and other audiovisual works. OJ C 332/1 of 15 November 2013. http://eur-lex.europa.eu/legal-content/EN/TXT/?uri=celex:52013XC1115(01). Accessed 8 Dec 2015

European Commission (2015a) Digital agenda for Europe. Audiovisual and other media content. https://ec.europa.eu/digital-agenda/en/audiovisual-and-other-media-content. Accessed 3 Dec 2015

European Commission (2015b) Vat rates applied in de member states of the European Union. Accessed 8 Dec 2015

Film Federation of India (2015) Entertainment tax in various states. http://www.filmfed.org/e-tax.html. Accessed 30 Dec 2015

Filming in Hungary (2015) 25 + 5% Tax Rebate. http://filminginhungary.com/255-tax-rebate. Accessed 30 Dec 2015

Filming in Hungary (2013) Why was The Borgias shot in Hungary? http://filminginhungary.com/uncategorized/the-borgias-shot-in-hungary. Accessed 30 Dec 2015

Finas (2015) Overview of the film in Malaysia incentive. http://www.filminmalaysia.com/index.php?option=com_content&view=article&id=93&Itemid=582. Accessed 30 Dec 2015

Goodfellow M (2015) Italy extends tax credit to TV. http://www.screendaily.com/festivals/cannes-news/italy-extends-tax-credit-to-tv/5088229.article. Accessed 30 Dec 2015

Hemels SJC (2010) Opkomst en ondergang van de belastingsubsidies voor de filmsector. Tijdschrift voor Mediageschiedenis 13(2):124–143

HM Revenue & Customs (2015) Corporation tax: creative industry tax reliefs. https://www.gov.uk/guidance/corporation-tax-creative-industry-tax-reliefs. Accessed 8 Dec 2015

HMRC (2014) Film tax relief summary, August 2014. https://www.gov.uk/government/uploads/system/uploads/attachment_data/file/405783/FTR_Monitoring_Summary_July_2014.pdf. Accessed 8 Dec 2015

Holdsworth N (2014) Hungarian ups film production tax rebate to 30 percent. http://www.hollywoodreporter.com/news/hungary-ups-film-production-tax-717663. Accessed 30 Dec 2015

Hungarian National Film Fund (2015) Brief presentation of the Hungarian Tax Relief. http://mnf.hu/en/filming-in-hungary.html. Accessed 30 Dec 2015

InfoComm (2014) The growing audiovisual industry. http://www.infocomm.org/cps/rde/xchg/infocomm/hs.xsl/32928.htm. Accessed 3 Dec 2015

Kemp S (2015) TV drama tax credit costs Treasury £79 m in first year. http://www.theguardian.com/media/2015/feb/24/tv-drama-tax-credit-costs-treasury-79m-in-first-year. Accessed 8 Dec 2015

KFTV, A to Z of countries. http://www.kftv.com/country/list. Accessed 29 Dec 2015

Kurp M (2004) Medienfonds als "Stupid German Money" Steuersparmodell unterstützt Hollywood statt deutsche Filmemacher. http://www.medienmaerkte.de/artikel/kino/040502_filmfonds.html. Accessed 30 Dec 2015
Mayaluna films (2015) The Hungarian tax incentive rebate for films. http://www.mayalunafilms.com/uploads/4/9/2/9/49293301/tax_incentives_for_films_in_hungary_2015.pdf. Accessed 30 Dec 2015
Mooij T (1996) Zusje. Hard werken aan spontaniteit. Filmkrant 163. http://www.filmkrant.nl/_titelindex_Z/1323. Accessed 4 Dec 2015
NCSL (National Conference of State Legislatures) (2014) State film production incentives & programs. http://www.ncsl.org/Portals/1/Documents/fiscal/2014FilmIncentivePrograms.pdf. Accessed 29 Dec 2015
Olsberg SPI (2015) A production incentive for Sweden, A report by Olsberg SPI. http://filmvast.se/wp-content/uploads/2015/05/A-Production-Incentive-for-Sweden-final-draft-2015-05-11.pdf. Accessed 13 Jun 2016
Ontario Ministry of Finance (2015) Ontario interactive digital media tax credit bulletin. http://www.fin.gov.on.ca/en/credit/oidmtc/bulletin-nov-2-2015.pdf. Accessed 29 Dec 2015
Povich ES (2015) Some states Yell "Cut" on film tax credits. http://www.pewtrusts.org/en/research-and-analysis/blogs/stateline/2015/5/18/some-states-yell-cut-on-film-tax-credits. Accessed 29 Dec 2015
Priot F, Julliard-Mourgues C, Chebance M (2015) Movies and TV production in France. The Incentives Guide. Film France, Paris. http://www.filmfrance.net/telechargement/IncentivesGuide2015.pdf. Accessed 28 Dec 2015
PwC (2015a) The big table. Film and video incentives in Canada 2015. http://www.pwc.com/ca/en/entertainment-media/publications/pwc-big-table-film-video-2015-09-en.pdf. Accessed 29 Dec 2015
PwC (2015b) The big table. Digital media and animation incentives in Canada 2015. http://www.pwc.com/ca/en/entertainment-media/publications/pwc-big-table-digital-animation-2015-09-en.pdf. Accessed 29 Dec 2015
Saas DR (2006) Hollywood east? Film tax credits in new England. Policy Brief 06-3. http://www.bostonfed.org/economic/neppc/briefs/2006/briefs063.pdf. Accessed 29 Dec 2015
Screen Australia (2015) Producer offset guidelines. http://www.screenaustralia.gov.au/getmedia/c83d96e6-d225-4270-847a-864b230759f0/Glines_ProducerOffset.pdf. Accessed 28 Dec 2015
Sinclair B (2013) Gaming tax credits: a developer's guide to free money. http://www.gamesindustry.biz/articles/2013-05-22-gaming-tax-credits-a-developers-guide-to-free-money. Accessed 29 Dec 2015
Vogel HL (2011) Entertainment industry economics: a guide for financial analysis. Cambridge University Press, New York

Chapter 9
Tax Incentives for the Art Market

Sigrid Hemels

Abstract Several countries apply tax incentives to promote the sale of certain works of art, such as works of contemporary artists and works of national importance. Examples include deductions for taxpayers who buy contemporary art, sometimes on the condition that the art be made accessible to the public. Although these incentives are not specifically designed to incentivize art dealers, the incentives can have that effect by reducing net or gross prices. If the price of art is reduced as a result of tax incentives, art dealers have a competitive advantage. Other examples include deductions that reduce the net price of works of significant cultural heritage. Tax incentives can also directly influence the gross price. Examples of such incentives include reduced VAT rates and customs duties, which are used in the European Union. However, the definition of "art" is problematic in this respect. Even bigger incentives are provided in so-called free ports, which have no customs duties or transfer taxes on works of art. However, these free ports may also provide opportunities for money laundering, tax evasion, and the fencing of stolen goods.

Keywords Art · Art dealers · VAT · Customs duties · Free ports

1 Introduction

Tax incentives can be used to promote the sale of certain works of art. For example, countries apply tax incentives to stimulate the sale of contemporary art or works of national importance. Tax incentives can also be used to promote the acquisition of national treasures. The effect of these incentives is that the net price of the work of art is reduced. Depending on price elasticity and the bargaining power of the parties

S. Hemels (✉)
Department of Tax Law, Erasmus School of Law,
Erasmus University Rotterdam, Rotterdam, The Netherlands
e-mail: hemels@law.eur.nl

S. Hemels
Allen & Overy, Amsterdam, The Netherlands

© Springer Science+Business Media Singapore 2017

S. Hemels and K. Goto (eds.), *Tax Incentives for the Creative Industries*,
Creative Economy, DOI 10.1007/978-981-287-832-8_9

involved in a transaction, whether it be the purchaser (e.g., a private collector, a company, or a museum), the seller (e.g., an art dealer or auction house), or the producer (the artist), everyone can effectively benefit from these incentives. Although the typical objective of these incentives is not necessarily to incentivize art dealers or auction houses, the incentives can have that effect by providing a competitive advantage. Rules of fair competition, as well as state aid in the EU (refer to Chap. 5), must therefore be taken into account when introducing such incentives.

Tax incentives can also reduce the gross price of art. This effect is typically achieved by indirect tax incentives applied to the value-added tax (VAT) and customs regulations. These types of incentives immediately reduce the price of an artwork, which can in turn promote its sale. In this chapter, I discuss incentives that have both deliberate and unintended effects on the art market. In this respect, economists make distinction between the primary and the secondary art market. The primary art market refers to when a work of art comes to the market for the first time, for example, when it is sold directly by the artist or an art gallery. If the artwork is purchased on the primary market and then resold, it enters the secondary market. This includes auction houses and art dealers. Tax incentives often do not differ between the primary and secondary art markets; some mainly affect the primary or secondary art market, while others affect both.

I begin with a discussion of tax incentives that provide deductions in personal or corporate income tax, thereby reducing the net price (i.e., the price after direct taxes have been levied) of works of contemporary art (Sect. 2) and works of significant cultural heritage (Sect. 3). I then discuss indirect tax incentives such as VAT and customs duties that reduce the gross price (i.e., the price including indirect taxes). I start with reductions in VAT rates and customs duties and exemptions from VAT and customs duties (Sect. 4). In this context, it is important to note that the definition of art used for these incentives is not always the same as the definition used by art experts and artists. I pay special attention to so-called free ports, where art can be stored and often sold free of VAT and customs duties (Sect. 5) before presenting my conclusion (Sect. 6).

2 Incentives that Reduce the Net Price of Contemporary Art

Several countries apply tax incentives for contemporary art through direct taxes such as corporate and personal income tax. These incentives benefit the market for this kind of art because they reduce net costs, which in this context refers to the cost remaining after taking direct taxes into account. In this section, I discuss some examples of these types of tax incentives.

If certain criteria are met, Canada grants a tax deduction, the so-called Capital Cost Allowance, for art bought by corporations or individuals who operate a business.[1]

[1]Section 1102(1)(e) ITR.

As a main rule, art cannot be depreciated in Canada because artworks are regarded as objects that do not depreciate. This view is also taken in many other countries. However, Canada does allow depreciation for certain works of art. First of all, the artwork must have been created by a Canadian. This incentive is, therefore, explicitly aimed at the market for national artists. Works with a value of less than CAD200 are excluded. Furthermore, the work must be related to the business's commercial activities. For example, it must be exhibited in a place of business where it will be seen by clients. If the work is rented instead of purchased, the rental expenses are also deductible, as long as they are for business purposes.

Through the Patronage Act,[2] France introduced a similar deduction in the French income tax for companies that acquire artworks from living artists and put them on permanent display at a location accessible to the public or the employees of the company,[3] such as a museum or a company's lobby or entrance foyer to which the general public is granted access. The offices of the employees do not qualify. If all requirements are met, the company may for tax purposes deduct one-fifth of the purchase price over a period of five years, with the maximum yearly tax deduction set at 0.5% of the annual turnover of the company. This possibility to deduct the costs of contemporary art reduces the purchasing costs and therefore benefits not only contemporary artists but also their dealers. It is important to note that this tax incentive not only gives artists the opportunity to sell their work, but also enables them to build a reputation. Furthermore, it enables the public to get acquainted with modern art. France grants a similar tax incentive to companies that buy musical instruments and give them on loan to musicians. This tax incentive enables talented artists to play valuable instruments, to the benefit of both the musician and audiences. Dealers in old instruments and manufacturers of new instruments also indirectly benefit because the incentives reduce the costs of these instruments.

In Singapore, individuals and organizations commissioning, displaying, and maintaining public art can get a tax incentive under the Public Art Tax Incentive Scheme (PATIS). Double tax deduction is granted on the initial installation cost, maintenance cost, and cost of conducting technical surveys for displaying public art. The National Heritage Board (2013) explains that public art is defined as any two- or three-dimensional work with artistic and/or heritage merit that can be a freestanding installation or integrated into a building façade, is not easily removed, and is located within a publicly accessible or publicly visible area. Publicly accessible or visible areas include through-block connections (pedestrian connections that pass through buildings) with 24-h public access, publicly accessible malls, underground pedestrian networks connected to the Mass Rapid Transit (MRT)/Rapid Transit Systems (RTS) stations that are open during the station's operating hours, circulation areas of the public transport system with mass commuter traffic, and lobbies of commercial developments open to the public from 7 AM to 10 PM.

---

[2]Loi n° 2003-709 du 1er août 2003 relative au mécénat, aux associations et aux foundations.

[3]Section 238 bis AB CGI.

Even though the incentives mentioned above are not aimed at the art market, they do exert an influence on both the primary and secondary art markets by making it cheaper to invest in certain forms of art, which gives the corresponding areas of the art market a competitive advantage.

3 Tax Incentives that Reduce the Net Price of Works of Significant Cultural Heritage

Individuals and companies may possess works of art deemed to be of national importance. If a private owner decides to sell a work of this type, it may be purchased by a rich foreign buyer and end up being taken out of the country. Countries can try to regulate this by refusing to grant export permits. Alternatively, they can provide tax incentives to keep the artworks in the country. Such tax incentives influence the secondary art market, as they make it cheaper for prospective buyers within the country to successfully compete with foreign buyers and purchase the artwork. In return for this type of incentive, the buyer is usually required to make the artwork available to the public. This makes sense as the incentive is publicly funded. For example, the French Patronage Act introduced several tax incentives into the income tax to retain works of significant cultural heritage (*trésors nationaux*) for France. If the owner of a work of significant cultural heritage wishes to export it, they must first acquire an export license, which the French government might choose to temporarily refuse while it attempts to obtain the funds needed to purchase the object from the buyer. If a company finances the acquisition on behalf of the French state, it receives a tax credit of 90% of the price of the artwork.[4] However, this tax incentive can only reduce the tax due to a maximum of 50%. For example, if the price is €40 million, the tax credit is in principle €36 million (90% of €40 million). However, if the total tax due is €50 million, the tax credit is reduced to €25 million (50% of €50 million). This tax incentive gives French companies a public relations opportunity: for 10% of the cost of the national treasure, they get positive publicity. This publicity might be well worth more than the 10% borne by the company, and thus represent a win-win situation for the company and the French government, which actually pays 90% of the price through the tax credit if the 50% maximum does not apply but has easier access to funding.

It will not always be possible for the French state to find funds to buy a national treasure. In such cases, companies operating in France may request approval of the French government to buy the object themselves by taking advantage of a specially designed tax incentive.[5] If approval is granted, the company may deduct 40% of the purchase price from its taxable profit. However, the company is obliged to loan the

[4]Section 238 bis-0 A CGI.

[5]Section 238 bis-0 AB CGI.

work to a French museum, public archive, or state library for a period of at least 10 years. During this 10-year period, the company is not allowed to transfer ownership of the cultural heritage.

Ministère de la Culture et de la Communication (2013), p. 7 reported that in the first 10 years of the French Patronage Act (2003–2013), several big companies, including Axa, Total, GDF Suez, LVMH and Yves Rocher, made use of these incentives. During this 10-year period, the French state acquired 67 major works worth approximately €170 million in total. Several French museums, including the Louvre, benefitted from this incentive.

4 Reducing the Gross Price of Art: VAT and Customs Incentives

Various countries directly reduce the gross price of art (i.e., the price including indirect taxes) by providing tax incentives. The sale of art is promoted under strict conditions by exempting artworks from customs duties, as is done in the US, or by applying reduced or zero rates for imports, as is done in the EU. This affects both the primary and secondary art markets. Several countries have also supported contemporary artists by reducing the consumer tax, such as VAT on sales of these artists, thereby incentivizing the primary art market. For example, under the harmonized EU VAT Directive, the general rate for the supply of goods and services must be at least 15%.[6] However, EU Member States are allowed to apply a reduced rate of at least 5% on the supply of certain goods and services.[7] Member States may apply this reduced rate on artworks that are imported or supplied by their creator or their successor(s) in title. Furthermore, the reduced rate may also be occasionally applied to the supply of art by a taxable person other than a dealer, when the artworks have been imported by the taxable person him/herself, when they have been supplied to that person by their creator or successor in title, or when they have entitled that person to a full VAT deduction.[8]

This incentive is very important for artists as they sell many of their works to customers who are not subject to or exempt from VAT. For these customers, the reduced rate means a real price difference. Those who are not taxable or exempt include private individuals, governments, and banks. These groups are very important for artists. For example, in 1995, artists in the Netherlands sold 77% of their uncommissioned and 69% of their commissioned work to private individuals, municipalities, and government institutions. As the regular and reduced VAT rates in the Netherlands are currently 21 and 6%, respectively, the tax incentive makes a significant price difference of nearly 15% (Meulenbeek et al. 1997).

---

[6]Article 97 VAT Directive.

[7]Article 99 VAT Directive.

[8]Article 103 VAT Directive.

Furthermore, EU Member States must apply the so-called margin scheme for second-hand goods, artworks, collectors' items and antiques.[9] This scheme also effectively reduces the price of artworks. Under this scheme, the regular rate is not applied to the price of the artwork, but rather to the margin of the art dealer, thereby reducing the price for consumers and exempt customers such as governments and banks. For example, if a Danish art dealer buys a painting from a collector for €15,000 and later sells it for €25,000, excluding VAT, the margin is €10,000. Denmark applies a VAT rate of 25%. Without the margin scheme, the price including VAT would be €31,250. Under the margin scheme, the price including VAT is €27,500.

4.1 Definition of "Works of Art"

Regarding tax incentives for the art market, the most difficult problem is that the definition of what qualifies as a work of art and, therefore, for the tax incentive remains unclear. The question of how to define art has kept art historians, sociologists, and critics, just to name a few, busy for quite some time. Up to now, they have not been able to come up with a consensus answer that is independent of time or place. For contemporary art, it has been even more problematic to define clearly the borders of what is and is not art. However, since 1995, the harmonized EU VAT has provided a detailed and closed definition of works of art. Currently, this definition is included in Annex IX to the VAT Directive, as follows:

> Works of art
>
> (1) Pictures, collages and similar decorative plaques, paintings and drawings, executed entirely by hand by the artist, other than plans and drawings for architectural, engineering, industrial, commercial, topographical or similar purposes, hand-decorated manufactured articles, theatrical scenery, studio back cloths or the like of painted canvas (CN code 9701);
>
> (2) original engravings, prints and lithographs, being impressions produced in limited numbers directly in black and white or in colour of one or of several plates executed entirely by hand by the artist, irrespective of the process or of the material employed, but not including any mechanical or photomechanical process (CN code 9702 00 00);
>
> (3) original sculptures and statuary, in any material, provided that they are executed entirely by the artist; sculpture casts the production of which is limited to eight copies and supervised by the artist or his successors in title (CN code 9703 00 00); on an exceptional basis, in cases determined by the Member States, the limit of eight copies may be exceeded for statuary casts produced before 1 January 1989;
>
> (4) tapestries (CN code 5805 00 00) and wall textiles (CN code 6304 00 00) made by hand from original designs provided by artists, provided that there are not more than eight copies of each;

[9]Chapter 4 (article 311-343) VAT Directive.

(5) individual pieces of ceramics executed entirely by the artist and signed by him;

(6) enamels on copper, executed entirely by hand, limited to eight numbered copies bearing the signature of the artist or the studio, excluding articles of jewellery and goldsmiths' and silversmiths' wares;

(7) photographs taken by the artist, printed by him or under his supervision, signed and numbered and limited to 30 copies, all sizes and mounts included.

This definition contains several references to the CN codes, which the goods nomenclature for the Common Customs Tariff, also known as the combined nomenclature.[10] The basis for the EU nomenclature is the Harmonized System (HS) Nomenclature run by the World Customs Organization.[11] This systematic list of commodities forms the basis for international trade negotiations, and is used by most trading nations. Chapter 97 is on "Works of art. Collectors' pieces, antiques" and reads as follows:

97.01 Paintings, drawings and pastels, executed entirely by hand, other than drawings of heading 49.06 and other than handpainted or hand-decorated manufactured articles; collages and similar decorative plaques.

9701.10 Paintings, drawings and pastels.

9701.90 Other.

9702.00 Original engravings, prints and lithographs.

9703.00 Original sculptures and statuary, in any material.

9704.00 Postage or revenue stamps, stamp-postmarks, first-day covers, postal stationery (stamped paper), and the like, used or unused, other than those of heading 49.07.

9705.00 Collections and collectors' pieces of zoological, botanical, mineralogical, anatomical, historical, archaeological, palaeontological, ethnographic or numismatic interest.

9706.00 Antiques of an age exceeding one hundred years.

It was logical to make the link in the VAT annex to the CN. Imports of certain works of art for exhibitions have been exempt from customs duties for a long time. Since 1987, this exemption has been included in Chapter 97 of the CN; therefore, many CN codes start with 97.

The European Court of Justice (ECJ) has had to interpret these CN code definitions on several occasions for the levy of customs duties. Because of the references to the CN codes in the VAT definition, the criteria developed for customs duties by the ECJ also apply in determining whether an object is a work of art for

[10]Council Regulation (EEC) No 2658/87 on the tariff and statistical nomenclature and on the Common Customs Tariff. An update is published regularly and can be accessed at http://ec.europa.eu/taxation_customs/customs/customs_duties/tariff_aspects/combined_nomenclature/index_en.htm. Accessed 14 November 2015.

[11]Online version: http://www.wcoomd.org/en/topics/nomenclature/instrument-and-tools/hs-online.aspx. Accessed 14 November 2015.

VAT purposes. Below I discuss several requirements that the ECJ did and did not deem relevant for the decision as to whether an object was a work of art under these definitions.

4.1.1 Materials or Technique Used not of Relevance

In 1985, the ECJ was asked how the expression "original sculptures and statuary, in any material" was to be understood.[12] A Berlin art dealer imported a three-dimensional work by an American artist entitled "Model, Motor Section, Giant Soft Fan" that consisted of a wall relief made of cardboard and polystyrene, sprayed with black paint and oil, and attached to a wooden panel by means of wire and synthetic resin (I assume it was one of Claes Oldenburg's sculptures). German customs authorities took the view that only objects having a sculptural form made by traditional techniques could be classified under the exemption for sculptures. In their view, other works of art, particularly contemporary works such as textile hangings, collages, assemblages and so on, could not be classified under this chapter and should be classified (and taxed at a rate of 14.2%) under the chapter for relevant materials (in this case "plastic").

The art dealer did not consider himself to be an importer of plastic and therefore challenged the tariff classification. The German *Finanzgericht* (Fiscal Court) asked the ECJ for a preliminary ruling. Insofar as original artistic productions are concerned, the European Commission advocated a liberal interpretation of the definitions and the embrace of new artistic techniques. The ECJ agreed with the European Commission. It stressed that parties agreed the object was an original work of art and that the dispute solely concerned the question of whether the characteristics of the work enabled it to be included within the classification "sculptures and statuary." The court ruled that this expression must be understood to refer to all three-dimensional artistic productions, irrespective of the techniques and materials used. As the definition of works of art in Annex I uses the same expression and refers to this CN code, in my opinion, the same liberal view must be taken for VAT purposes.

Subsequently, in November 1990, the ECJ defined the difference between a painting and a sculpture.[13] The case was as follows. In 1988, the director of an art gallery in Cologne purchased a work by the artist Laszlo Moholy-Nagy for US $400,000. This work was entitled *Konstruktion in Emaille I (Telefonbild)* and consisted of a steel plate with a fused coating of enamel glaze colors. The German tax authorities wanted to apply the rate for "other ornaments, of base metal." That classification meant that the work was subject to the full rate of German turnover tax on imports instead of the reduced rate for works of art. This art dealer rejected

[12]ECJ 15 May 1985, Case 155/84, Reinhard Onnasch v Hauptzollamt Berlin - Packhof.

[13]ECJ 8 November 1990, Case C-231/89, Krystyna Gmurzynska-Bscher, Galerie Gmurzynska v. Oberfinanzdirektion Köln.

being treated as an ironmonger. The *Bundesfinanzhof* referred to the ECJ for a preliminary ruling regarding the question of whether this work constituted a painting or sculpture and whether it should be classified according to its material composition as an ornament of base metal. The ECJ first noted that it was clear the national court had no doubt that the object was an original work of art. The court stated that an object of that kind cannot be regarded as being for decoration, which constitutes the essential feature of articles classified under the heading "other ornaments, of base metal." I doubt the practicality of this is criterion, as a very important function of art for centuries has been decoration.

Regarding the question of whether this work of art had to be classified as a painting or a sculpture, the court noted that although both headings cover entirely personal creations in which an artist expresses an aesthetic ideal, each refers to a specific category of artworks. Paintings are all pictorial works executed entirely by hand on a support of any kind of material, whereas sculptures are all three-dimensional representations in a material to which the artist has given a specific form, regardless of the technique and materials used. Accordingly, the criterion the ECJ gave for distinguishing between the two lies in the dimensions of the work. According to the ECJ, the artistic nature of the Moholy-Nagy resided not in its three-dimensional form, but in the fact that paint had been applied by hand by the artist upon a steel support, which was in itself of no artistic value.

4.1.2 An Impossible Criterion: Art Is not Competitive

In 1990, the ECJ again had to interpret the term "works of art."[14] The German *Finanzgericht* wanted to know if paperweights, which were produced entirely by hand, in limited editions, signed by well-known glassware artists, collected by collectors and displayed in museums without ever being used as paperweights, had to be regarded as articles of a commercial character and consequently classified by reference to their constituent material, or whether they were to be classified as works of art. In the latter case, the national court also wanted to know whether the paperweights should be classified as "paintings, etc." or as original sculptures and statuary, in any material.

The ECJ observed that sculptures that are commercial in character, and in particular works of craftsmanship, are not works of art. The fact that an article may be recognized as being of an artistic nature does not necessarily mean that it is to be classified as art. Even if certain objects are to be regarded as works of art, that fact cannot determine their customs classification. For me, it is difficult to understand the ECJ at this point. Art is a commodity that has been traded for centuries and is, in that regard, always commercial in character. Especially if an object is regarded as a work of art by independent experts (it is not clear whether this was the case with the

[14]ECJ 18 September 1990, Case C-228/89, Farfalla Flemming und Partner v Hauptzollamt MünchenWest.

paperweights, but the court seemed to give a general rule), it would be very strange not to recognize it as such for VAT or customs purposes. This is even more so if the purpose of the exemption the ECJ defined in 1985 is taken into account:

> The exemptions [...] are intended to facilitate international trade in objects of cultural and educational value and that aim is decisive for the interpretation of the heading in question.[15]

In the view of the ECJ, works of art are entirely personal creations through which the artists express an aesthetic ideal. Furthermore, according to the ECJ, these do not compete economically with each other or with other articles. For that reason, the ECJ does not want to apply the customs exemption on articles that, at least potentially, compete economically with similar articles manufactured industrially or as works of craftsmanship. This does not make sense from an economic point of view, as artworks compete not only with each other, but also with other commodities, such as jewels, expensive cars, and holidays. The consumer can spend his or her money only once. The art dealer who purchased Claes Oldenburgh's work could have also purchased a work by Andy Warhol, Pablo Picasso, or Johannes Vermeer. Works of art do compete economically with each other or with other articles. Therefore, in my view, the ECJ introduced a completely useless criterion in this judgment.

4.1.3 Made by the Artist Expressing Their Aesthetic Ideal: A Criterion Which Already Lost Its Relevance Through Duchamp's Urinal

In the Moholy-Nagy judgment discussed in Sect. 4.1.1, the ECJ deemed it important that the artist make the work of art himself. Apparently, neither the court nor the German tax authorities had checked art history books on the *Telefonbild*. The characteristic of these works is that the artist did not apply the paint; indeed, this is where the works derive their name. Moholy-Nagy (1947, p. 79) described how these works were made:

> In 1922 I ordered by telephone from a sign factory five paintings in porcelain enamel. I had the factory's color chart before me and I sketched my paintings on graph paper. At the other end of the telephone, the factory supervisor had the same kind of paper, divided into squares. He took down the dictated shapes in the correct position. (...) True, these pictures do not have the quality of the "individual touch" (...) But my belief is that mathematically harmonious shapes, executed precisely, are filled with emotional quality, and that they represent the perfect balance between feeling and intellect.

In an unsigned editorial in Marcel Duchamp's journal *The Blind Man* (1917, p. 5), this point was already covered in relation to Duchamp's urinal (*Fountain*, 1917), which he signed R. Mutt:

[15] ECJ 10 October 1985, Case 252/84, Collector Guns GmbH & Co. KG v Hauptzollamt Koblenz, consideration 12.

Whether Mr. Mutt with his own hands made the fountain or not has no importance. He CHOSE it. He took an ordinary article of life, placed it so that its useful significance disappeared under new title and point of view-created a new thought for that object.

These two examples show that even at the beginning of the 20th century, the definition of the ECJ, requiring the artist to make the work himself, was already obsolete.

The observation in the paperweight case of Sect. 4.1.2 that works of art should be entirely personal creations through which the artist expresses an aesthetic ideal, is problematic as well, especially for modern and contemporary art. It is questionable whether Duchamp used the urinal, Damien Hirst used his shark,[16] or Tracy Emin used her tent[17] to express an aesthetic ideal. Artists often have a message that is not necessarily shared through their aesthetic ideal. Sometimes the purpose of art is to make the audience think about, for example, violence, overconsumption, or inequality; this is a goal that artists do not always try to reach through aesthetic means. Also, in this respect, the ECJ seemed to have had a narrow, conservative, and very outdated view on art.

4.2 *Closed Definition of Art: Video and Light Art Excluded*

The EU definition of art for VAT purposes is limited to the categories summed up in Annex IX of the VAT Directive. Forms of art not mentioned in this annex are excluded. This is problematic as art, especially contemporary art, is continuously renewing itself. Even when the definition was introduced in 1995, it was already outdated. The theatrical scenery that Marc Chagall painted for the Jewish Theatre in Moscow just after the Russian Revolution and that has been displayed in several museums across the world, is, for example, not art according to this definition, which explicitly excludes scenery.

Another example is video art. Even though almost every museum of contemporary art houses this kind of art by artists such as Bill Viola, Pipilotti Rist, and Bruce Nauman, and although video art will celebrate its 45th birthday in 2018, it is not art for VAT purposes. On 11 August 2010, the European Commission published a regulation[18] in which video and light art were explicitly denied the status of sculpture, and therefore of a work of art under the European CN. A work of video art is described as follows in the regulation:

A video-sound installation consisting essentially of the following components:

10 video reproducing apparatus of the digital versatile disc (DVD) type,

[16]The Physical Impossibility of Death in the Mind of Someone Living, Damien Hirst 1991.
[17]My Bed, Tracey Emin 1998.
[18]Commission Regulation (EU) No 731/2010 of 11 August 2010.

10 projectors using matrix liquid crystal display (LCD) technology, of a kind also capable of displaying digital information generated by an automatic data-processing machine,

10 single self-powered loudspeakers, mounted in their enclosures, and

20 digital versatile discs (DVDs) containing recorded works of 'modern art' in the form of images accompanied by sound.

The appearance of the video reproducing apparatus, the projectors and the loudspeakers has been modified by an artist with a view to appear as a work of 'modern art' without altering their function. The installation is presented disassembled.

A light art installation is described as:

A so-called 'light installation' consisting of six circular fluorescent lighting tubes and six lighting fittings of plastics. It has been designed by an artist and operates in accordance with instructions provided by the artist. It is intended to be displayed in a gallery, fixed to the wall. The fittings are separate from each other and are intended to be mounted vertically. The tubes are to be placed into the fittings, providing two alternating shades of white. The product is presented disassembled.

The European Commission decided that both works could not be classified as a sculpture. The reason given in relation to video art is that:

none of the individual components or the whole installation, when assembled, can be considered as a sculpture. The components have been slightly modified by the artist, but these modifications do not alter their preliminary function of goods of Section XVI.[19] It is the content recorded on the DVD which, together with the components of the installation, provides for the 'modern art'. The video-sound installation is neither composite goods, as it rather consists of individual components, nor goods put up in sets for retail sale [...]. Consequently, the components of the installation are to be classified separately.

Video art was therefore classified as a combination of a video recording or reproducing apparatus, projector, loudspeakers and DVDs. Light art was dismissed as being "wall lighting fittings" and not a sculpture:

as it is not the installation that constitutes a 'work of art' but the result of the operations (the light effect) carried out by it.

Valentin (2011) points out that the two works described in the regulation correspond to the works of two renowned artists: the video installation *Hall of Whispers* by Bill Viola and *Six Alternating Cool White/Warm White Fluorescent Lights Vertical and Centered* (1973) by Dan Flavin. In 2008, the London VAT and Duties Tribunal had classified both works as sculptures that could be imported under the reduced VAT import rate of 5% on their import value, instead of the standard rate of 17.5%.[20] The tribunal allowed for expert witnesses, including a museum director, a curator, and an art critic, to give evidence on the character of the

[19]The heading of Section XVI is "Machinery and mechanical appliances; electrical equipment; parts thereof; sound recorders and reproducers, television image and sound recorders and reproducers, and parts and accessories of such articles".

[20]Haunch of Venison Partners Limited v HM Revenue and Customs, C 00266, 11 December 2008.

works. According to Adam (2010), the director of the National Portrait Gallery in London observed in court:

> We have a history of well over 100 years of art that can appear to be made of ordinary things that have other uses. It is very common for sculptures to be shipped in parts. The fact that the work in transit is not like a work of art could apply to a large bronze figurative sculpture – an Anthony Caro piece would not necessarily travel as a whole sculpture in a single box.... The question of 'is this the sculpture?' is not to do with what it looks like when it is in customs but what it looks like assembled.

Furthermore, the judges went to the Tate Modern Museum to view a similar Flavin work (para 16 of the judgment). According to the Tribunal (para 51), it stretches the objective characteristics principle too far to say that a work is no longer a work of art if it is dismantled for transportation. The Tribunal regarded it (para 49):

> as absurd to classify any of these works as components ignoring the fact that the components together make a work of art.

The Tribunal dismissed the fears of the UK tax authorities that importers might declare just anything as works of art as being "grossly exaggerated" (para 50). It pointed out that the burden of proof would be on the importer, and that the tax authorities could call expert evidence.

The UK tax authorities did not appeal this decision, but it seems to have inspired the EC Customs Code Committee to put video art on the agenda. According to Valentin (2011), some Member States expressed the view that components of video installations should be taxed individually as video projectors. Other than the UK Tribunal, the Committee does not seem to have involved expert witnesses in coming to its conclusion in the Regulation mentioned previously. In any case, this decision was not made out in the open, but behind closed doors.

This Regulation underpins the fact that the EU uses a rather conservative definition of art for VAT and customs purposes. Tischler (2012), p. 1685 rightly points out that non-art components are necessary components of certain artworks. She observes:

> If a court accepted the Commission's standard, any work that uses infrastructure upon its completion—pressurized water for a fountain, electrical plugs for a neon sculpture, wind for chimes—may not be classified as art, but rather a composition of non-art components. A work would only become art in its intended context or ultimate form—when the play button is pressed or the electrical current is live. This is akin to legislating that artworks that are intended for a particular context are "not art" until they are actually placed in that context. Under this standard, a fully assembled Flavin work would cease to be an artwork once the gallery closed for the night and the janitor turned off the lights. This standard thus requires that an artwork be continually connected to every element of its context in order to remain art.

The EU art definition favors traditional forms of art over more unconventional and new art forms that cannot be classified in one of the existing categories. This is problematic not only from an artistic point of view, and probably contrary to the direct subsidies policy of many member states' Ministries of Culture, but also from the perspective that it is not in line with the neutrality idea of VAT, as certain art forms are taxed at a lower rate than others. Therefore, the EU definition of art distorts fair competition in the art market.

4.3 Involvement of Art Experts Is Important

In the EU, independent art experts do not seem to have been involved in drafting the definition of art. Furthermore, they were not consulted by the ECJ or the European Commission when classifying works. In a famous American court case on the question regarding whether an object had to be considered a work of art, the judge involved art experts.[21] In 1926, the photographer Edward Steichen wanted to import one of the statues of the sculptor Brancusi to the US. This statue, *Bird in Space*, represented for Brancusi the idea of flight and the essence of a bird's take-off. However, for the US customs authorities, it was a mere arch of raw metal (they called it a propeller blade) that should be taxed accordingly. Other works of Brancusi intended for a sales exhibition in the US were treated in the same way (categorized as kitchen utensils and hospital supplies). Edward Steichen purchased *Bird in Space*, paid the duty, and then went to court to appeal the levy of the tax (Giry 2002; Rowell and Paleologue 1999). Many experts gave evidence before the court. Sculptor Jacob Epstein, the editors of *The Arts* and *Vanity Fair*, the director of the Brooklyn Museum of Art, and the art critic Henry McBride testified for Brancusi. The witnesses for the government included the sculptors Robert Aitken and Thomas Jones, a professor at Columbia University. Tischler (2012), p. 1688 observes that the court applied a three-part test: (1) Was this the work of a professional?; (2) Was this an original work?; and (3) Was this an article of utility? The first two questions were easily answered by the court in the affirmative. The last question, rephrased as to whether the sculpture was actually a work of art, was more problematic for the court. However, in recognizing the "so-called new school of art," the court accepted an art movement "whose exponents attempt to portray abstract ideas rather than to imitate natural objects," and held that it must recognize the change. As a result, *Bird in Space* was categorized as art and could be imported tax-free. Tischler (2012), p. 1688 points out that the court relied on the principle of "objective acceptance," which subordinates conflicting subjective responses of the court to expert testimonials and recognizes shifting trends within the art world. This also seems to have been the approach of the UK Tribunal in the 2008 case mentioned in Sect. 4.2 on the Flavin and Viola works. Interestingly, the Tribunal even mentioned the Brancusi case in para 30 of its judgment:

> That case is not authority binding on us but it is interesting to note that the Court made the following remarks:

---

[21]Brancusi vs. United States, US Customs Court, 26 November 1928.

> "... the man who produced the importation is a professional sculptor, as is shown by his reputation and works and the manner in which he is considered *by those competent to judge upon that subject*".
>
> We emphasize those words because they show that expert evidence was regarded as relevant.

I agree with Tischler (2012), p. 1688 that the European Commission should have done the same and relied on the principle of "objective acceptance" when assessing whether video and light art were to be considered art for EU VAT and customs purposes.

In my opinion, it is important to give art experts a role in the interpretation of the definition of art for VAT and Customs purposes. National art councils involved in the assignment of direct subsidies and other art experts can be consulted by judges before they reach a judgment. This might also prevent tax incentives from supporting objects that would have never been considered works of art for direct subsidy purposes, and, on the other hand, from not supporting unconventional works of art highly valued by experts. The negative effect on competition in the European art market caused by the fact that traditional forms of art are favored over new forms could also be solved by these adaptations.

5 Free Ports

Several countries have so-called "free ports" where imported works of art may be stored. As long as the works do not leave the free port, no VAT/transaction taxes or customs duties are imposed, hence the word "free." This affects the secondary art market by reducing the gross price of artworks in the free port.[22] Technically, goods in free ports are in transit; however, free ports do not usually impose limits on the period the goods can be kept in the free port. Free ports can therefore be used as semi-permanent tax-free havens for valuable goods such as art. The *Economist* (2013) quotes the managing director of the Luxembourg free port stating that the idea is to turn free ports into "places the end-customer wants to be seen in, the best alternative to owning your own museum."

Often, no VAT or other local taxes are due when the work is sold within a free port. The increasing number of art buyers who buy art as an investment can therefore buy and sell VAT-free art. This can be regarded as a tax incentive for the art market as the gross price of art stored and sold in free ports is lower than that of art imported or sold outside free ports.

Switzerland already opened a free port in the 19th century, not for art, but for temporary storage of agricultural goods (Segal 2012). Later, the Swiss free ports branched out into the storage of art. For example, the Swiss free ports are very

---

[22]In Switzerland, the German word for these free ports is *Zollfreilager*, and the French word is *dépôts francs*. Section 175 ZV.

important for Art Basel, a famous art fair. Many countries have such free ports, some of which have facilities for the storage and sale of art. For example, in the Singapore art free port, which opened in 2010, the auction house Christies operates "Christie's Fine Art Storage Services."[23] Other countries that have free ports with facilities for art include Monaco (Monaco Freeport, since 2012), Luxembourg (Le Freeport, since 2014), and China (Beijing Free Port of Culture, since 2014). Beijing's free port is the only one in China that allows foreign investors to set up art businesses without any limitations (Zhangyu 2014). It consists of warehouses, showrooms, and trade centers, and houses art fairs such as the Beijing International Fine Art Fair and Sotheby's auctions. As long as foreign art remains in the free port, no Chinese import taxes are due and no VAT is levied upon sale (Zhangyu 2014). In 2015, the Delaware free port opened in the US. This is a different facility as it makes use of the fact that Delaware does not impose sales or use tax, and is therefore aimed at domestic as opposed to foreign art. In addition, it does not have a special customs status. Bowley (2015) observes that where before, US collectors had to send their art to free ports in Switzerland, they can now obtain the same advantages—discretion, security, and tax savings—in Delaware.

Private collectors are not the only ones who use free ports. *The Economist* (2013) mentions that clients of free ports also include museums, galleries, and art investment funds. Segal (2012) mentions that some galleries use the free port not only for storage, but also for viewing rooms. In some cases, art can be temporarily imported into the host country without losing the tax exemption, therefore encouraging collectors to lend pieces to local museums or have them restored locally. For example, in Monaco, temporary tax-free exit of goods is allowed for exhibitions, restorations, and expert assessment. In the EU, no import duties are levied if goods are to be exhibited or used at a public event, or if works of art, collectors' items, or antiques are imported for the purposes of exhibition with a view toward a possible sale.[24]

However, these free ports are criticized, not so much because of the VAT/customs-free status of the goods, but because of the secrecy around what is stored and who is storing it. Free ports provide opportunities for money laundering, tax evasion, and the fencing of stolen goods. Segal (2012) mentions that in 2003, hundreds of antiquities stolen from excavation sites in Egypt were discovered in a Swiss free port. For those reasons, free ports remain controversial.

---

[23]http://www.cfass.com/singapore-freeport/en/ Accessed 12 November 2015.

[24]Article 576 CCIP.

6 Conclusion

The art market is highly commercial and competitive. By reducing the net or gross price of certain works of art, tax incentives for the art market can easily distort fair competition both in the primary and secondary art markets. In the EU, the state aid prohibition and the fundamental freedoms discussed in Chap. 5 must always be considered carefully when introducing tax incentives for this sector of the creative industries. It is easier to introduce such incentives outside of the EU. For example, it would be difficult to introduce an incentive similar to the Canadian incentive discussed in Sect. 2 into the EU. The requirement that the incentive only applies to works created by a domestic artist would probably infringe upon the fundamental freedoms of the TFEU. In the EU, such incentives should probably apply to all EU artists, not only those of a single Member State.

VAT and customs incentives directly decrease the price of art. These levies are harmonized in the EU. However, the conservative definition of art that is used for the purpose of these incentives actually distorts competition in the art market. Conventional forms of art are favored over modern and contemporary ones. The lack of involvement of art experts in defining art for EU purposes is, in my view, problematic and leads to strange results. The EU should, in this respect, learn from the willingness of US and UK courts to hear witness evidence when deciding on whether something is art for tax purposes. Furthermore, as opposed to the exhaustive list used by the EU, which was already outdated when introduced in 1995, a more open and modern definition is needed.

References

Adam G (2010) Flavin and viola light works ruled "Not Art". Art Newspaper 219:59

Bowley G (2015) Art Collectors Find Safe Harbor in Delaware's Tax Laws. http://www.nytimes.com/2015/10/26/arts/design/art-collectors-find-safe-harbor-in-delawares-tax-laws.html. Accessed 12 Nov 2015

Culture Communication (2013) La loi "Aillagon" a 10 ans. Mécénat: le temps du développement et des mutations, 210: 6–11. http://www.culturecommunication.gouv.fr/content/download/76195/580168/version/1/file/Mag+210+dossier+m%C3%A9c%C3%A9nat.pdf. Accessed 23 Oct 2015

Economist (2013) Freeports. Über-warehouses for the ultra-rich. http://www.economist.com/news/briefing/21590353-ever-more-wealth-being-parked-fancy-storage-facilities-some-customers-they-are. Accessed 3 Nov 2015

Giry S (2002) An odd bird. Legal affairs.http://www.legalaffairs.org/issues/September-October-2002/story_giry_sepoct2002.msp. Accessed 23 Oct 2015

Meulenbeek H, Hop JP, Webbink D (1997) De financiële positie van beeldend kunstenaars 1993–1995. Ministerie van Onderwijs, Cultuur en Wetenschappen, Zoetermeer

Ministère de la Culture et de la Communication (2013) Dix ans de mécénat 2003/2013. http://www.culturecommunication.gouv.fr/content/download/76179/580075/version/1/file/DP%2Btimbre%2Bm%C3%A9c%C3%A9nat%5B1%5D.pdf. Accessed 23 Oct 2015

Moholy-Nagy L (1947) The new vision and abstract of an artist. Wittenborn, New York

National Heritage Board (2013) Public Art Tax Incentive Scheme. http://www.nhb.gov.sg/~/media/nhb/files/support%20us/patis_more_info.pdf?la=en. Accessed 12 Nov 2013
Rowell M, Paleologue A (1999) Brancusi vs. United States the historic trail 1928. Vilo International, Paris
Segal D (2012) Swiss Freeports Are Home for a Growing Treasury of Art. www.nytimes.com/2012/07/22/business/swiss-freeports-are-home-for-a-growing-treasury-of-art.html?_r=0. Accessed 12 Nov 2015
Tischler RJ (2012) "The power to tax involves the power to destroy" how avant-garde art outstrips the imagination of regulators, and why a judicial rubric can save it. Brooklyn Law Rev 77 (4):1665–1705 http://practicum.brooklaw.edu/sites/default/files/print/pdfs/journals/brooklyn-law-review/volume-77/issue-4/blr_v77iv_6.pdf. Accessed 2 Nov 2015
The Blind Man (1917) The Richard Mutt Case. The Blind Man 2:5–6. http://sdrc.lib.uiowa.edu/dada/blindman/2/. Accessed 10 Nov 2015
Valentin P (2011) UK: The European Commission Says It's Not Art. Mondaq. http://www.mondaq.com/x/135086/Music+and+the+Arts/The+European+Commission+Says+Its+Not+Art. Accessed 2 Nov 2015
Zhangyu D (2014) Beijing Culture Free Port poised for art market. http://www.chinadaily.com.cn/culture/art/2014-09/23/content_18643138.htm. Accessed 12 Nov 2015

Chapter 10
Tax Incentives for Copyright

Dick Molenaar

Abstract Copyright belongs to the creative industries as the legal result of the creative process. It can be sold or licensed and often creates income. By its nature, copyright is highly mobile and can easily cross borders, because it can be split off from normal business activities and held as a separate asset. States are interested in stimulating or attracting copyright, as they believe this has a positive effect on their economic activities or because they want to support their artists. States may implement a broad range of tax incentives, which may focus on low-earning creatives, major companies with high copyright income, or anything in between. Copyright income can easily be taxed twice in cross-border situations, a situation that states try to prevent through the use of tax treaties. This leads to opportunities for international structuring. Limits on this structuring are currently being set internationally with the Anti Base Erosion and Profit Shifting (BEPS) program. However, this should not necessarily affect well-intended copyright tax incentive schemes.

Keywords Copyright · BEPS · IP boxes · R&D incentives · Bilateral tax treaties · Harmful tax competition

1 Introduction

Copyright, a key factor in the creative industries, is the result of the creative process, in which a new and unique product or service comes into existence. The creator of this product or service is the owner of the copyright. He or she may sell this copyright, or may retain ownership and only license the copyright for use by others. Copyright is sometimes strictly personal and remains always connected to

D. Molenaar
Department of Tax Law, Erasmus School of Law,
Erasmus University Rotterdam, Rotterdam, The Netherlands

D. Molenaar (✉)
All Arts Tax Advisers, Rotterdam, The Netherlands
e-mail: dmolenaar@allarts.nl

© Springer Science+Business Media Singapore 2017

S. Hemels and K. Goto (eds.), *Tax Incentives for the Creative Industries*,
Creative Economy, DOI 10.1007/978-981-287-832-8_10

the creator, such as in the case of image rights and the copyrights of composers and authors. In those cases, licensing is the only possible way for others to use the copyright legally.

Copyright often generates income in the form of royalties based on the proceeds of the product or service, for example, as a percentage, where proceeds will continue as long as the copyright is used, or in other forms, such as fixed income or lump sum payments in one or more installments.

Income from copyright is taxed in its country of origin, the source state. For residents and permanent establishments of non-residents, this will be normal company income, which is taxed on the profit after the deduction of all business expenses and at the normal company tax rates of the state. However, it can also be foreign-source income for non-residents without a fixed base in that state, which is often taxed on a gross basis or, at a lower tax rate, with limited deductibility of expenses.

Copyright can be highly mobile, because it can be easily split off from normal business activities and usually does not require much maintenance. This means that copyright is more responsive to (corporate) income tax rates and is therefore more likely to move to low-tax jurisdictions than normal business activities.

States often use preferential tax regimes such as IP Boxes and R&D tax deductions to attempt to attract and develop copyright and other intellectual property. These tax incentives are the main subject of this chapter.

Foreign income from copyright will also be taxed in the state of residence of the owner of the copyright as part of his worldwide income. This can lead to double taxation of copyright income, since it is taxed in both the source state and in the residence state. To prevent such double taxation, states may conclude bilateral tax treaties. The OECD in Paris coordinates this through the Model Income Tax Convention, in which Article 12 is devoted solely to royalties and comparable income from copyright and other IP income. The OECD recommends allocating taxing rights to the residence state and exempting income in the source state, but it also gives countries some room for implementing source taxes. This, for example, might be preferred by countries which are mainly royalty-exporting states. The state of residence must then allow a tax credit to eliminate double taxation.

The UN Model Double Taxation Convention between developed and developing countries and the US Model Income Tax Convention also employ these same principles, meaning that almost every bilateral tax treaty includes a section like Article 12 of the OECD Model for royalties.

Within the EU, a special Directive for interest and royalties allocates the taxing right solely to the state of residence of the copyright holder, when certain conditions are met, without the option for a source tax.[1] In contrast to the optional status of the OECD Model, the EU Directive is binding for all EU Member States.

[1]Council Directive 2003/49/EC of 3 June 2003 on a common system of taxation applicable to interest and royalty payments made between associated companies of different Member States (OJ L 157, 26.6.2003, p. 49), as amended (latest amendment: 13 May 2013, OJ 2013, L 141).

The mobility of copyright, the national tax rules and Article 12 of the bilateral tax treaties create options for international structuring, which owners of copyright use to ensure that copyright income falls into the lowest possible tax rate. The international economic world has taken action against abuse through the Anti Base Erosion and Profit Shifting (BEPS) program, led by the OECD. In particular, Actions 5 and 6 from the BEPS Package of October 2015[2] concern the mobility of royalties and other copyright income and seek to reduce avoidance while preserving the positive economic impact of the tax incentives for copyright income.

It has also been debated whether these tax incentives for copyright could be classified as state aid and harmful tax competition within the EU. The European Commission decided that this was not the case with the Spanish IP Box, as this tax incentive is not explicitly selective in favoring certain undertakings based on objective factors such as region, sector, size or legal form. EU Member States must always take into account state aid law and EU soft law on harmful tax competition when implementing tax incentives for copyright. EU state aid law is discussed in Chap. 5 of this book. Harmful tax competition is also discussed in Sect. 7 of this chapter.

2 Definitions

A copyright is an intangible property right that protects an original artistic or literary work. The owner of a copyright has the exclusive right to reproduce the copyrighted work, to prepare derivative works, to distribute copies or phonographic records of the copyrighted work, to perform the copyrighted work publicly or to display the copyrighted work publicly. Copyright regularly protects the following:

- literary, dramatic, musical and artistic works (traditionally called the "classical" copyrights);
- film, sound recordings, broadcasts and the typographical arrangement of published editions (often called "related rights", because they involve the exploitation of "classical" works);
- computer software and non-original databases (despite their modest credentials as "creative" works) and
- performances.

Copyright does not protect ideas, concepts, styles, techniques or information. For example, a person may write an outline of an idea for a TV show, which would itself be protected by copyright. Another person could write his own script using the same general ideas without necessarily infringing the copyright of the first person. This other person would only be infringing the copyright in the outline if he were to copy enough of the way the first person had structured the plot, scenes or conversations.

---

[2] http://www.oecd.org/ctp/beps-2015-final-reports.htm (Accessed 7 June 2016).

Some "works" are too small or unoriginal to be protected under copyright. For example, single words, names, titles, slogans and headlines are unlikely to be protected by copyright—although they may be protected in other ways, for example as trademarks.

Normally, a work is protected automatically from the time it is first written or recorded in some way, provided that it has resulted from the creator's skill and effort and is not simply copied from another work. In most cases, copyright lasts for the creator's lifetime plus seventy years.

Copyright gives the creator the right to prevent others from exploiting the work without permission. The form of restricted exploitation includes the following: copying the work; making the work available to the public; distributing the work; renting or lending it (excluding public lending); and translating, arranging or adapting the work. These restrictions enable the creator to charge a fee or royalty for the reproduction of the work.

Copyright owners can assign or license their rights. Assigning rights mean someone else becomes the owner; while licensing means another person can use the copyright material. Assignments and licenses can apply to all the rights in the material or to just one or some of the rights. For example, an author may give an assignment or license to reproduce his story in an anthology but retain all other rights.

A copyright is a property right that is separate from the copyrighted work. For example, one person might own the copyright to a manuscript and another person may own the manuscript itself.

Copyright is a form of intellectual property, together with patents and trademarks. A patent is an intangible property right that protects an invention. A patent gives its owner the right to exclude others from making, using, offering for sale or selling an invention without their permission in the countries for which the patent has been granted. A patent generally lasts for 20 years and is not renewable.[3]

A trademark is a recognizable sign, design, or expression which identifies products or services of a particular source from those of others. The trademark owner can be an individual, a business organization, or any legal entity. A trademark may be located on a package, a label, a voucher, or on the product itself. For the sake of corporate identity, trademarks are often displayed on company buildings.

Income from copyrights is often paid as a royalty. A royalty is a portion of the income from or share in the profits generated by a copyright, patent, trademark, or other similar asset or intellectual property. This income can also be fixed in one or more installments.

---

[3]Definition according to the European Patent Office (see www.epo.org and search for "glossary").

3 National Tax Rules: Deductions, Exemptions and Tax Rates

3.1 National Source Rules

3.1.1 Normal Tax Rules for Residents

Copyright income is often taxed under the normal rules for income or corporation tax for residents. Most states do not have separate rules or rates, but consider royalty income as business income for corporations, partnerships, sole proprietorships and other legal entities. This also applies to permanent establishments of non-residents in the state. Expenses are deductible, whether they are specific to the copyright or for overhead expenses.

Expenses incurred in the creation of a copyright (i.e. materials, utilities, and wages) as well as the on-going expenses for managing, improving and financing investments in the copyright are generally immediately deductible as business expenses. Capital expenditures such as the acquisition costs for machinery and buildings used for creating the copyright as well as for the acquisition of a copyright are not immediately deductible but instead subject to capital allowances or tax depreciation.

It is rarely required to capitalize self-developed intangible assets for tax accounting purposes, although many countries provide an option to do so upon meeting certain requirements (often similar to IAS 38: identifiably, probability of future economic benefits and the power to obtain these benefits, and the ability to measure the costs of the asset reliably). In some cases, this only applies to development expenses whereas research expenses may not be capitalized (Spengel and Zöllkau 2012, p. 58).

3.1.2 Source Withholding Tax for Non-residents

Most states do not only tax their residents, but also tax the income of non-residents which originates from the state (source income). This is either because the state wants a share of the pie from non-residents, as non-residents use the public infrastructure of the state to a certain extent, or because the state wants to prevent tax evasion should the income go to a low-tax territory or non-compliance should the income not be reported in the residence state.

The source tax will normally be levied as a withholding tax, for which the resident payer of the copyright income will be held liable. For many years this withholding tax was a lower rate than the regular rate, but without the possibility to deduct expenses. In addition, a normal tax settlement at the end of the year was not possible, meaning that the gross withholding tax became the final tax obligation. Rates varied from 10 to 30%, but were effectively higher because of the non-deductibility of the expenses.

This system has changed over the last decade, beginning with decisions by the European Court of Justice in cases about gross taxation within the EU. The Gerritse,[4] Scorpio[5] and Centro Equestre[6] cases made it clear not only that expenses should be deductible at the moment of the payment of the income, but also that the regular tax rates can then be applied on the net taxable income. EU Member States have mostly implemented these decisions in their national legislation and offer non-residents regular taxation for source income. States outside the EU have also made the tax rules for non-residents more flexible. A drawback of this is the increased administrative burden that accompanies the deduction of expenses and regular taxation, because tax returns must then be filed in many different states. Gross taxation at a lower rate reduces the administrative burden, but can be unfair when expenses are considerable.

3.2 *Tax Exemption in Ireland*

A full exemption was introduced in Ireland in 1969 with the Artists Tax Exemption Scheme. This scheme allowed the earnings of artists from the sale of original and creative works to be exempt from income tax. It applied to visual artists, composers of music, and writers. In order to qualify, the Revenue Commissioners had to make a determination that the works were original and generally recognized as having cultural or artistic merit. The Irish Income Tax Law specifically listed these works as: a book or other writing, a play, a musical composition, a painting or other like picture and a sculpture.[7] Those categories were interpreted in a broad enough manner to accommodate most of what comprises contemporary practice in the visual arts. For example, artists working in video, performance and other emerging experiential modes of practice were also listed as recipients of the tax exemption on the Revenue Commissioners website. The Irish tax authority was assisted in the interpretation of the act by guidelines drawn up by the Arts Council and the Arts Minister. The exemption was on income tax only—artists were still liable for VAT and PRSI. Artists were also liable for tax on income derived from other activities, such as teaching. Artists had to be resident in Ireland and not resident elsewhere, but were allowed to leave the state for a period of time and still retain the tax-exempt status, so that they could travel outside of Ireland to promote their work and widen their experience. Interpretative artists such as dancers, actors and performers were not eligible for tax exemptions.

The Scheme resulted in many artists, musicians and writers locating in Ireland to take advantage of its benefits. A small number of big acts and writers were said to

---

[4]ECJ 12 June 2003, C-234/01 (Arnoud Gerritse).

[5]ECJ 3 October 2006, C-290/04 (FKP Scorpio Konzertproduktionen GmbH).

[6]ECJ 15 February 2007, C-345/04 (Centro Equestre da Lezíria Grande Lda).

[7]Section 195 TCA.

benefit hugely from the scheme with their income from music publishing for example (but not sales of CDs etc.) being totally exempt from tax. These artists were, however, a high earning minority, and the average income of most qualifying artists was relatively low. In 1994, the cost was recorded as IEP5.1 million. This rose steadily to IEP36.8 million in 2000 but dipped to IEP23.9 million for 2002. While this may seem high, these figures must be seen in context, as the artists exemption represented just 0.15% of all tax expenditures in 2002.

Based on the Tax Returns received for 2001, the Revenue Commissioners were able to calculate that 694 artists claimed the exemption against sales for incomes of less than IEP10,000. A total of 456 artists claimed exemption on incomes between IEP10,000 and IEP50,000, while 114 artists claimed exemption on incomes of between IEP50,000 and IEP200,000. Only 59 artists claimed the exemption against income over 200,000.

The total income of this latter group of 59 artists (individuals earning over IEP200,000) which was exempted from tax was over 56 million. The total income exempted for tax by those 1,264 artists who earned under IEP200,000 was just over 23 million. The total income exempted from tax of those 694 artists who earned under IEP10,000 amounted to just IEP 2.7 million.

Since the scheme was initiated, over 8,400 applications for exemption have been received, of which over 6,300 have been granted. In 2004, 407 exemptions were issued of which 231 were for visual artists.

In 2004, Ireland began a debate over the need to review certain tax incentive schemes, including the Artists Tax Exemption Scheme. The government believed that the concept of unlimited or unrestricted relief was no longer acceptable to the general tax-paying public. However, a survey also noted that many visual artists live below the poverty line: 67% earn less than €10,000 from their creative works and a further 24% earn between €10,000 and €25,000, which means that they are dependent on other work and support to make ends meet.[8]

Influenced by a recommendation of the European Commission, in 2006 the tax exemption was subsequently capped at €250,000 per year. Because of the economic crisis, this was lowered in 2011 to a maximum of €40,000 per year and then raised to €50,000 in 2015.

More information about the conditions of the current exemption scheme is included in Chap. 11, Sect. 7.

3.3 *Tax Deduction in Quebec, Canada*

In 1995, the Province of Quebec in Canada introduced a tax exemption and deduction for copyright income of individuals. Artists with a professional status in the performing arts, recording, film, visual arts, crafts and literature are entitled to a

[8]Information comes from the website http://visualartists.ie, search for "artists tax exemption".

deduction for income from copyright. The copyright (or public lending right) must be for work of which the individual is the creator, for an exclusive right for a performance, for a sound recording of a performance or for the reproduction for private use of sound recordings.

The tax deduction applies to the Province tax of Quebec and not to the federal Canadian income tax. The tax rates vary from 16% (up to CAD42,000) to 25.75% (over CAD103,000). The schema allows a full exemption up to CAD30,000 copyright income per year and is descending above that amount, up to CAD60,000 per year, at which the deduction is nil. Above this amount, copyright income is taxed normally.[9]

The reason for the tax deduction is that it provides an incentive to those who create the nation's cultural products. Setting a reasonable upper limit of copyright income ensures that only those writers and artists most in need of the incentive benefit from the deduction.

3.4 Fixed Deduction and Flat Rate in Belgium

In 2009, Belgium introduced a fixed deduction and flat tax rate for copyright income for individuals and non-profit organizations. The Belgian government seeks to support the creation of copyright, strengthen the financial position of copyright holders and take into consideration the fact that the creation of the copyright may take many years, while the income can be received in a short period of time, in which the progressivity of the tax rates is heavier than over the total period. Therefore, Belgium has introduced a special tax regime for copyright income. This applies to original copyright from literature, art, music, choreography, sculptures, paintings, drawings, databases, computer software and such.

The special tax scheme goes up to approx. €57,000 gross copyright income per year. Above this amount the copyright income is taxed normally using the progressive tax rates.

First, the individual or non-profit organization can deduct a fixed amount for deemed expenses, regardless of whether real expenses have been made or to what amount. There is a 50% deduction of up to €15,000 of copyright income per year, a 25% deduction for income between €15,000 and €30,000 per year and no deduction above approximately €30,000 per year. The taxable amount after this deduction is taxed at a fixed rate of 15% per year.

Until 2012 this special tax was levied with a final withholding tax for which the payer of the copyright income was responsible and the income did not have to be mentioned in the annual income tax return. This was changed in 2012. Although the withholding obligation for the payer and the tax rate remained the same, the income must now be mentioned in the income tax return, so that the municipal surcharge

[9]Quebec Taxation Act, Section 726.26.

and other levies can also be based on this income.[10] This leads to a slightly higher effective tax rate.

3.5 *IP Boxes*

A growing number of developed economies have recently implemented intellectual property (IP) Box regimes. These give royalties and other income from intellectual property, such as copyright, a preferential tax treatment.

3.5.1 Eleven States with Special Tax Regimes, but not Always for Copyright

At the moment 11 states have regimes which can be classified as IP Boxes, as shown below in Table 1.[11] The last column shows whether copyright is included in the IP Box.

These IP Box regimes are all in European countries and fall broadly into two groups. One group (including Belgium, Luxembourg, the Netherlands, and the United Kingdom) has elements that are targeted at incentivizing R&D investment and innovation, which means that they focus on patents and other trade intangibles and do not apply to acquired IP. The second group (including Cyprus, Hungary, Malta, and the Swiss Canton of Nidwalden) focuses on attracting mobile IP income, in particular by not requiring any original R&D activity on behalf of the taxpayer.

Only five states facilitate copyright in their IP Box. These include Cyprus, Hungary, Liechtenstein, Malta and the Swiss Canton of Nidwalden.

3.5.2 Specific Aspects

The taxable amount for the IP Box rate is in most states the net income, which means that expenses should be allocated and then deducted from the qualifying IP income to come to the taxable IP profit. This is the case in Cyprus, France, Liechtenstein, Luxembourg, the Netherlands, Spain, Nidwalden (Switzerland) and the United Kingdom. Some other states, however, tax the gross income at the lower tax rate of the IP Box and allow the deduction of expenses against the other, normal earnings, which are taxed at the normal tax rate. This the case in Belgium and Hungary. This means that with considerable expenses, the net result can be higher

[10]Article 17, §1(5) and Article 37(2) WIB92.

[11]The special tax exemption for creative income in Ireland was discussed separately, because of the special scope and conditions.

Table 1 European IP boxes

State	Year	IP Box rate(%)	Normal tax rate(%)	Copyright
Belgium	2007	6,8	34	No
Cyprus	2011	2.5	10	Yes
France	2000	15.5	34	No
Hungary	2003	9.5	19	Yes
Liechtenstein	2011	2.5	12.5	Yes
Luxembourg	2008	5.8	29	No
Malta	2010	0	35	Yes
Netherlands	2007	5	25	No
Spain[a]	2008	12	30	No
Swiss Canton of Nidwalden	2011	8.8	13	Yes
United Kingdom	2013	10	20	No

[a]For an overview see Ibañez and Velasco (2013)

than the profit of the IP activities, because the tax due on the gross earnings is less than the tax advantage from the deductible expenses.

States may have a different approach towards R&D expenses which have been incurred in the past. Some states want these expenses to be recaptured and then deducted from the IP income, such as Liechtenstein, Luxembourg, Malta, the Netherlands and the United Kingdom. Other states leave the expenses as they have been deducted and do not want a recapture, such as Belgium, Cyprus, France, Hungary Spain and Nidwalden, Switzerland.

In some countries the benefits of the low IP Box tax rate are capped. This may be designed in absolute terms or in relation to the R&D expenses or the overall profits. In Hungary, the notional deduction of 50% of qualifying IP income is limited to 50% of the overall profits.

3.6 R&D Tax Deductions

The normal rules for expenses for creating copyright are that they can be written off directly as tax-deductible expenses (see Sect. 3.1.1). But sometimes, expenses must be capitalized, put as an asset on the balance sheet and deducted from the later sale of the copyright or from other taxable earnings.

Many states offer tax incentives for investment in R&D and innovation in the form of tax credits and additional deductions (i.e. super deduction, enhanced deduction) for R&D expenses. As a consequence, the tax deductions exceed the amount which has actually been incurred. Besides this, some countries offer immediate or accelerated depreciation for assets used for R&D activity. Among the eleven countries only Cyprus, Liechtenstein and the Swiss Canton of Nidwalden do not have R&D tax credits, super deductions or accelerated depreciation for R&D assets in place.

4 Income from Copyright and Tax Treaties

4.1 Tax Treaties, OECD Model Income Tax Convention

Double taxation is very likely when copyright income is taxed both in the source state and in the residence state. This would be a barrier to international trade and therefore states concluded bilateral agreements with each other over one-hundred years ago. These tax treaties include a separate article on royalties, the collective term for copyright income. In 1963, the OECD began to coordinate these bilateral tax treaties with a Model Income Tax Convention. Not only the Member States but also other states are following this Model, sometimes with adjustments. Also, the UN Model Double Taxation Convention between developed and developing countries and the US Model Income Tax Convention have a special clause for royalties, with comparable wording.

Eliminating international double taxation can also be regarded as a tax incentive for the creative industries, since most states only concluded between 30 and 70 bilateral tax treaties, meaning that for most states there is a high risk of double taxation. Other states, however, are very active in concluding and renegotiating their bilateral tax treaties, which means that there is a tax advantage for their residents when receiving copyright income when compared to other states.

4.2 Article 12 for Royalties

The OECD recommends the use of Article 12 of its Model Income Tax Convention for royalties. This article eliminates possible double taxation by allocating the taxing right solely to the state of residence of the beneficial owner of the royalties. This is where the owner of the copyright or the person to which the copyright has been licensed has his or her residence[12] or permanent establishment.[13] The source state of the royalties must allow a full tax exemption when this wording of Article 12 has been adopted in a bilateral tax treaty.

The term royalties for Article 12 is defined as follows[14]:

> payments of any kind received as a consideration for the use of, or the right to use, any copyright of literary, artistic or scientific work including cinematograph films, any patent, trade mark, design or model, plan, secret formula or process, or for information concerning industrial, commercial or scientific experience.

---

[12] Art. 12(1) OECD Model Tax Convention. A definition for the term "resident" has been given in Art. 4 of the OECD Model Tax Convention.

[13] Art. 12(3) OECD Model Tax Convention. This is under the condition that the copyright is effectively connected with the permanent establishment.

[14] Art. 12(2) OECD Model Tax Convention.

This definition covers the term copyright as discussed in this chapter. The term "beneficial owner" is not used in a narrow technical sense. Rather, it should be understood in its context and in light of the object and purposes of the tax treaty, including avoiding double taxation and the prevention of fiscal evasion and avoidance.[15]

The beneficial owner is not an agent or nominee receiving royalties on behalf of someone else, which means that this representative will be taxed in the source state when he does not identify the real beneficial owner.[16] This is also the case with conduit companies, which only want to receive the royalties because of preferential tax treatment, but pay them (almost) completely through to the beneficial owner, most often in a low-tax jurisdiction. Such a conduit company is not the beneficial owner, and the source state will not allow an exemption for the source tax.[17]

When the payment of the royalties is made to a person in a state other than that of the beneficial owner, the source tax can still be exempted when the state of residence of the beneficial owner and the source state of the royalties have included a royalty article comparable to article 12 of the OECD Model in their bilateral tax treaty.[18]

4.3 *Use of Article 12 in Bilateral Tax Treaties*

Most states follow the OECD recommendation completely and exempt outgoing royalties at the source in treaty situations. Other states, however, still wish to tax royalties arising in their state at the source. Some have mentioned this as a reservation on Article 12 OECD Model, such as Australia, Chile, Greece, Czech Republic, Canada, Italy, Korea, New Zealand, Poland, Portugal, Slovak Republic, Spain and Turkey. But there are differences in the types of copyright they wish to tax at particular source tax rates. Royalties from, for example, music copyrights can be taxed at a different rate than royalties from industrial design. Almost always, the payer of the royalties will then be responsible for the withholding of the tax at the source. The rates vary from 5 to 30%.

In order to obtain the tax exemption or the lower tax rate, most source states require non-residents to file an application form. The form must be completed with information about the payer and recipient, the type of copyright and the amount of royalties. It will most often also have to be signed and stamped by the tax

---

[15]Para. 4 of the Commentary on Art. 12 OECD Model Tax Convention.

[16]Para. 4.1 of the Commentary on Art. 12 OECD Model Tax Convention.

[17]Para. 4.2 of the Commentary on Art. 12 OECD Model Tax Convention. See also the report from the Committee on Fiscal Affairs entitled "Double Taxation Conventions and the Use of Conduit Companies", OECD (1986).

[18]Para. 4.3 of the Commentary on Art. 12 OECD Model Tax Convention.

authorities of the resident state, which confirms that the recipient is resident there and can make use of the royalty article of the relevant tax treaty.[19]

The state of residence of the recipient of the royalties will also tax the income, but will allow a tax credit to eliminate international double taxation. This tax credit method[20] is regularly used for passive income with only a low source tax, such as interest, dividend and royalties.

When the tax treaty provides for an exemption or lower rate in the source state, it is important to apply for that benefit and not leave the original national source withholding tax in place. The state of residence will not allow a tax credit when an exemption has been agreed or only allow a tax credit for the lower tax rate mentioned in the tax treaty. When the exemption or lower tax rate is not applied for, the recipient will end up with international double taxation on the copyright income.

5 EU Directive for Income from Copyright

The common market principle has caused the European Union to introduce its own regulation for cross-border royalties between affiliated companies.[21] Provided certain requirements have been met, the Royalty and Interest Directive obliges EU Member States to exempt certain royalty income from source taxation. The main purpose of this Directive is to prevent double taxation. This is also the purpose of bilateral tax treaties and the OECD Model Tax Convention. Furthermore, the definition of royalties in the EU Directive is comparable to the definition in Article 12 of the OECD Model Tax Convention; it completely covers income from copyright. However, the EU Directive is restricted to royalty (and interest) payments between companies (or persons) in the same group. Affiliated companies for the EU Directive refers to ownership of at least 25% of the shares of the subsidiary in another EU Member State. States have the option to change this criterion to 25% of the voting rights. As a binding Directive for all EU Member States and with the European Court of Justice as appeal institute, this directive is stronger than a bilateral tax treaty. It eliminates cash flow problems stemming from the deduction of source withholding tax first and refund procedures after the taxable year, which means that it also reduces administrative expenses. The recipient of the royalties must be the beneficial owner of the copyright to qualify for the source tax

---

[19]Within the EU, this exemption application procedure is not against the freedom principles of the TFEU, because a state is allowed to certify that a treaty exemption really applies. This was decided in ECJ 3 October 2006, C-290/04 (FKP Scorpio Konzertproduktionen).

[20]See Article 23B OECD Model Tax Convention.

[21]Royalty and Interest Directive 2003/49/EU (as amended with Directives 2004/76/EU and 2006/96/EU).

exemption under the Royalty and Interest Directive, under the additional condition that this must be already so two years before the application for the exemption. This EU Directive also applies to Switzerland.[22]

6 International Structuring

Copyright owners or licensees may experience international double taxation when there is no tax treaty with the source state and the EU Directive does not apply. This problem can be solved with international structuring of the copyright, in which it is licensed to a company in a state with tax treaties with both the source state of the royalties (and many other states) and the residence state of the original copyright owner. When this license company has enough substance and activities in its residence state, such as its own office in which the exploitation of the copyright and audit of the royalties is initiated, it will be recognized in the source state as the beneficial owner of the royalties and therefore qualify for the tax treaty exemption or lower rate. Under the license agreement the license company can pay royalties to the original copyright holder. However, it can also keep the profit, be taxed in its resident state, and pay dividends to its shareholder. This is a legal and acceptable way of preventing international double taxation and is often used in the creative industries.

Structuring can also be set up as a tax avoidance scheme. When the state of residence of the license company does not impose a source tax on outgoing royalties (or even dividend), it is relatively easy to transfer a large portion of the royalties to a low-tax jurisdiction. Many tax firms have dealt with these structures and tax administrations of some states are willing to confirm the substance of the license companies and the transfer pricing arguments for the royalty payments to the foreign copyright owners.

7 The BEPS Report

7.1 International Action

Preferential tax regimes and international structuring have been criticized for years, even when they are technically legal according to the tax laws of the states involved. The critics focus not only on the use of low-tax jurisdictions, but also on the transfer of income from a state with the real activity to a state with a lower tax rate.

Acting under the initiative of the G20, the OECD began to address the issue in 2012 with the action plan "Addressing Base Erosion and Profit Shifting" (BEPS). In

[22]EU 20 December 2004, nr. L385/36.

addition to the 30 OECD Member States, 80 developing states and other non-OECD and non-G20-states took part in this project. International tax issues have never been so high on the international political agenda. This led to the final BEPS Report of 8 October 2015 on Action 1 to 14.[23] The leaders of the G20 states confirmed this report on 15 and 16 November 2015 in Antalya, Turkey.

Together the Actions form a comprehensive and cohesive approach to the international framework, influencing domestic law, tax treaties and transfer pricing guidelines. The conclusions can be divided into minimum standards, common approaches and guidance based on best practices. Most states have committed themselves to the results of the BEPS report and are now working on implementation. The EU Member States also have a joint approach and adopted coordinated measures regarding several Actions.

7.2 Action 5 and Preferential Tax Regimes

The OECD has devoted part of Action 5 of the BEPS report to copyright income. Entitled "Countering Harmful Tax Practices More Effectively, Taking into Account Transparency and Substance", the first part of this report concerns income from intellectual property (IP) rights. The report introduces minimum standards for determining whether there are substantial activities under preferential regimes and whether there is enough transparency on rulings, and for domestic law provisions for IP regimes. With these measures Action 5 should avoid harmful tax competition.

The OECD has achieved consensus on the so called "nexus approach", which uses expenditure as a proxy for activity. This means that preferential regimes may grant benefits to a taxpayer only when the taxpayer undertook the activities required to produce the income covered by the preferential regime. The result is that income is taxed where the economic activities take place and the value is created, but it will not take away the opportunity for states to have an IP regime with lower tax rates.

This means that tax incentives for copyright are still possible under Action 5 of the BEPS package. However, a direct link between the development of the copyright and the copyright income is required. It seems that the tax exemptions (or deductions) in Ireland, Quebec and Belgium can be continued. However, the IP boxes for copyright in Cyprus, Hungary, Liechtenstein, Malta and the Swiss Canton of Nidwalden may now be problematic since it is unlikely that all copyrights were created there.

---

[23]http://www.oecd.org/ctp/beps-2015-final-reports.htm (Accessed 7 June 2016).

7.3 Action 6 and International Structuring

The OECD has devoted Action 6, "Preventing the Granting of Treaty Benefits in Inappropriate Circumstances", mainly to international structuring. Its main purpose is to set minimum standards against treaty shopping. Treaty shopping can be defined as the artificial creation of conduit companies without relevant substance in a state to make use of tax treaties and avoid taxation in the source state of the income. Action 6 comprises three measures: the principal purpose test, the limitation on benefits clause and a clear statement in tax treaties against tax avoidance and treaty shopping. When these measures are implemented, it will become harder for copyright owners to set up international structures with conduit companies to take away the risk of double taxation or to relocate copyright income to a low-tax jurisdiction.

8 Conclusion

Copyright is important for the creative industries and can be very mobile and therefore international. Some states try to attract copyright (and other IP assets) with preferential tax regimes, including special deductions and lower tax rates. Examples can be found in Ireland, Canada and Belgium, but also in the IP Boxes in eleven European states. When states expect to receive more tax revenue from these incentives, they may be disappointed. Because of tax competition the net tax result is most often lower than forecasted. But states also want to use the lower tax rates for copyright income as incentives for R&D activities, which can lead to more economic activity and employment, which in turn generates more tax revenue. States may also use as an argument for lower (and fixed) tax rates that the creation of the copyright may have taken years, while the copyright income may come in peaks. This is also one of the findings from the Mirrlees Review (2011), p. 473:

> We should try to assess the progressivity of the tax system in terms of people's lifetime resources, not just in annual snapshots.

Copyright income, such as royalties, can come from foreign sources, which means that taxation of the income may be taxed in both the source state and the state of residence. Most tax treaties follow Article 12 of the OECD Model and allocate the taxing right to the residence state, although many tax treaties also give the source state the right to levy tax at a relatively low tax rate. The residence state must then allow a tax credit to eliminate double taxation. The differences between states make international structuring possible, either to take away the international double taxation because of the lack of tax treaties, or to transfer most of the copyright income to low-tax jurisdictions. The second activity in particular has caused the G20 to instruct the OECD to study opportunities to counteract these tax-avoidance schemes. This has resulted in the 2015 BEPS Project, of which Action 5 and 6 are important for copyright.

The final conclusion is that there are still interesting tax incentives available for copyright, but that the international community has become more aware of unfair tax competition and abuse and has taken actions against it. The BEPS project will not be the final step in making the tax rules fairer and more transparent, but after that states may still use tax incentives to stimulate and attract copyright in their territory.

References

Alstadtsaeter A, Barrios S, Nicodeme G, Skonieczna AM, Vezzani A (2015) Patent boxes design, patents location and local R&D. Working Paper N. 57, European Commission, DG TAXUD

de Wilde M (2016) OESO – Actiepunten BEPS, Nederlandse Documentatie voor Fiscaal Recht, The Hague

Directorate-General for Internal Policies (2015) Intellectual property box regimes, European Commission

Eastaway N, Gallafent R, Dauppe V, Kimber J (2013) Intellectual property law and taxation. Sweet & Maxwell, Thomson Reuters, London

Evers L, Miller H, Spengel C (2013) Intellectual property box regimes: effective tax rates and tax policy considerations. Zentrum für Europäische Wirtschaftsforschung (ZEW), Mannheim

Ibañez A, Velasco S (2013) Spain—government publishes draft tax reforms. Tax Notes Int 788–789

Mirrlees Review (2011) Reforming the tax system for the 21th century. Oxford University Press, p 473

OECD Model Income Tax Convention (2014) Paris

OECD (2015) Final BEPS package for reform of the international tax system to tackle tax avoidance http://www.oecd.org/ctp/beps-2015-final-reports.htm. Accessed 7 Jun 2016

Spengel C, Zöllkau Y (eds) (2012) Common Corporate Tax Base (CC(C)TB) and determination of taxable income: an international comparison. Springer, Heidelberg

Chapter 11
Tax Incentives for Artists

Dick Molenaar

Abstract Artists are key players in the creative industries who create and perform the work. Many of them are in an economically vulnerable situation and some countries prefer to have more artists than the market would otherwise allow. This desire leads those countries to enact financial support measures, such as tax incentives. In addition, goals such as preserving national culture and stimulating the economic impact of artists may also be reasons for these tax incentives. This chapter examines several examples of tax incentives, including the value-added tax exemption and reduced rate in the EU, the Theatre Tax Relief and Orchestra Tax Relief in the UK, the Theater Tax Benefit in the USA, the option for artists to pay taxes with artwork in Mexico, and the income tax exemption for authors, composers, painters and sculptors in Ireland. In the conclusion, these tax incentives are compared with the criteria for fairness, effectiveness, complexity and visibility outlined in Chap. 4 and for state aid in Chap. 5.

Keywords Artist · VAT exemption · Reduced VAT rate · Orchestra tax relief · Theatre tax relief · Theatre tax benefit · Pago en especie · Artist's exemption

1 Introduction

Artists are important players in creative industries because they create what can be seen and used by others. Some artists are very successful, become well-known and can have considerable earnings, while others are not directly commercially profitable, because not every piece of art has sufficient demand to generate enough income for an artist to live on. Developed societies, though, find it important that

D. Molenaar
Department of Tax Law, Erasmus School of Law,
Erasmus University Rotterdam, Rotterdam, The Netherlands

D. Molenaar (✉)
All Arts Tax Advisers, Rotterdam, The Netherlands
e-mail: dmolenaar@allarts.nl

© Springer Science+Business Media Singapore 2017

S. Hemels and K. Goto (eds.), *Tax Incentives for the Creative Industries*,
Creative Economy, DOI 10.1007/978-981-287-832-8_11

there are enough artists to generate experimentation, new directions, developments, opinions, discussions and insights. These societies believe that their quality level is related to the amount of freedom in which artists can work and create their art and present their work to the public. This preference for having more artists than the economic balance of the market would allow therefore creates the need for funding for artists, either through subsidies or tax incentives.

Another reason for these tax incentives may be that governments find the market position of artists vulnerable, which leads to lower income than wanted. Tax incentives, other than subsidies, will create more economic activity by the artists in order to obtain a financial advantage.

In addition, the protection and stimulus of a country's own culture and heritage may also serve as a reason for tax incentives. In a globalizing world, the cultural expression from other countries may become overpowering and a country can take measures to protect its own culture with tax incentives. This can be combined with the acknowledgement of the contribution of artists and culture to the economy, which may potentially be increased with tax incentives, not only in the country itself, but also as an export product abroad.

Elements from previous chapters are important to consider for this chapter. Some tax incentives for artists have common ground with tax incentives in the other chapters of Part II of this book, but overlap should be avoided. In such cases, the tax incentive will only briefly be discussed.

The theoretical context in Part I, such as the economic theory (Chap. 3), and the theory of tax incentives (Chap. 4) and state aid (Chap. 5) will be used as the measuring staff for the conclusion of this chapter. This chapter will approach tax incentives from the perspective of the artist.

2 Terminology and Definitions

For this chapter, an artist can be either a performing or creating artist. Or both, given that many musicians and comedians themselves create the work that they perform.

For a performing artist the word "artiste" is very often used and various dictionaries give the following meanings to that word:

- "A professional person in any of the performing arts; a person very skilled in his work; often humorous or facetious" (Webster's New World Dictionary 2014);
- "An artist, especially an actor, singer, dancer, or other public performer" (Random House Webster's Unabridged Dictionary 2001); and
- "A public performer who appeals to the aesthetic faculties, as a professional singer, dancer, etc." (Oxford Dictionary of English 2010).

However, the word "entertainer" is also a key word to consider, as it is very often used instead of "performing artist", such as in Article 17 of the OECD Model

Tax Convention. The dictionaries give the following meaning for the word "entertainer":

- "Professional provider of amusement" (Concise Oxford Dictionary 2011);
- "A person whose job is amusing or interesting people, for example, by singing, telling jokes or dancing" (Oxford Advanced Learner's Dictionary 2010); and
- "A person, such as a singer, dancer, or comedian, whose job is to entertain others" (Oxford Dictionary of English 2010).

The word "entertainer" seems to cover the lighter versions of the performing arts, comparable with the term *Unterhaltungskunst* (*U-Kunst*) in the German language, while the word "artiste" seems to cover the more serious expressions of performing arts, such as classical dance, music, theatre and opera, comparable with the term *Hochkunst (H-Kunst)* in the German language.

For the word "artist", the various dictionaries give the following meanings:

- "A person who works in or is skilled in the techniques of any of the fine arts, especially in painting, drawing, sculpture, etc." (Webster's New World Dictionary 2014);
- "A person who creates paintings or drawings as a profession or hobby" (Oxford Dictionary of English 2010); and
- "A person who creates works of art, especially paintings or drawings" (Oxford Advanced Learner's Dictionary 2010)

Composers and authors are also artists because they are creating art. This makes the definition broader than in the various meaning listed in the dictionaries.

3 EU: VAT Exemptions and Reduced Rate

The EU recognizes in the Treaty on the Functioning of the European Union (TFEU) that culture is important in society and that the EU shall contribute to the "flowering of the cultures, while respecting their national and regional diversity and the same time bringing the common cultural heritage to the fore".[1] This recognition leads to many measures in directives and council regulations for financially supporting culture and allowing exceptions to the general principles, such as for state aid, to promote culture.[2]

Also, artists are profiting from this through VAT exemptions and reduced VAT rates, which are specified in the VAT Directive. These policies classify artists and their work in the list of basic necessities, which may completely shield them from VAT or only apply a low rate for VAT. The EU VAT is a consumption tax but it is levied on businesses, which are required to charge the VAT on goods and services.

---

[1]Art. 167 TFEU.

[2]Art. 107(3)(d) TFEU.

The VAT can be refunded by other businesses but not by consumers. The net effect of this is that each supplier in the business chain remits the tax on the value that each has added, while ultimately the tax is paid by the end consumer.

The harmonization of the EU VAT is an important aspect of the single market. VAT is mentioned in the TFEU[3] and has been worked out in VAT Directives. It started in 1977 with the Sixth Directive, while currently the EU VAT Directive 2006/112/EC applies. Under this directive, the Member States apply a normal VAT rate between 17 and 27% (cannot be lower than 15%),[4] but they may also carve out exemptions and have the option of applying reduced rates for specific goods and services (cannot be lower than 5%).[5]

The VAT has been criticized in the past because of its heavy burden on people with lower income. Even at the introduction of the first turnover tax in the German city of Bremen in 1862, Lasalle (1873) commented that this indirect tax was unfair because it did not tax people on the basis of their income but on the basis of their needs. Therefore, in the EU VAT system, exemptions and a reduced rate were introduced to take away this disadvantage for goods and services that are considered to be basic necessities and most often are used by people with a lower income.

3.1 VAT Exemptions

The exemptions from the VAT Directive are obligatory for the Member States to implement. For artists, the following exemption is applicable:

> the supply of certain cultural services, and the supply of goods closely linked thereto, by bodies governed by public law or by other cultural bodies recognized by the Member State concerned.[6]

There is no official explanation from the EU for this exemption. Some guidance can be found in decisions of the European Court of Justice, which has issued several decisions about this exemption and comparable exemptions in the VAT Directive. To qualify, services should be in the public interest, which differs from a commercial interest.[7] However, this does not mean that services resulting in a profit should be excluded, as long as services as a whole do not have a commercial purpose.[8] This means that an exempt organization can have a business, but the proceeds must be used for a cultural, and thus public, interest.[9]

---

[3]Art. 113 TFEU.

[4]Art. 97 EU Directive 2006/112/EC.

[5]Art. 99 EU Directive 2006/112/EC.

[6]Art. 132(n) EU Directive 2006/112/EC.

[7]ECJ 21 March 2002, C-174/00 (Kennemer Golfclub).

[8]ECJ 26 May 2005, C-498/03 (Kingcrest).

[9]ECJ 21 January 2016, C-225/14 (Les Jardins de Jouvence).

Unfortunately, the ECJ to date has not issued a clear definition of "cultural services". It had the chance in two decisions about artists, authors, photographers, composers and play writers and about the importation of works of art, but did not go further than deciding in both cases that the exemption did not apply.[10] There were also two ECJ decisions in which the exemption was accepted, but in those cases the cultural aspect of the services was not under discussion.[11]

As a result, despite the obligatory status of the exemption, the EU Member States have much room to maneuver with this exemption and to decide which cultural goods and services they want to exempt and which conditions must be met.

3.2 VAT Reduced Rate

Reduced VAT rates are mentioned both in in the Directive itself and in an Annex to the Directive. In both situations the use of a reduced rate is optional, so that Member States have the freedom to choose whether and how to implement it in their national VAT legislation. Also, these provisions are not "all or nothing", meaning that Member States can use as many or as few of these options as they want, and they can even make use of just parts of the options. The only restriction is that comparable goods and services have to be treated equal.[12]

3.2.1 Works of Art, Collector's Items and Antiques

The optional reduced VAT rate can be implemented by EU Member States for works of art, collector's items and antiques in the following three situations:[13]

- the importation of works of art, collector's items and antiques;
- the supply of works of art by their creator or his successor in title; and
- the supply of works of art by a person other than a taxable dealer, where the works of art have been imported by the taxable person himself, or where they have been supplied to him by their creator or his successors in title, or where they have entitled him to full deduction of VAT.

This reduced rate is discussed extensively in Sect. 4 of Chap. 9, and will not be explained further here. The definition of "works of art" is very interesting, as it was

[10]ECJ 17 October 1991, C-35/90 (Commission/Spain) and ECJ 7 March 2002, C-169/00 (Commission/France).

[11]ECJ 3 April 2003, C-144/00 (Matthias Hoffman) and ECJ 21 March 2002, C-267/00 (Zoological Society of London).

[12]ECJ 3 May 2001, C-481/98, ECJ 8 May 2003, C-384/01, ECJ 23 October 2003, C-109/02 and ECJ 6 May 2010, C-094/09 (Commission/France). The ECJ decided that comparable goods and services that are competing directly should have the same VAT rate to avoid unfair competition.

[13]Art. 103 of EU Directive 2006/112/EC.

written in 1995 and has not been changed since then. It has many restrictions and exclusions and is not open for new artistic developments. This is strange for a sector that thrives on change and development and very often leads the way for other sectors. This definition is discussed in Sect. 4.1 of Chap. 9.

3.2.2 Admission and Services

The optional reduced VAT rate can also be implemented by EU Member States for two artistic and cultural services:[14]

(1) admission to shows, theatres, circuses, fairs, amusement parks, concerts, museums, zoos, cinemas, exhibitions and similar cultural events and facilities; and
(2) supply of services by writers, composers and performing artists, or of the royalties due to them.

The events for which the admission may fall under the reduced rate are very different from each other; they vary from culture to mere entertainment. There seems to be no logic behind it; the EU appears simply to want to give its Member States the opportunity to bring down the tax burden for these events. It is an important and effective measure because almost only consumers make use of these events and for them the VAT is the final tax.

This differs from artistic services, which normally are rendered to other taxable persons, so that the VAT can be reclaimed as input tax and does not lead to a tax burden. Still, the artists' services may potentially be subject to the reduced VAT rate in situations where these services are provided to consumers or exempted organizations.

3.2.3 Use of the Reduced VAT Rate in the EU

Many EU Member States apply the reduced rate for works of art and artistic and cultural services mentioned above, but often not in the same way. An overview is available on the EU website[15] and is provided in Table 1.

Table 1 shows that there is no common approach among the EU Member States for how to use the three options for the reduced VAT rate. Within the Member States, variations also exist within a specific category. These differences make this tax incentive very uncertain in the EU even as it seeks to be a single market without borders.

---

[14] Annex III to EU Directive 2006/112/EC.

[15] Search for "VAT rates", "EU", "2016" (http://ec.europa.eu/taxation_customs/resources/documents/taxation/vat/how_vat_works/rates/vat_rates_en.pdf).

Table 1 VAT rate for works of art, admission and services of artists

	Work of art VAT rate	Admission VAT rate	Services VAT rate
Austria	13	10/ex[#]	13/20
Belgium	6	6/ex	6/21/ex
Bulgaria	20	20/ex	20
Croatia	25	5/13/25	25/ex
Czech Republic	21	15	15
Cyprus	5	5/ex	5
Denmark*	25	25/ex	ex
Estonia	20	20	20
Finland	10	10	10/ex
France	5.5	5.5/20	5.5
Germany	7	7/ex	7
Greece	23	6/23	23
Hungary	27	18/27	27
Ireland	13.5	9/ex	23
Italy	10	10	22/ex
Latvia	21	21/ex	ex
Lithuania	21	21/ex	21
Luxembourg	8	3	17
Malta	18	5/18	18
Netherlands	6	6	6/ex
Poland	8	8	8/ex
Portugal	6	13/23/ex	23/ex
Romania	20	5	20
Slovakia	20	20/ex	20
Slovenia	9.5	9.5	9.5
Spain	10	21/ex	21
Sweden	12	6	6
United Kingdom	20	20	20

[#]'ex' means exempt
[*]These Member States do not use a reduced tax rate

3.2.4 Comparison of VAT Exemptions and Reduced Rate

A major difference between a VAT exemption and a reduced VAT rate is the effect on the reclaim of the input tax. When a taxable person or the supply of the good or service is exempted, there is no right to reclaim the input tax on the expenses. With mixed activities, thus partly taxable and partly exempted, the effect on the input tax is as follows:

- direct expenses for the taxable activities can be fully reclaimed;
- direct expenses for the exempted activities cannot be reclaimed; and
- overhead expenses can be partly reclaimed (pro rata taxable/total activities).

However, when the reduced VAT rate applies, there is no negative effect on the input tax because it can be fully reclaimed. When the balance is negative, this will lead to a VAT refund.

Whether a VAT exemption or a reduced rate is more profitable depends on the amount of the input tax. This is an important aspect for governments when they decide on their tax policy and the use of tax incentives. Regardless, it is clear that when an exemption is used within the business chain, the non-deductibility of the input tax will have a cumulative effect and is most often very negative. This may be different at the end of the business chain, when the exemption would replace the normal VAT rate. On the other hand, the low VAT rate may lead to a better result when the input tax is considerable.

4 UK: Theatre Tax Relief and Orchestra Tax Relief

The UK has introduced two tax incentives for artists in 2014 and 2016, the Theatre Tax Relief and the Orchestra Tax Relief, respectively. These incentives are part of the Creative Industry Tax Relief (CITR). The other CITR items are aimed at audiovisual industries and have been discussed in Sect. 3.4.3 of Chap. 8.

4.1 Theatre Tax Relief

The Theatre Tax Relief (TTR) is a creative industry tax incentive to encourage and support both touring and non-touring theatrical productions in the UK. The reason for the introduction of the TTR is that public funding has declined under the Conservative government, but that theatre is a big part of people's lives and is a big driver of UK tourism. According to Osborne (2014), the TTR can make theatre more attractive for potential investors, helping to boost investment in new shows, especially for riskier productions.

The TTR entered into force on 1 September 2014, after a consultation and preparation period and is available to production companies that are responsible for the production, operation and closing of a theatre production. Eligible production companies can be a commercial company, but may also be a charity or charity's trading subsidiary.

To qualify, the production company must

- be actively engaged in the decision making at all stages of the production;
- make an "effective" creative, technical and artistic contribution to the production; and
- directly negotiate for, contract for, and pay for rights, goods and services in relation to the production.

The maximum claim for qualifying companies is either

- an additional tax deduction (the enhancement) of 100% of enhanceable expenditure; or
- if a loss is surrendered: for touring performances 25% and for static performances (a performance which remains in the same place) 20% of the loss up to the amount of enhanceable expenditure.

The conditions for the Theatre Tax Relief are

- at least 25% of the production costs are incurred in the European Economic Area (EEA);
- a theatrical production includes a ballet, play, opera, musical, circus or other dramatic piece;
- performances must be live for an audience, including performances in schools;
- a production may be a touring production or static production;
- only professional theatrical productions qualify, because it is the intention that the performances are given to paying members of the public or provided for educational purposes. However, there is no cultural test to pass to qualify for and claim TTR.

No relief will be allowed when

- the performance is for an advertising or promotional purpose;
- the performance consists of or includes an element of competition or contest;
- a wild animal is to be used in any performance;
- the production is of a sexual nature;
- making a relevant recording is one of the main objectives of the production.

The enhanceable expenditure is the lesser of

- the EEA qualifying expenditure; or
- 80% of the total qualifying expenditure.

The expenditure qualifies if it is incurred in relation to the producing and closing of the production, such as casting costs, equipment rental, visual and sound effects, costumes and props and rehearsal costs. Expenditures for the ordinary running of the production do not qualify, although a substantial recasting or set redesign during the run of the production may qualify.

TTR can be obtained through the normal UK corporation tax return[16] Most UK theatre production companies will be liable to pay corporation tax but for those which are not, such as charities, or those otherwise not required to pay corporation tax because of losses, the relief can be obtained by means of a cash payment from the UK tax authorities.

---

[16]Part 15C CTA.

The following two examples highlight the application of the TTR.

1. Tax relief for taxable touring theatre production: income from the production £4 million; total expenditure £3 million, of which £1.5 million is qualifying expenditure. Tax relief will be 1.5 million × 80 × 25% = £300,000. The corporation tax of 20% from the profit of 1.0 million = £200,000 will then be brought down to nil and a cash payment of £100,000 for the remainder will be given.
2. Cash payment for non-taxable non-touring opera production: income from the production £1.5 million; total expenditure £2.5 million, of which £2 million is qualifying expenditure. Cash payment will be £2 million × 80 × 20% = £320,000.

In 2015, theatre companies across the UK have benefited from an estimated £25 million of tax relief from this tax incentive.[17] The regular government funding from Arts Council England is £310 million per year. The UK culture minister has emphasized that TTR is not a substitute for core public funding, but an encouragement for producers to make more shows.

There is a specialist unit of the UK tax authorities, HM Revenue and Customs (HMRC), dealing with the claims for TTR called the Creative Industries Unit in Glasgow.[18]

4.2 *Orchestra Tax Relief*

Orchestra Tax Relief (OTR) was created along the same lines as TTR. The reason for this tax incentive is that the UK orchestras are heard across the country and around the world, and provide enrichment and education to millions of people each year. The UK government wants to encourage orchestras to promote British culture in a sustainable way and to boost economic activity in the creative sector. The new tax relief recognizes the artistic importance and cultural value of British orchestras and its objective is to support orchestras so they can perform for a wide range of audiences. The UK government (2015) expects that the tax incentive will cost £10 million per year. OTR began on 1 April 2016, after a consultation and preparation period.

The maximum claim that may be filed, up to a maximum relief per company of £50 million, is calculated for qualifying companies as either

- an additional tax deduction (the enhancement) of 100% of enhanceable expenditure; or

---

[17]HMRC data.

[18]HMRC published a Theatre Tax Relief Manual on 12 December 2015 with detailed information on definitions, conditions, exclusions, application and appeal procedures.

- if a loss is surrendered, 25% of the loss up to the amount of enhanceable expenditure.

The conditions for Orchestra Tax Relief are as follows:

- qualifying companies must be directly engaged in the production of live orchestral performances;
- performances must be played by a musical ensemble of 12 or more performers;
- most of the instruments used are not directly or electronically amplified;
- players in the orchestra must be the primary focus of each performance;
- all sorts of music can be played, thus not only classical but also pop and rock;
- no distinction is made between touring and static productions;
- the performance must be given to paying members of the general public or provided for educational purposes; and
- each performance must be live with the players actually present before their audience.

No relief will be allowed when

- the entertainment has a competitive element;
- advertising is the sole or main purpose of the performance; or
- the performance is intended solely or mainly for recording or broadcast.

The enhanceable expenditure is the lesser of

- EEA qualifying expenditure; or
- 80% of total qualifying expenditure.

Tax relief is given for creative and production costs incurred in producing live orchestral performances or commissioning new musical work. Rehearsal costs are included but performance costs are not.

When a company claims OTR, it will not be able to claim relief under another tax credit scheme, such as film, theatre or research and development tax relief. The practical examples for OTR are comparable to TTR.

5 USA: Theatre Tax Benefit

The USA has also introduced a theatre tax incentive as of 2016. In December 2015, the US Congress passed changes to the tax law that provides tax relief to Broadway theatre producers.[19] This law creates the same tax treatment for theatre as for film and television production, both of which already had such tax benefit.

[19]Protecting Americans From Tax Hikes Act of 2015.

Under the benefit, a deduction of 100% of an investment is allowed in the year of the investment,[20] while income from the theatre project is tax-free up to 9% of the value of the investment.[21]

This legislation creates an incentive to invest in live theatrical productions by accelerating deductions and by ending the requirement that theatres pay income tax on what producers refer to as "phantom profits", which is money returned to investors that is less than the amount they had initially invested. Investment in theatre is highly risky; most Broadway shows fail financially. Therefore, the industry wants to make it as attractive as possible. The US Congress declared in the legislation that Broadway is an important cultural and economic export product, which the country cannot afford to lose.

The provision applies to a qualified live theatrical production, which is defined as a live stage production of a play (with or without music) that is derived from a written book or script and is produced or presented by a commercial entity in any venue with an audience capacity of less than 3.000. It also applies to short-term series of performances lasting no longer than 10 weeks in a taxable year in a venue with a capacity of less than 6.500. Sexually explicit productions are excluded. At least 75% of the production budget must be spent within the USA and the tax credit cannot exceed $15 million per production.

In addition, many US states have tax benefits for theatre, music and other performing arts, which can often be used together with this federal tax incentive.

6 Mexico: Artists Can Pay Taxes with Their Artwork

In Mexico, the tax law allows painters, sculptors and other artists to donate part of their annual production of artwork as an alternative means of paying taxes. This program is called Payment in Kind (*Pago en Especie*) and started in 1957 after an agreement between artist David Alfaro Siqueiros and secretary of state Hugo Margain. In return, Mexico now has a huge collection of contemporary art.

A rotating committee of seven artists and curators evaluates proposed donations to see whether they fairly represent the body of the work of a give artist. The collection of more 7,000 works of art is shown on walls and in open spaces of public buildings across Mexico. If the art is of a particularly high caliber, it becomes part of the "national-heritage collection", which is displayed in a permanent exhibition in Mexico City. Certain pieces are also sent abroad to foreign museums.

The program entails that donations are made according to reported sales. If an artist sells between one and five pieces of art in a given year, he donates one piece to the federal government. If the artist sells between six and eight pieces, he donates

[20] Section 181 IRC.

[21] Section 199 IRC.

two, and so on, with an annual cap of six donations. Only painters, sculptors and graphic artists can participate, although program administrators are considering whether to include performance art as an acceptable means of payment.

Mexican artists are proud of the program, knowing that their art becomes part of a historic collection that reflects Mexico's creative heritage (Hershaw 2014; Wood 2014).

7 Ireland: Exemption from Income Tax for Artists

Since 1969, Ireland provides for a tax exemption for artists developing specific original and creative artistic works. These works should be recognized as having cultural or artistic merit.[22]

For 2015 and subsequent years, the first €50,000 in profits or gains per year earned by writers, composers, visual artists and sculptors from the sale of their work is exempt from income tax in Ireland under certain circumstances. For the years 2011 to 2014, the maximum amount that may be exempted was €40,000. From 2006 to 2010, €250,000 was exempt. Prior to 2006, a full exemption applied.

The Arts Council and Minister for Arts Heritage and the Gaeltacht has developed guidelines for the exemption, with the consent of the Minister for Finance, for determining whether a work is an original and creative work for the purposes of Section 195 of the tax code and whether it has, or is generally recognized as having, cultural or artistic merit. The Revenue Commissioners may consult with a person or group of persons, such as The Arts Council, for assistance in reaching decisions in relation to Artists' Exemption.

The scheme provides that the Revenue Commissioners can make determinations with respect to artistic works in the following categories only:

1. books or other writings;
2. plays;
3. musical compositions;
4. paintings or other like pictures; and
5. sculptures.

Claimants for Artists' Exemption must be resident or ordinarily resident and domiciled in an EU Member State or in an EEA State and not be resident elsewhere. Previously, residency in Ireland was obligatory. Especially under the full exemption that existed prior to 2006, it was questionable why Irish resident artists got a full exemption, whereas all other income earners were required to pay taxes. At that time, many foreign artists moved to Ireland to benefit from the exemption, including pop artists such as Lisa Stansfield and Elvis Costello, authors Irvine Welsh and Michel Houellebecq and rock band Def Leppard. Furthermore, the

[22]Section 195 TCA 1997.

exemption was not only used by artists, but also by sportsmen, politicians and journalists who published best sellers. This effect was criticized and this critique, together with the financial crisis, lead to a drastic reduction in the exemption. The exemption is less attractive now for big earners, but there is still an issue of fairness as the exemption is still significant and artists thus pay less tax than other taxpayers.

The Revenue Commissioners are prepared to give advance opinions regarding the work of prospective claimants residing outside of the EU/EEA. In the event that a favorable advanced opinion is given, the prospective claimant will be advised to make a formal application for a determination on taking up residence in the EU/EEA.

Grants, awards and prizes are generally taxable as income, but may qualify for an exemption if it is determined that they are related to a qualifying work by the artist. In such cases, an exemption may be claimed up to the maximum amount allowed in law.

In addition, some other specific sources of income are determined by the Revenue Commissioners as qualifying for the Artists' Exemption scheme, such as grants directly received from the Arts Council, annuity grants for 5 years received from the Aosdana Scheme and sale of qualifying works abroad (Comhairle Ealaion 2015).

8 Conclusion

This chapter discussed examples of tax incentives for artists. The first conclusion is that they are quite focused at the national level, rather than cross-border focused. Even in the EU, Member States use (or do not use) the VAT exemption and reduced VAT rate in very different ways and the exemptions are not aimed at stimulating more EU-wide economic activity. As explained in the introduction, the protection and promotion of each country's own culture and heritage can be seen as one of the primary reasons for a tax incentive for artists, beyond the importance of artists for the economy both within the country and as an export product abroad.

The exemption and reduced VAT rate of the EU are quite simple, but other tax incentives are more complex. Neutrality seems to be secured when the macro-economic picture is considered, but within the sector itself, not qualifying for the tax incentive may have a major impact on the results for the producer. It is difficult to calculate the costs of the VAT exemption and reduced rate, while it is relatively easy to determine the financial impact of the other tax incentives. Mixed thoughts may come up about the effectiveness and efficiency, but the measures are quite visible because they attract much attention and are widely used in the sector. Compared with other tax measures, abuse and fraud may happen at a similar rate for these incentives. These tax incentives quite likely encourage commercial success.

Considering state aid within the EU, these tax incentives can most often make use of the approval for aid for culture, as described in Sect. 4.1 of Chap. 5, but applications must be made to determine whether the conditions are met.

References

Comhairle Ealaion, Minister of Arts Heritage, the Gaeltacht and the Minister for Finance (2015) Artists' exemption information and guidelines, Dublin
Concise Oxford Dictionary (2011) 12th edn. Oxford University Press, Oxford
Lasalle F (1873) Die indirekte Steuer und die Lage der arbeitenden Klassen. Julius Röthing, Leipzig (Freihandbuch)
McAndrew C (2002) Artists, taxes and benefits, an international review. Arts Council of England
Molenaar D (2006) Taxation of international performing artistes. IBFD, Amsterdam
Nederlandse Documentatie voor Fiscaal Recht (NDFR). Sdu Uitgevers, The Hague
Sandler D (1995) The taxation of international entertainers and athletes — all the world's a stage. Kluwer Law International, The Hague
Hershaw E (2014) Mexico, artists can pay taxes with artwork. The Atlantic, Washington, DC
Osborne G (2014) Tax relief encouraging theatre productions launched by chancellor. www.gov.uk
Oxford Advanced Learner's Dictionary (2010) 8th edn. Oxford University Press, Oxford
Oxford Dictionary of English (2010) 3rd edn.
Random House Webster's Unabridged Dictionary (2001) 2nd edn. Random House, New York
HMRC (2015) Theatre tax relief manual, London
UK Government (2015) Orchestra tax relief, policy paper, London
Webster's New World Dictionary (2014) Fifth college edition. Houghton Mifflin Harcourt, New York
Wood RW (2014) Paying tax with art is legal in mexico, why not in US? Forbes, Jersey City

Part III
Conclusion

Chapter 12
Conclusion

Sigrid Hemels

Abstract In this chapter, the theoretical framework presented in Part I of this book is discussed in relation to the cases presented in Part II to arrive at some general conclusions regarding tax incentives for the creative industries.

Keywords Tax incentives · Creative industries · Cultural policy · Economic policy

1 Introduction

In this chapter, we discuss the theoretical framework developed in Part I of this book in relation to the cases presented in Part II to arrive at some general conclusions regarding tax incentives for the creative industries. To what extent are the three defining characteristics of the creative industries reflected in the tax incentives for the various sub-sectors of these industries? Which market failures are addressed by these tax incentives? Which designs do governments use for their tax incentives, and are the conditions for successful tax incentives met? Lastly, is a regulatory influence on the design of tax incentives discernible?

S. Hemels (✉)
Department of Tax Law, Erasmus School of Law, Erasmus University Rotterdam, Rotterdam, The Netherlands
e-mail: hemels@law.eur.nl

S. Hemels
Allen & Overy, Amsterdam, The Netherlands

© Springer Science+Business Media Singapore 2017
S. Hemels and K. Goto (eds.), *Tax Incentives for the Creative Industries*,
Creative Economy, DOI 10.1007/978-981-287-832-8_12

2 Tax Incentives and the Three Characteristics of the Creative Industries

In Chap. 2, Kazuko Goto identified three defining features of the creative industries:

1. They have cultural and economic aspects relating to cultural policy goals as well as economic policy goals.
2. They are a combination of art and commerce.
3. They contain both nonprofit and for-profit organizations.

From this definition, we identified five different sub-sectors of the creative industries, which we used in Part II to analyze the various forms of tax incentives:

1. Museums and cultural heritage
2. The audiovisual industry
3. The art market
4. Copyright
5. Artists

While the three defining characteristics occur in various combinations within all of these sub-sectors, their proportions differ. Tax incentives for these sub-sectors are never driven by cultural policy motivations alone, nor are they driven by economic policy motivations alone. Similarly, they are not targeted exclusively at art in the narrow sense or at commerce, nor are they exclusively targeted at non-profit organizations or for-profit organizations. However, there are clear distinctions between the sub-sectors regarding their locations on these three scales. If we examine the characteristics of the creative industries in relation to the motivations underlying the introduction of tax incentives within these five sub-sectors, the following picture emerges. Tax incentives for museums and cultural heritage are predominantly motivated by cultural policy goals, and are mainly aimed at art in the narrow sense and at nonprofits. At the other end of the spectrum, tax incentives for the audiovisual industry are predominantly motivated by economic policy considerations and are, to a significant degree, aimed at the commercial products of for-profit organizations. Tax incentives for the art market mainly have a cultural policy motivation, free ports being a clear exception because of their dominant economic policy motivation. Furthermore, these incentives are mostly aimed at art in the narrow sense. However, in contrast to tax incentives for museums and cultural heritage, most of these incentives are aimed at for-profit entities and persons. Tax incentives for copyrights are more or less equally motivated by cultural and economic policy objectives, and are also more or less equally aimed at art in the narrow sense and commercial products. These tax incentives are predominantly aimed at for-profit entities and persons. If one defines income support for artists as an economic policy goal (income redistribution), then tax incentives for artists are mainly motivated by economic policy goals. However, cultural policy goals such as promoting excellence are important as well. These incentives are to a large extent

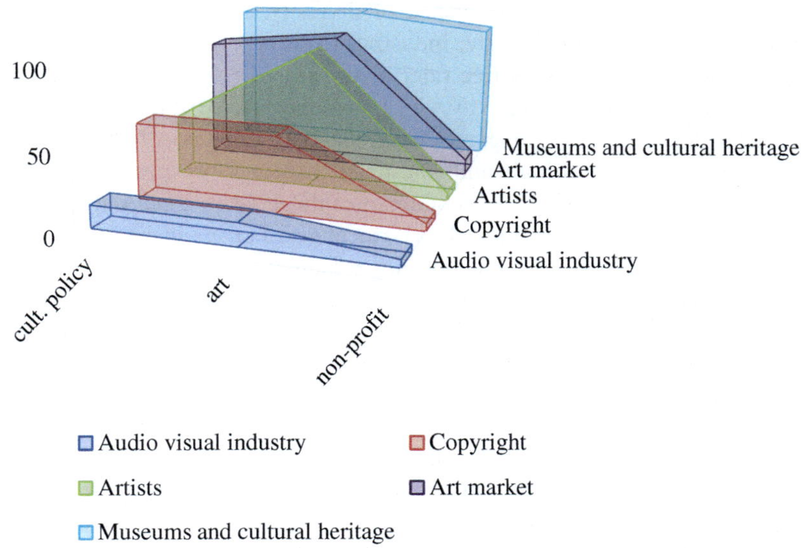

Fig. 1 Tax incentives for the sub-sectors in relation to the three characteristics of the creative industries

aimed at art in the narrow sense. For-profit entities and persons are predominantly targeted by these incentives.

While the picture is of course not all black and white, it can be plotted graphically, as shown in Fig. 1. In this figure, it is the ratios between the five sub-sectors rather than the absolute figures, which are very rough estimates, that are of key significance. The tax incentives for the five sub-sectors are scored on a scale of 0–100 along three dimensions: cultural policy motivation (0 = only economic policy motivation; 100 = only cultural policy motivation); aimed at art in the narrow sense (0 = exclusively aimed at commercial products; 100 = exclusively aimed at art in the narrow sense) and aimed at nonprofits (0 = exclusively aimed at for-profits; 100 = exclusively aimed at nonprofits). None of the sub-sectors scored 0 for any of the three characteristics. As the creative industries are characterized by a hybrid nature, it is not surprising that tax incentives also follow a hybrid pattern. It is also clear that there are variations between the sub-sectors and that a number of tax incentives are aimed at the for-profit sector.

3 Which Market Failures Do Governments Address Through Tax Incentives for the Creative Industries?

In Chap. 3, Kazuko Goto identified as cultural policy reasons brought forward for financial support of the creative industries the furtherance of excellence, innovation, and access; recognition and celebration of national, regional, or local identity;

promotion of continuity; and furtherance of diversity. Economic policy reasons include the contribution of the creative industries to the economy, perceived positive externalities, the wish to redress free rider behavior and difficulties some creative industries have to increase productivity whilst costs increase (Baumol's cost disease) and the reduction of the negative effects of the cost structure of many creative industries: a combination of high sunk and fixed costs and low marginal costs.

From the cases discussed in the second part of this book, we can see that not all of the above rationales are used for all tax incentives. For tax incentives targeting museums and cultural heritage, cultural policy reasons such as promotion of access, identity, diversity and continuity and, to a lesser degree, Baumol's cost disease, appear to be the most important. For some of these incentives, especially those relating to cultural heritage, redressing free rider behavior is also a motivating factor. For the audiovisual industry, the promotion of identity, diversity, innovation, and high fixed and sunk costs seem to provide supporting rationales. For tax incentives related to the art market, the most important rationales seem to be generation of public benefit from artistic activities and furtherance of excellence. Tax incentives for copyright seem to be motivated by cultural policy reasons such as promoting innovation, excellence and diversity. In some cases, such as special IP regimes and R&D tax incentives, high fixed and sunk costs also provide a rationale for government support. Regarding tax incentives for artists furtherance of excellence, and the promotion of identity and diversity can be identified as rationales for providing tax incentives.

4 Design of Tax Incentives

Sigrid Hemels discussed the various possible designs of tax incentives in Chap. 4. The chapters in Part II showed that tax incentives are, in fact, designed in many different ways. Even tax incentives targeting the same object, for example, those for donations and those for films are designed differently in different countries. Thus, there does not seem to be any "one size fits all" design. While it is beyond the scope of this book to compare the effectiveness of differently designed tax incentives targeting the same object, this would definitely be of interest, from both academic and policy perspectives.

On the other hand, we see many similarities between the tax incentives of different countries for the same object. In the EU, this can explained, at least in part, by the fact that EU Member States have to meet certain requirements laid down in the TFEU (e.g., fundamental freedoms and the prohibition of state aid), directives (e.g., the VAT Directive and the Interest and Royalty Directive) and regulations (e.g., the GBER). However, there are also many similarities that cannot be explained by an overarching regulatory framework. Countries seem to copy tax incentives from other countries. Especially when such incentives are used to compete with other countries, for example, in the case of film incentives, this could lead to a "race to the bottom," leaving all countries worse off than they were before.

In Chap. 4, the OECD conditions for successful tax incentives (1–4 below) and cultural policy conditions (5–8 below) were also discussed:

1. Administrative economies of scale and scope
2. Limited probability of abuse or fraud
3. An appropriately wide range of tax payer choices
4. Measurement of tax-paying capacity
5. Taking public preferences into account to align those who care and those who pay
6. Encouragement of commercial success
7. Empowerment of creative industries
8. Rapid raising of funds to preserve cultural heritage

It is clear from the chapters in Part II that none of the tax incentives meet all of the above conditions. The OECD conditions do not seem to have always been applied when deciding on implementing tax incentives for the creative industries. In several cases, specific information must be reported to the tax administration to establish whether the incentive applies, for example regarding the audiovisual industry incentives, acceptance in lieu of tax, theatre and orchestra tax benefits, and IP and R&D incentives. This would suggest that economies of scale and scope, limited probability of abuse and fraud, or an appropriately wide range of tax payer choices were not applied as conditions for introducing the tax incentives. This does not mean that this was never the case. General exemptions, including those for artists' incomes and works of art given on loan to museums, special tax regimes for copyright income, and reduced VAT rates appear to meet the OECD conditions.

The fourth OECD condition is somewhat problematic. Tax incentives targeted at artists earning low incomes could be regarded as meeting this criterion, as these incentives usually have a redistributive effect. However, a closer examination of deductions from progressively taxed income raises some questions. At first glance, such deductions may appear to satisfy the ability to pay concept. However, in a progressive tax rate system, high-income groups benefit more from these deductions because of the "upside-down" effect discussed in Chap. 4. This is not necessarily in line with the ability to pay principle. The Canadian solution of linking progressiveness not to income but to the amount of expenditure (e.g., the gift) seems to be more in line with this principle. An alternative solution applied by some countries is a deduction from tax (a tax credit), instead of a deduction from income. Reduced VAT rates for products of the creative industries seem to be even more problematic from an ability to pay perspective. These goods and services, including works of art and theatre and museum tickets are usually consumed more by individuals belonging to groups with higher education and incomes. Consequently, these incentives can go against the ability to pay principle. The same applies to other tax incentives related to the acquisition or transfer of works of art. A final consideration is that tax incentives aimed at corporations are not usually linked to the ability to pay principle. Whether this is problematic can be debated, as in many cases tax incentives for the creative industries will not have a redistributive purpose (except for those aimed at low-income artists).

The conditions that are linked to cultural policy objects seem to be less problematic. This might be explained by the fact that cultural policy considerations play at least some role during the introduction of a tax incentive for the creative industries. Again, not all conditions are met by all tax incentives. Empowering the creative industries seems to apply to many, if not all, tax incentives for the creative industries. Examples include tax incentives for artists; reduced VAT rates; IP, R&D, and other copyright incentives; and incentives for the audiovisual industry. Such incentives also encourage commercial success. Incentives for museums and cultural heritage specifically encourage consideration of public preferences and alignment of those who care and those who pay. Raising funds quickly to preserve cultural heritage is clearly a characteristic of the various acceptance in lieu incentives.

5 Influence of International Regulations

In Chap. 5, Raymond Luja discussed international regulatory frameworks that influence the freedom countries have when designing tax incentives for the creative industries. The influence of these regulations was evident in several tax incentives discussed in Part II.

Regulatory influences are clearly seen in EU Member States' tax incentives aimed at commercial products of for-profit entities and persons. The prohibition of state aid and the leeway given by, for example, the GBER, have had an important influence on the design of tax incentives for the audiovisual industry, theatre and orchestra productions, and IP and R&D within the EU. The latter incentives have also been influenced by discussions on harmful taxation and by international action against tax evasion and tax avoidance, specifically the anti-base erosion and profit shifting project. This also applies to tax incentives relating to royalty income.

Incentives that are primarily aimed at nonprofit entities and art in the narrow sense are less affected by these state aid rules. However, the fundamental freedoms are important for the design and use of these incentives as Renate Buijze showed in her discussion of tax incentives for charitable giving in a cross-border context in Chap. 6. The fundamental freedoms must also be considered when designing tax incentives aimed at a national culture or resident artists. For example, limiting the Irish exemption for artists to only those artists who are Irish nationals would not be allowed under EU rules.

Directives also influence the design of tax incentives within the EU. Examples include reduced VAT rates, which are regulated by the VAT Directive, and the exemption of royalty income, which is regulated by the Interest and Royalty Directive. Moreover, outside the EU, taxation of royalty income is influenced by international regulations, more specifically, bilateral tax treaties that reduce the tax rate applied on royalty income.

6 Conclusion

This book's comparative study of countries as well as sub-sectors of the creative industries has demonstrated the diversity of tax incentives that have been developed for these industries. The design of tax incentives for this sector is influenced by various factors, including cultural policy objects, economic policy objects, and external regulations. We hope that this book can deepen understanding of these tax incentives and that it will prove valuable for both academics and students studying the creative industries and tax incentives, as well as for policy makers whose task it is to design these incentives and make decisions regarding their introduction, retention, and abolishment.

Index

© Springer Science+Business Media Singapore 2017

S. Hemels and K. Goto (eds.), *Tax Incentives for the Creative Industries*,
Creative Economy, DOI 10.1007/978-981-287-832-8

Printed by Printforce, the Netherlands